GLOBAL FINANCE, CASES AND NOTES

To my parents. To Teodoro, Gustavo, Lilia,
Lilia del Carmen, Maria Elena and Patricia.

Global Finance, Cases and Notes

FRANCISCO CARRADA-BRAVO
Department of World Business
Thunderbird, The American Graduate
School of International Law

Ashgate

Aldershot • Burlington USA • Singapore • Sydney

Published by
Ashgate Publishing Ltd
Gower House
Croft Road
Aldershot
Hants GU11 3HR
England

Ashgate Publishing Company
131 Main Street
Burlington,
Vermont 05401
USA

Ashgate website:http://www.ashgate.com

Reprinted 2000

British Library Cataloguing in Publication Data
Carrada-Bravo, Francisco
  Global finance, cases and notes
  1. International finance 2. International business
  enterprises – Management
  I. Title
  332'.042

Library of Congress Catalog Card Number: 98-074634

ISBN 1 85972 573 2

Printed and bound in Great Britain by Biddles Limited,
Guildford and King's Lynn.

Contents

List of Tables		vi
Acknowledgments		ix
Preface		x
Introduction		xii

1	Managing globalization	1
2	Comparative advantages and international trade	8
3	Theories of international trade and production	21
4	The instruments of trade policy	35
5	Tendencies in global financing, some stylized facts	55
6	Interest rate parity and the foreign exchange market	59
7	Purchasing power parity and the foreign exchange market	71
8	The foreign exchange market	77
9	SKF in Poland: Foreign exchange rate corporate reporting	92
10	The fundamentals of the time value of money	97
11	The present value of annuities and perpetuities	104
12	Wendy's franchising in Argentina	112
13	Transnational investment	128
14	Cuetara in Morocco	141
15	Exchange rate risk management	152
16	Cemex: Debt and exchange rate risk	156
17	Managing transaction exposure with spot and forward contracts	168
18	Managing transaction exposure with futures and options	177
19	Controlling economic risk	188
20	Giant manufacturing and globalization	199
21	International arbitrage	208
22	Note on international currency swaps	217
23	The balance of payments	228
24	National income and the balance of payments	242
25	Monetary and fiscal policy, output and exchange rate	251
26	The collapse of the Mexican peso	267
27	The international monetary system	275

List of Tables

Table 1.1	Top industries, 1997	6
Table 1.2	Top international companies by profit margin, 1997	6
Table 1.3	Top companies by profit growth	6
Table 1.4	Top companies by dollar sales, 1997	7
Table 2.1	The theory of absolute advantages: A numerical example	9
Table 2.2	Illustration of the theory of comparative advantages	10
Table 2.3	Comparative advantages, exchange rate and international terms of trade	11
Table 2.4	Comparative advantages, wages, exchange rate and the international terms of trade	13
Table 3.1	The trade balance of NAFTA	29
Table 5.1	American Depository Receipts listed in the New York Stock Exchange	58
Table 6.1	Dollar-returns on a yen savings account	66
Table 8.1	CME futures, currency contract highlights	82
Table 8.2	Futures quotations	83
Table 8.3	CME options, currency contract highlights	85
Table 8.4	Option quotations	86
Table 10.1	The present value of a changing cash flow	101
Table 11.1	Present value of the cost of running machine one	108
Table 11.2	Annual cost equivalence of machine two	109
Table 11.3	Annual equivalence revenues of the South African projects	110
Table 12.1	Population of major cities of Argentina, 1996	122
Table 12.2	Wendy's average net dollar sales per domestic restaurant, 1993 – 96	122
Table 12.3	Wendy's cost of sales and its distribution, 1995	122
Table 12.4	Operating profit margin, 1994 – 1996	123
Table 12.5	International Wendy's, 1996	123
Table 12.6	Wendy's domestic and international restaurants	124
Table 12.7	Fast food restaurants financial statistics, 1996	124
Table 12.8	Exchange rate, 1991 – 1996	125
Table 12.9	Country statistics, 1996	125

Table 12.10   Wendy's international consolidated income statement   126
Table 12.11   Average sales per restaurant and number of restaurants   127
Table 13.1   Estimating cash flows   131
Table 13.2   Cash flows and exchange rate forecast   135
Table 13.3   Net present value of the Malaysian project under option one 135
Table 13.4   Net present value of the Malaysian project under option two 136
Table 14.1   Industrial evolution of the biscuit industry   148
Table 14.2   Leading producers in the Spanish biscuit industry   148
Table 14.3   Regional per capita consumption of biscuits in Spain, 1990   149
Table 14.4   Cost structure of the alimentary industry in Spain, 1990   149
Table 14.5   Cuetara, composition of sales, 1993   149
Table 14.6   Comparative cost structure, 1994   150
Table 14.7   Professional salaries in Morocco, 1994   150
Table 14.8   Urban population in Morocco, 1993   150
Table 14.9   Summary data of the Spanish biscuit industry, 1989 – 1992   151
Table 14.10   Key competitors in the Spanish bakery industry, 1991   151
Table 16.1   Distribution of assets and sales, December 1996   162
Table 16.2   Mexico, inflation, exchange rates and interest rates   162
Table 16.3   Spain, inflation, exchange rates and interest rates   162
Table 16.4   The US, inflation and interest rates   163
Table 16.5   Short-term loans, and other short-term liabilities   163
Table 16.6   Debt structure, 1966   163
Table 16.7   Maturity of long-term debt, 1996   164
Table 16.8   Long-term liability by type of currency   164
Table 16.9   Foreign exchange rate position, 1996   164
Table 16.10   Key financial figures   165
Table 16.11   Performance ratios   165
Table 16.12   Net sales, net income, and total assets   165
Table 16.13   Consolidated income statement, December 1995 and 1996   166
Table 16.14   Consolidated balance sheet, December 31, 1995 and 1996   167
Table 17.1   Foreign exchange and interest rate quotes   169
Table 17.2   Hedging imports with spot contracts   172
Table 20.1   Major bicycle exporters   203
Table 20.2   Taiwan, bicycle exports, 1984-1996   203
Table 20.3   Taiwan, bicycle exports, main markets, 1996   204
Table 20.4   Giant manufacturing exports, 1995   204
Table 20.5   Giant manufacturing exports, 1995-1996   204
Table 20.6   Financial performance, Giant manufacturing, 1994-1995   205
Table 20.7   Country statistics, Taiwan and main world markets, 1996   205
Table 20.8   Exchange rates   206
Table 20.9   Foreign exchange rates trends, December 1997   206
Table 20.10   Eurocurrency rates, December 1997   206
Table 21.1   Exchange rate quotations (DM/$)   209
Table 21.2   Cross rates and triangular arbitrage   209

vii

Table 21.3   Identifying covered interest arbitrage opportunities   211
Table 22.1   Case of absolute advantages   218
Table 22.2   Description of the dollar – German mark swap agreement   220
Table 22.3   Borrowing interest rates   220
Table 22.4   Description of the dollar – franc swap agreement   222
Table 22.5   Description of the dollar – yen swap agreement   223
Table 22.6   Dollar present value of the 3-year semi-annual coupon
             payments of a $/¥ swap   224
Table 26.1   Savings and investment   270
Table 26.2   Total external debt and interest payments on Mexico's
             external debt   270
Table 26.3   3-month interest rates   271
Table 26.4   Inflation and exchange rate changes, peso/dollar   272
Table 26.5   Financing of current account deficits   272
Table 26.6   Mexico, balance of payments, 1993-1994   273
Table 26.7   Policy alternatives and outcomes   273
Table 26.8   Monetary base and its components   274

Acknowledgments

This book was made possible thanks to the assistance provided by many institutions, colleagues, staff, and former students. Some of them provided financial and technical support. Others reviewed the manuscripts and contributed with valuable insights.

At the risk of missing some names, I like to express my appreciation to Robert Grosse and Dale Davison, World Business Department Chairs in different periods at Thunderbird, The American Graduate School of International Management. Both of them relieved me from some of my teaching duties to allow me to spend time writing this book. To my colleagues in the World Business Department at Thunderbird, especially Taeho Kim and Bryan Heathcotte. The former provided some guidance and advice on how to approach the writing of a book. The latter reviewed some of the material and suggested technical corrections and valuable insights. To John Boyll, who as a student first and editor later, contributed many suggestions and corrections that improved the style and content. To Mauricio Gruener, who reviewed and corrected all the solutions to the problems and cases. To Anamarie Sabbagh, who helped edit and kept the office running. To Georgia Lessard, Center for Authoring and Presentation Support (CAPS) also at Thunderbird, who turned raw drafts into carefully edited chapters. To Maureen Mansell-Ward, Desk Editor at Ashgate for her valuable comments, corrections, and insights, to the final draft. To all of them, I give my gratitude.

As is customary, any remaining shortcomings and oversights in the text are mine alone.

Preface

This book is intended for use in international master of business administration (international MBA), master of international management (MIM), and upper-level courses in international finance. It is the fruit of many hours of work dedicated to the creation of teaching materials that I felt were appropriate to train business executives and graduate students of a master in international management. The content of this book is directed to instruct students on how to apply the principles of global finance to the challenges posed by the world trading system. This focus is a reflection of the pedagogy that I use to teach international finance.

To fulfill the pedagogical objectives set for this manual, I have divided it into twenty-seven modules. Each unit, which is either a technical note or a case, is organized logically in sets explaining diverse subject matters. International trade theory, commercial policy, theories of exchange rate determination, foreign exchange market, fundamentals of transnational investment, exchange rate risk management, swaps, balance of payments, output and the exchange rate, and the international monetary system.

To maintain continuity throughout the book, all of the technical notes share the same structure. They begin with a brief introduction justifying their teaching objectives. It follows a short statement describing the aim of the note in detail. Subsequently, there is a description of the theory needed to fulfill the purpose of the note and a large number of exercises designed to illustrate the theory applications to specific business conditions. At the end, there is a summary that wraps up all the key aspects. To help the students to further master the content of each technical note, there is a closing section containing sets of problems designed to extend the pedagogical value of this teaching material.

The cases are placed strategically throughout the text. Their purpose is to provide, under a rich variety of circumstances, an unstructured learning environment. Their discussion can precede or follow the study of the notes. The first method encourages the students to use their intuition to find reasonable solutions to the queries and challenges posed by the case. The second method helps the student to develop a gradual understanding of global finance.

The success of either method will depend on how the instructor focuses the discussion of the cases. To help in this endeavor, I have prepared teaching notes for each case. These teaching notes start with an executive summary followed by teaching objectives, assignment questions, a suggested teaching approach, and a detailed analysis of the solutions to each question. They are available upon request to the instructors using this book. They can also be obtained by checking into my home page at *My Thunderbird* or by requesting them by e-mail at carradaf@t-bird.edu.

To facilitate the use of the material included in this volume, I have prepared electronic presentations for each one of the technical notes and cases. The instructors may want to use these presentations to facilitate the delivery of their lectures. The students can utilize them to supplement their lecture notes.

Instructors can apply the presentations in a variety of circumstances. They can project them in a distance learning environment, in a computerized classroom, or simply via conventional overhead projectors. These presentations are available upon request or through my Internet address at Thunderbird.

The material included in this volume has been tested in the classroom at least three times under many different circumstances in institutions around the world. Some of the places where the material contained in this volume was used include classrooms in Chile, Argentina, Mexico, the United States, Spain, Indonesia and Japan.

Introduction

The domain of global finance

While tradition dictates that we differentiate between corporate, and international finance, the practice indicates that all finance has turned global. Today, with few remaining barriers to international trade and the transfer of financial flows, all the financial markets are closely linked and globally integrated. This integration has standardized the problems faced by companies and individuals all over the world.

Even though most if not all finance must be viewed as global, there are still specific problems that can be traced to the economic relations existing between nations. The key aspects of this relationship are associated to the volume and value of exports and imports, the transfer of real and financial resources, the payment mechanism to settle international transaction, the international data collection system, and the level and variability of the exchange rate.

The study and solution of the problems associated to the economic interaction between residents of two or more nations, is the specific subject matter of this book.

The importance and benefits of studying global finance

For international managers and government officials engaged in global affairs, the knowledge of global finance is very important in several ways. First, it helps them to judge how external shocks may affect the economy of a country or the finance of a firm. Second, global finance will provide them with guidance regarding what steps should be taken to profit from the external disturbance. Otherwise, it will suggest ways of how to isolate institutions from the harmful aspects of an external shock.

To build the judgement required to take wise international finance decisions, the managers need to know how to anticipate variations in the exchange rate and understand how these variations will affect local inflation, domestic interest rates, exports, imports, the home capital markets, and the level of national income. Also, they need to grasp how the disturbance created at home by either changes in the exchange rate or other external shocks can be transmitted across nations. Equally important is that these managers comprehend the possible consequences of the economic radiation of both changes in the exchange rate and external shocks.

Who should read this book

The nature of global finance of focusing on the world character of a local event leads every manager and government official, and each individual aspiring to be one of them, to be continuously involved in the thrill of analyzing world events.

The personal stimulation of applying global finance to understand corporate performance is not limited only to managers of very large and sophisticated multinational corporations or government officials of rich nations. Rather, it extends to managers of small, medium, and large size businesses.

Regardless of location, size, and economic activity, the manager of any institution, whether private or public, can apply the guidance provided by global finance to improve the net worth of the institution. For instance a small company selling handicrafts in a Mexican market can be affected, positively or negatively, by changes in the exchange rate. By spending time reading through the content of this book, the manager of this company, similarly to the executive of a very large multinational corporation, can find guidance of how to benefit from the change in the peso parity.

Likewise the Mexican manager, Argentineans holding their own government bonds, denominated in their own currency, and spending all their money at home, can find in the pages of this book useful advise of how to manage local assets.

It appears obvious from the previous discussion that global finance is a useful and important subject matter that can be applied to every aspect of the cross border relation between individuals, firms, and nations. Thus, the material contained in this book is recommended for any person interested in either international business or world affairs. Also, international business executive and government official interested in world affairs, should read it.

The importance of exchange rates, the Asian crisis

This Asian crisis began in Philippines and Thailand in July of 1997 when these two countries, due to a host of variables, were forced to devalue their currencies. Very soon, the effects of the devaluation in Philippines and Thailand extended to Indonesia, South Korea, Malaysia, Taiwan, Singapore and Japan. See Table 1.

The exchange rate adjustments resulted in tremendous financial hardships for the Asian economies, but also provided them with badly needed competitive advantages in world markets since the Asian products became cheaper in terms of non-Asian currencies. The reduction in the price of the Asian goods, placed a downward price pressures on domestically produced goods in markets outside the continent. The first sector to succumb to the Asian downward price pressure was the industrial commodities sector. In six months, the world prices of oil, lumber, metals, and petrochemicals fell substantially. Later, this downward spiral extended to the aerospace, semiconductors, computer, footwear and other.

Table 1
Asian Currencies, July 1, 1997—March 2, 1998
Percent Change

Country	Currency	Variations in the Exchange Rate %
Japan	yen	-8.5
South Korea	won	-42.6
Indonesia	rupiah	-72.6
Malaysia	ringgit	-30.5
Philippines	peso	-33.6
Singapore	dollar	-11.5
Thailand	baht	-44.2
Taiwan	dollar	-12.7
Hong Kong	dollar	-0.1

In the initial stage, the Asian crisis affected severely the level of reserves of Thailand, Korea, and Indonesia. The International Monetary Fund (IMF), suggested as the first order of business for the governments of these three nations was to restore confidence in the currencies. To achieve this goal, the IMF insinuated a temporary increase in interest rates to increase the attractiveness of holding local currency.

Another important IMF suggestion was to restructure the government budget to make room for the savings needed to meet the future cost of rescuing the badly hurt banking systems of the three countries. And depending on the balance of payments situation of each nation, the rewriting of the budget should also focus on the reduction of government expenditures to liberate the financial resources required to reduce current account deficits. The current account is a statement of a country's international transactions of goods, services, gifts, net interest payments, and net repatriation of profits.

Ultimately, the fiscal adjustment for Indonesia turned out to be one percent of gross national product (GDP); in Korea it was 1.5 percent of GDP; and in Thailand —reflecting a large current account deficit—the initial adjustment was 3 percent of GDP.[1]

The IMF policy suggestions did not receive a universal acclaim on the part of either the governments or the residents of the Asian countries. To some, the approach was too tough. The IMF critics suggested instead, a policy mix contemplating lower interest rates and more devaluation. They considered their suggestion a kinder, gentler Asian way.

Topics covered in this book

To understand the implications of the two policy alternatives presented to solve the Asian crisis, the reader needs to have a theoretical framework of reference, and a clearly defined set of concepts. This helps to identify the meaning of the notion used to describe the economic conditions of the Asian nations in 1998.

To provide the theoretical tools and the concepts used in global finance, this book has been integrated into seven sections.

The first section runs from Chapters 1-4. It is related to international trade theory and the instruments of trade policy. Chapter one provides a useful guidance of how to extend the activity of a firm overseas. If the foreign demand for local products abroad is small, and if the local firm possesses excess capacity at home, exporting is the most viable strategy. Under different circumstances, licensing or investing may be a better alternative. Chapter 2 and 3, consider the theory of international trade and production and barriers to trading.

The second segment goes from Chapters 5 to 7. They introduce two central principles of global finance, the purchasing power parity (PPP) and interest rate parity theories of exchange rate determination. These two theories are widely applied, under a variety of circumstances, throughout the pages of this book.

The third part, ranging from Chapters 8 to 9, lets the reader find a thorough description of the foreign exchange market as well as a case exposing the student to data covering all the angles of this market.

The fourth section, that extends from Chapters 10 to 14, furnishes the reader with the tools required to evaluate cross border investment opportunities. These Chapters also contribute with two cases presenting the appropriate corporate and country data needed to evaluate transnational investment. This data include financial information, and discount and tax rates. The cases also confront the student with the decision of choosing the appropriate capital structure as well as the best source of capital funding.

Section five stretches out from Chapters 15 through 22. These chapters cover the different aspects of exchange risk management. This material confronts the reader with the challenge of how to reduce a firm's exposure to unanticipated changes in the exchange rate. It also includes a fair amount of readings dealing with the consequences of different hedging techniques. These include spot, forward, futures, and options contracts, as well as swaps. The financial engineering techniques required to hedge and speculate are described in detail, and in a manner that can be easily accessible to readers whose background in global finance is limited to the readings included in this manuscript. In addition, there are two cases suited to let the reader to practice exchange rate risk management in the context of loose business environments.

The sixth segment is limited to Chapter 23. This chapter looks at the structure and meaning of the different aspects of the balance of payments accounts.

The seventh and last section, that includes Chapters 24 through 27, provides a structured framework to study the macroeconomic relation between output and the exchange rates. It also explores the role of monetary and fiscal policy in the determination of output and the exchange rate.

The preceding overview of the context of this book, along with the earlier parts of this chapter, indicate the broad range of fascinating issues addressed within international finance, which is by far the most globalized of all subject matters of business. Having provided a brief sketch of what is ahead, let us begin our journey.

Note

1. Fisher Stanley, "The Asian Crisis, the IMF, and the Japanese Economy," speech delivered in Tokyo, Japan, April 8, 1998, International Monetary Fund (IMF), www:imf.org/external/speeches/1998/0400898.htm.

1   Managing globalization

Introduction

Globalization of industry refers to the transnational operations undertaken by multinational corporations. These actions are aimed at sourcing, manufacturing, marketing, financing, and organizing the development of new products.[1]

A distinctive characteristic of globalization is the partition of the firm's operations into separate company divisions implemented simultaneously in different countries. The most peculiar features of globalization are international trade, transnational investment, and cross-country alliances.[2]

Historically, the expansion of multinationals was instrumented mainly through international trade. In the 1980s, international trade was replace by foreign direct investment and inter-firm collaboration as the main engine of world growth. Most recently, firms have been employing trade, investment, and inter company alliances as the tools to globalize.

Purpose

The aim of this note is to provide the student with the analytical tools required to identify, design, and evaluate business opportunities in the global market place.

Factors shaping the globalization of industries

Globalization has been characterized by easier access to overseas factors of production and markets —especially for US, Japanese, and European multinationals— and the facilities granted to multinationals to transfer technology between parent companies and their subsidiaries.

Easier access to factors of production and foreign markets has been the direct consequence of both deregulation and the agreement reached at the end of the Uruguay Round to lower trade barriers.[3]

Deregulation has taken place all over the world, leading to a reduction of investment restrictions virtually everywhere. Since 1991, there have been around the globe some 570 liberalization changes in regulations that govern foreign direct investment. By 1998, there were more than 1,330 bilateral investment treaties involving 162 countries. This number represented a 300 percent increase in treaties of this nature in half a decade.[4]

The process of liberalization also got rid of duties and exchange controls on imported goods and services. Between 1994 and 1997, the duties existing in the emerging nations fell from 34 to 14 percent. Between 1970 and 1997, the number of countries reducing restrictions on imports of goods and services grew from 35 to 137.

Under the Uruguay Round agreement, the tariffs imposed by the advanced nations on imports of manufactured goods will be reduced to less than 4 percent by the year 2001.

Technology transfer has been also the direct result of improvements in infrastructure. Computing costs are lower, software is better and cheaper, and international communications are easier and faster. For instance, between 1960 and 1990, the cost of a unit of computer power declined 99 percent. In the period between 1930 and 1990, average revenue per mile in air transport fell from $0.68 to $0.11. In a similar fashion, the cost of a three-minute telephone call between New York and London fell from $244 to $3.25.[5]

The process of globalization

International expansion starts with the evaluation of demand in overseas markets for the firm's products. If the demand exists, the next step is to identify the most efficient way to serve the foreign market. The effectiveness of a new operation is measured based on how much it contributes to cut costs, to improve international coordination, to diversify the firm's business activities, to expand the firm's presence in foreign markets. But more importantly, perhaps, is by how much the new operation contributes to raise the stock price of the parent company.

The analysis of demand conditions in foreign markets

To evaluate demand conditions overseas, firms must consider the degree of distinctiveness of corporate products (δ), the price of corporate products abroad relative to the price of substitute products overseas (Ph/Pf), and per capita purchasing power abroad measured by gross domestic product per capita (γ). That is:

$$Qf = f(\delta, Ph/Pf, \gamma)$$

Once international demand is believed to exist, a firm must decide on the most efficient way to serve the foreign market.

Domestic globalized operations

A domestic globalized operation is best described by a transaction where a local firm supplies foreign firms at home. In this instance, the supplying local firm is acting as a supporting or related industry of a large multinational corporation.[6] Transactions between Japanese firms and the non-Japanese motor vehicle industry often fall in this classification.

Limited to moderately globalized operations

A limited to moderately transnational operation is the preferred form of expansion for multinationals belonging to the fast food industry, This type of transactions involve sales of corporate products through foreign intermediaries or marketing affiliates. Licensing rights to foreign competitors to produce corporate products overseas and the final assembly of electronic items in plants belonging to these competitors also fall within the range of this classification.

Globalized operations

This way to expand is preferred by companies heavily involved in the design, development, financing, and manufacturing of key core products. Firms belonging to the computer industry are the best example of companies using this approach.[7]

Rules to globalize

There are no established rules to internationalize the business of a firm. Transnationalization does not begin with exports and end up with the establishment of a full-fledged subsidiary. In many instances, the process starts with foreign investment and concludes with exports. In the 1960s, Chrysler initiated operations in Spain with an assembly plant in Villaverde, near Madrid. In the 1970s, due to the poor performance of the Spanish subsidiary and the overall financial conditions of the parent company, Chrysler shut down the plant and left the Spanish market. In the late 1980s, the US auto maker returned to Spain. In its second venture, however, the company's strategy was to export from the US to the European nation.

Exporting

Exporting is a viable strategy to internationalize the operations of a company, if the ratio of the difference between the price of the product in foreign markets (P_f) and the average cost of producing at home (AC_h) to the cost of transportation (TC) is greater or equal to one.[8] That is:

$$(P_f - AC_h)/TC \geq 1$$

Licensing and franchising

Licensing and/or franchising are adequate alternatives to enter into a new market if the average cost of producing abroad (AC_f) by a wholly-owned subsidiary is greater than or equal to the price of the domestic product overseas (P_f).[9] That is:

$$AC_f \geq P_f$$

Foreign direct investment

A cross-border investment is a convenient alternative for international expansion when this investment yields a net present value. This happens when the average cost of production abroad is less than or equal to the price of the company's product in a foreign market. That is:

$$AC_f \leq P_f$$

This happens when intellectual property rights, organizational and managerial skills, and marketing networks can be exploited abroad with appropriate economies of scale.

Foreign direct investment is also feasible when the relocation of manufacturing assets from the home market to overseas leads to substantial savings in manufacturing costs due to the availability of comparative advantages in the foreign country.

Foreign direct investment also makes sense when potential profits from "internalizing" the exploitation of the firm's assets is greater than the cost resulting from managing a larger and more geographically dispersed organization.[10]

Foreign direct investment may take the form of a joint venture, a strategic alliance, or a wholly-owned subsidiary.

Joint ventures refer to equity contributions by two or more partners to establish a foreign ancillary.

Global strategic alliances are formal, short or long-term coalitions between two or more firms (belonging to different countries) that link some aspects or lines of business, but fall short of merging.[11] These alliances are engineered to reduce manufacturing costs, to improve international market share, and to trade complementary technologies.

4

A wholly-owned subsidiary refers to equity contributions by one firm to acquire or establish a foreign subsidiary.

The relative importance of Foreign Direct Investment (FDI)

During the eighties and nineties, FDI has been the preferred form to globalize and the most important aspect of international business. For instance, from 1980 to 1997, the flow of foreign direct investment grew at a rate of 12 percent while exports increased at a rate of only 7 percent. For the same period, FDI also outpaced domestic capital formation since it grew twice as fast as local gross capital formation.[12]

Other reasons to invest abroad

Foreign direct investment, which amounted to $3 trillion in 1997, is not always related to efficiency or ruled by net present value considerations. Often, FDI is aimed to avoid trade protection measures. This form of international investment, which is practiced widely by Japanese, German, and US companies, and is known as tariff-jumping foreign direct investment.

Notes

1   Organization for Economic Co-Operation and Development, *Globalization of Industry, Overview and Sector Reports*, 1996, p. 15.
2   Ibidem.
3   The Results of the Uruguay Round of Multilateral Trade Negotiations were adopted at Marrakesh on April 15, 1994. For further details, see World Trade Organization, *Annual Report 1996*, vol. 1, 1996, p. 162.
4   Ibidem.
5   Wolf, Martin, "Perspective: The Heart of the New World Economy," *The Financial Times*, Wednesday, October 1, 1997.
6   See appendix, Top International Companies by Profit Margin, 1997.
7   Ibidem.
8   Karrenbrock, Jeffrey, "The Internationalization of the Beer Brewing Industry," The Federal Reserve Bank of St. Louis, November/December, 1990, pp. 3-18.
9   Ibidem.
10 World Trade Organization, *Annual Report 1996, Special Topic: Trade and Foreign Direct Investment*, Vol. 1, p. 50, 1996.
11 Porter, M., *Competition in Global Industries*, Harvard Business School Press, Boston, MA, 1986.
12 World Trade Organization, *Annual Report 1996, Special Topic: Trade and Foreign Direct Investment*, Vol. 1, p. 50, 1996.

Table 1.1
Top industries, 1997

World Rank	Industry
1	Food
2	Chemicals
3	Electronic/Electric
3	Metals
5	Industrial Equipment

Source: Industry Week 1,000, www.businesswire.com/emk/wtop/10htm, August 9, 1997.

Table 1.2
Top international companies by profit margin, 1997

World Rank	Name	Profit Margin	Country
923	News International PLC	91.24	UK
930	Vorwek and Co.	44.91	Germany
428	Time Mirror	35.38	USA
223	Eli Lilly	33.87	USA
926	UST, Inc.	32.42	USA

Source: Industry Week 1,000, www.businesswire.com/emk/wtop/10htm, August 9, 1997.

Table 1.3
Top companies by profit growth

World Rank	Name	Profit Growth	Country
875	Cartiere Burgo	9,709	Italy
128	Nippon Paper Industries	7,325	Japan
914	KM-Kabelmetal AG	5,028	Germany
854	Methanex Corp.	4,027	Canada
435	Quantum Corp.	2,915	USA

Source: Industry Week 1,000, www.businesswire.com/emk/wtop/10htm, August 9, 1997.

Table 1.4
Top companies by dollar sales, 1997

World Rank	Name	Industry	Country
1	General Motors Corp.	Motor Vehicles and Parts	USA
2	Ford Motor Co.	Motor Vehicles and Parts	USA
3	Toyota Motor Corp.	Motor Vehicles and Parts	Japan
4	Hitachi Ltd.	Electronic/Electric	Japan
5	Matsushita Electric Co.	Electronic/Electric	Japan
6	International Business Machine	Computer/Office Equipment	USA
7	Daimler Benz AG	Motor Vehicles and Parts	Germany
8	General Electric Co.	Electronic/ Electric	USA
9	Nissan Motor Co.	Motor Vehicles and Parts	Japan
10	Phillip Morris Co.	Tobacco	USA

Source: Industry Week 1,000, www.businesswire.com/emk/wtop/10htm, August 9, 1997.

2 Comparative advantages and international trade

Introduction

In the summer of 1989, BMW decided that it needed a new production facility outside Germany. The ideal location was defined as a site close to the US market, within the area of NAFTA, with easy access to ports for exporting and importing, in an Eastern time zone, and with an abundant and well-trained labor force. The final choice was the State of South Carolina in the United States.

The factors listed as major elements in the final decision suggest that the choice of the site was based, to a great extent, on the comparative advantages offered by South Carolina to the German corporation.

The purpose of this technical note is to explain the relationship between absolute and comparative advantages and international trade.

To lay the grounds for the framework required to explain these two relationships, several simplifying assumptions need to be made. First, only a two-country world economy will be considered. Second, labor is the only cost of production. Third, trade is barter (this assumption will be relaxed later to allow the introduction of money). Fourth, free trade is allowed and is made up mainly of undifferentiated products of similar quality known as "commodities". Fifth, the base of international trade is efficiency, that is, each country can produce one or more commodities at a lower real cost than its trading partners.

The theory of absolute advantages

Consider two countries, Germany and China, each having different endowments of labor and different skills. Given this skill differential, each country can produce one or more commodities at a lower real-labor-cost than its trading partner. Since labor is the only cost of production, each country will benefit from specializing in those commodities in which it has an "absolute labor-based cost advantage." To illustrate this concept, consider the information presented in Table 2.1. The German workers appear more skilled than their Chinese counterparts in the production of cars. In contrast, the Chinese workers are showing better skills in the production of pottery.

Table 2.1
The theory of absolute advantages: A numerical example

Country	Input	Output Cars	Pottery	Terms Of Trade Domestic	International	Gains
Germany	100	40	80	1C:2P	1C:4P	+2P
China	100	20	120	1C:6P	1C:4P	-2P

In the absence of international trade, the German car producer can exchange one car for two units of pottery. Similarly, the producers of pottery in China, in order to have a car, have to give away six units of pottery. These relationships are known as *the domestic terms of trade.*

If trade barriers are eliminated, it is only logical that both Germany and China specialize in the production of cars and pottery respectively because in these products each country holds an absolute cost advantage. Since trade is based on barter, then each country shows a zero trade balance; therefore, exports are equal to imports.

To trade profitably, the terms of trade have to lie between one German car for two to six units of Chinese pottery. Less than two units of pottery per one car will turn international trade unprofitable for Germany. Terms of trade exceeding six units of pottery in exchange for one car will not be beneficial to China for the same reason.

If the terms of trade fall within the feasible region of trading, let us say, one German car in exchange for four units of pottery, then both the German and the Chinese producers will gain from international trade.

The German car producers will obtain two more units of pottery for each car produced and traded as compared with how much they could get selling their cars domestically. The Chinese producers of pottery will be able to "purchase" a car from the Germans with only four units of pottery, which will provide them with a savings of two units of pottery per car purchased. These gains of international trade for both Germans and Chinese are presented in the last column of Table 2.1.

These gains lead to the conclusion that International trade based on absolute advantages may improve the welfare of the two trading nations by making their producers better off. This case of trading is interesting, but it is too limited. It does not explain the paradoxical export of some commodities produced relatively more inefficient in the home country. This case can only be explained by the logic of comparative advantages.

Comparative advantages

In contrast to absolute advantages, international trade based on comparative advantages depends only on the difference in comparative costs. This means that nations can still trade with each other even if one country has cost superiority on every commodity. To explain this idea, this note will resort to the information presented in Table 2.2.

Table 2.2
Illustration of the theory of comparative advantages

Country	Input	Output		Terms Of Trade		Gains
		Cars	Pottery	Domestic	International	
Germany	100	40	80	1C:2P	1C:4P	+2P
China	100	10	50	1C:5P	1C:4P	-1P

Germany is depicted in Table 2.2 as a country with absolute cost advantages in the production of both cars and pottery. That is, with the same amount of labor, Germany can produce more of each one of the commodities. This German superiority in the production of the two goods does not prevent international trading. The two countries can still be better off if they specialize and trade based on their relative cost strengths. For instance, Germany can specialize in cars where it has a four-to-one superiority over China, and let the Chinese specialize in pottery.

This relocation of production will allow the German workers, specialized in the production of pottery, to relocate to the production of automobiles. This will permit them to increase their productivity against the Chinese from 1.66 to 1 that they have in pottery to 4 to 1 in cars.

The Chinese will also benefit from the re-engineering of production. They will move their workers out of the production of automobiles, where they hold a one-to-four disadvantage, to pottery, where the relative disadvantage is only 1 to 1.66.

Profitable international terms of trade for both countries are again limited by their respective domestic terms of trade. To gain from international trade under comparative advantages, the international terms of trade should be more than two units of pottery in exchange for one car and less than five units of pottery in exchange for the same car. As explained before, a relationship beyond the boundaries of the domestic terms of trade will make the exchange of goods between Germany and China economically inefficient.

The benefits of international trade based on comparative advantages can again be illustrated by choosing a ratio located in the "feasible zone" of profitable terms of trade. For instance, if the ratio is one car to four units of pottery, the German car producers will have two more units of pottery for each car produced as compared to how much they could get if they were limited to domestic trade. In turn, the Chinese producers of pottery will be able to import cars from the Germans at a cost of only four units of pottery. This trade agreement will allow the Chinese to save one unit of pottery on each car purchased —domestically, they have to pay five units of pottery to obtain a car of similar quality. The gains of trade for each party are shown in the last column of Table 2.3.

Table 2.3
Comparative advantages, exchange rate and international terms of trade

Country	Input	Output		Terms Of Trade		Prices	
		Cars	Pottery	Domestic	International	Cars	Pottery
Germany	100	40	80	1C:2P	1C:4P	DM4	DM2
China	100	10	15	1C:5P	1C:4P	Y10	Y2

Exchange Rate = Y2/DM

Money prices, exchange rate, and international terms of trade

If the assumption of barter trade is relaxed and money prices are introduced, it is possible to determine the specific terms of international trade.

Calculating international terms of trade

To estimate the international terms of trade, under the assumption of a zero trade balance, it is necessary to take the following steps. The first is to standardize the domestic prices of both cars and pottery in terms of a single currency, the second is to assume a zero trade balance and equate export revenues with the import bill, and the third and final step is to determine the terms of trade.

Step One

Country	Domestic Prices		International Prices	
	Cars	Pottery	Cars	Pottery
Germany	DM4	DM2	DM4	DM2
China	Y10	Y2	Y10*(DM1/Y2) = DM5	Y2*(DM1/Y2)= DM1

Step 2

$$\text{EXPORTS} = \text{IMPORTS}$$
$$(P_{,c},DM)*Q_{,c} = (P_{,p},Y)*(\text{exch rate})*Q_{,p}$$
$$DM4*Q_{,c} = DM1*Q_{,p}$$

11

<u>Step 3</u>

$$DM4 * Q_{,c} = DM1 * Q_{,p}$$
$$Q_{,c}/Q_{,p} = DM1/DM4$$
$$Q_{,c}/Q_{,p} = 1/4$$
$$\text{One car} = \text{four units of pottery}$$

The ratio of one car to four units of pottery is known as *the international terms of trade*.

Note: $P_{,c,}DM$ is the price of the German car exports to China measured in marks; $Q_{,c}$ is the quantity of German car exports to China; $P_{,p,}Y$ is the price of Chinese pottery exports to Germany; exch rate is the exchange rate between the German mark and the yuan; $Q_{,p}$ is the quantity of pottery imports of Germany from China; $[P_{,c,}DM)*Q_{,c}]$ is the mark value of the German exports; and $[(P_{,p,}Y)*(\text{exch rate})*Q_{,p}]$ is the German import bill.

Comparative advantages in practice

Multinationals recognize two forms of comparative advantages: structural and responsive.

Structural advantages are built into the nature of the business. For example, in the introduction of this note, it was mentioned that BMW was planning to build a plant in South Carolina. As the company has complied with the proposed plan, this plant will enjoy two structural advantages: geographic location and abundance of a well-trained labor force, both of which lead to lower production costs as compared to producing cars in other competing locations.

Responsive advantages refer to positions of comparative advantage that a firm builds over time as a result of a sequence of appropriate managerial decisions. Using again the example of BMW, it is known that the State of South Carolina offered the German company generous financing terms, an excellent package of worker's training programs, and the promise to build the appropriate infrastructure to improve the State's international transportation system. The negotiation for these concessions by BMW management created responsive advantages which will help to lower the cost of producing cars in South Carolina even further as compared to other competing sites.

Comparative advantages and competition

Comparative advantages can be applied to different stages of the business cycle. Examination of a business' operating system with comparative advantages in mind is useful to gain sustainable comparative advantages. It may enable a firm to discover the source of greatest economic leverage because it allows for identifying

12

stages in the business system where the firm may build cost advantages against competition. The use of comparative advantages in the context of a business system also may be used to analyze a competitor's costs and to gain insights into the sources of a competitor's current advantage in either cost or economic value to the customer.

Comparative advantages, wages, and the exchange rate

To capitalize on the comparative advantages of a skilled labor force and to be able to benefit from these advantages in the international market, a business has to maintain the wage rates of its labor force consistent with the productivity of that labor. The purpose of this section is to develop a procedure to estimate the maximum and the minimum wage rates which are consistent with international trade given an exchange rate and a set of comparative advantages.

Table 2.4
Comparative advantages, wages, exchange rate
and the international terms of trade

Country	Input	Output		Wages	
		Cars	Wine	Daily	Total
Portugal	150	20	80	E3	E450
Germany	150	80	240	DM2	DM300

Domestic Unit Cost		Exchange Rate	International Unit Cost		Terms of Trade	
Cars	Wine		Cars	Wine	Domestic	International
E22.5	5.56	E5/DM1	DM4.5	1.112	1C:4W	1C:3.3W
DM3.75	1.25		DM3.7	1.25	1C:3W	1C:3.3W

Note: Labor input, output, total wages, and the exchange rate are given; daily wages = total wages/labor force; unit cost = total cost/output; international Portuguese unit costs are expressed in German marks.

Estimation of the maximum wage in Germany consistent with the international terms of trade

Assuming the information provided in Table 2.4, Germany will continue to export cars to Portugal as long as the unit cost of producing cars in Germany is less than or equal to the unit cost of producing cars in Portugal (assuming that the cars produced are of similar quality). The unit cost of producing cars in Germany, in turn, is equal to the wage rate (W) times the number of workers (L) used to produce the cars, divided by the number of cars produced (Q), that is:

Unit Cost = W*L/Q

Given that the cost of producing cars in Portugal is 4.5 German marks, the maximum wage rate in Germany is 2.4 marks. Any wage rate above this rate will eliminate the comparative advantages of the German labor force in the production of cars. The procedure used to estimate the maximum wage rate in Germany is presented below.

Unit Cost = W*L/Q = DM4.5

Solving by the wage rate (W), we have that:

W = [(DM4.5)*80]/150 = DM2.4

Estimation of the minimum wage in Germany consistent with the international terms of trade

Using the information of Table 2.4 again, it is possible to determine what maximum German wage will permit the trading of goods between Germany and Portugal. Germany will import wine from Portugal as long as the unit cost of producing wine in Germany is greater than or equal to the unit cost of producing wine in Portugal (assuming that the wine produced in Portugal is similar in quality to the German wine), that is:

Unit Cost = W*L/Q

Given that the cost of producing wine in Portugal is 1.112 marks, Portugal can remain a viable competitor in wines as long as the German wage rate does not fall below 1.78 marks. Otherwise, any German rate below 1.78 marks will eliminate the comparative advantages of the Portuguese labor force in the production of wine.

The procedure used to estimate the minimum wage rate in Germany is presented below.

Unit Cost = W*L/Q = DM 1.1125

Solving by the wage rate (W), we have that

W = [(DM1.1125)*240]/150 = DM1.78

Relationship between wages and international trade

International trade between Germany and Portugal will continue as long as the wages in Germany remain between the maximum wage of DM2.4 and the minimum of DM1.78. A higher or lower rate will hinder trade between the two nations.

Problems

1. Suppose that money prices of two goods are as follows:

Country	Meat	Cloth	Domestic Terms of Trade
Brazil	Cr30	Cr10	M_____ = C_1_____
Canada	Can$40	Can$20	M_____ = C_1_____

The spot rate is Cr 12/Can$1

What are the limits to international trade between Brazil and Canada?

2. You are given the following information:

	Labor Cost	
Country	Apples	Wheat
Italy	1	10
France	5	20
Productivity Ratio	_____	_____

> **Note:** Labor costs are given in terms of the number of hours of work required to produce one unit of product.

Based on the information provided, which country has a comparative advantage in the production of apples?

3. Pakistan and South Korea have 480 hours of labor each. Labor can be allocated to produce bracelets, cloth, TV's, or rice or a combination of them. In the table below, you have information regarding the number of hours of labor required to produce each one of the commodities.

Information

	Hours of Labor			
	Bracelets	Cloth	TVs	Rice
Pakistan	4	8	5	3
South Korea	6	9	9	4

a) In which commodity does Pakistan have the greatest comparative advantage?

b) In which commodity does South Korea have the highest comparative advantage?

c) If each country is going to specialize in the production of two commodities, indicate in which commodities should Pakistan specialize?

4. Suppose that the prices of capital and labor in Venezuela and Canada are as follows:

Country	Capital	Labor
Venezuela	B4	B20
Canada	Can$10	Can$20

The exchange rate is B4/Can$1.

What is the country with a higher abundance of capital relative to labor?

5. You are given the following information:

Country	Labor	Rice	Cloth	Domestic Terms of Trade	Gains
Burma	25	75	100	_____	_____
Taiwan	25	50	25	_____	_____

a) Does Taiwan have a comparative advantage?

b) What are the domestic terms of trade for each country?

c) If the international terms of trade are between 1.5 units of rice in exchange for one unit of cloth, what are the gains of international trade for Burma and Taiwan?

6. Suppose that money prices of two goods are as follows:

Country	Meat	Cloth
Argentina	P30	P10
Bolivia	BP40	BP40

The exchange rate is BP2.5=P1

a) In what product should Argentina and Bolivia specialize to trade?

b) What are the international terms of trade?

c) What are the gains from international trade for each country?

7. You are given the following information:

Country	Labor Input	Output Wine	Cars	Wages Daily	Total	Unit Cost Wine	Cars
Germany	50	120	60	DM___	DM 90	___	___
France	50	80	20	Ff ___	FF 60	___	___

Domestic Terms of Trade	International Unit Cost	
	Wine	Cars
France _____		
Germany _____	DM ___	___
	DM ___	___

a) Fill in the "daily wages," the "unit cost," and the "domestic terms of trade."

b) In which commodity does Germany have an absolute advantage?

c) In which commodity does Germany have a comparative advantage?

d) What is the range for the possible terms of trade?

e) If the exchange rate is as follows: FF1.5 = DM1, what are the exact terms of international trade?

f) Given the French wage rate and the exchange rate between the two countries, what is the maximum wage in Germany which is consistent with a two-way trade?

g) Given the French wage rate and the exchange rate between the two countries, what is the minimum wage in Germany consistent with a two-way trade?

h) Find out the gains of trade for each country.

8. Assume a world of only two countries, Brazil and Japan, with coffee and steel the only commodities.

Country	Labor Input	Output Coffee	Steel	Wages Daily	Total	Unit Cost Coffee	Steel
Brazil	300	10	60	3	___	___	___
Japan	300	4	40	5	___	___	___

18

Domestic Terms of Trade
Brazil _____
Japan _____

a) Fill in the "total wages," the "unit cost," and the "domestic terms of trade."

b) In which commodity does Brazil have an absolute advantage?

c) In which commodity does Brazil have a comparative advantage?

d) What is the range for the possible terms of trade?

e) If the exchange rate is as follows: Cr0.3 = 1 Yen, what are the exact terms of international trade?

f) Given the Japanese wage rate and the exchange rate between the two countries, what is the maximum wage in Brazil consistent with a two-way trade?

g) Given the Japanese wage rate and the exchange rate between the two countries, what is the minimum wage in Brazil consistent with a two-way trade?

h) Find out the gains of trade for each country.

9. Assume the following information:

Country	Labor Input	Output Tires	Output Shoes	Wages Daily	Wages Total	Unit Cost Tires	Unit Cost Shoes
Venezuela	100	40	120	B ____	360	____	____
Germany	100	120	240	DM ____	480	____	____

Domestic Terms of Trade
Venezuela _____
Germany _____

a) Fill in the "daily wages," the "unit cost," and the "domestic terms of trade."

b) In which commodity does Germany have an absolute advantage?

c) In which commodity does Germany have a comparative advantage?

d) In which commodity does Venezuela have a comparative advantage?

19

e) What is the range for the possible terms of trade?

f) If the exchange rate is as follows: DM0.5 = B1, what are the exact terms of international trade?

g) Find out the gains of trade for each country:

h) Given the wage rate in Venezuela, indicate what is the maximum wage rate in Germany consistent with international trade?

i) Given the wage rate in Venezuela, indicate what is the minimum wage rate in Germany consistent with international trade between the two countries.

10. You are given the following information:

Country	Labor Input	Output Oil	Output Coffee	Wages Daily	Wages Total	Unit Cost Oil	Unit Cost Coffee
Venezuela	10	50	200	B20			
Ecuador	10	10	100	S5			

The spot rate is B1.2 = S1, where the Bolivar is the Venezuelan currency and the Sucre is the currency of Ecuador.

a) Given the Venezuelan wage rate and the exchange rate between the two countries, what is the maximum wage in Ecuador consistent with a two-way trade?

b) Given the Venezuelan wage rate and the exchange rate between the two countries, what is the minimum wage in Ecuador consistent with a two-way trade?

c) What are the gains of trade for each country?

3 Theories of international trade and production

Introduction

In recent years, trade theory has evolved at a very fast pace. The changes have centered upon sophistication in the analysis of demand, the refinement of the production side, the inclusion of the relationship between intra-trade and specialization, and the increasing role of the multinational corporation in the promotion of international trade.

Purpose

The purpose of this technical note is to provide students, business executives, and government officials engaged in international affairs with a frame of reference to analyze international trade and competition.

Consumer's behavior

The basic tools used to analyze the behaviors of consumers in the market place are the *indifference curve* and the *budget constraint*. The indifference curve shows the various combinations of two goods that provide the same level of satisfaction to the consumer. Figure 3.1 shows an indifference curve.

A budget constraint is necessary to determine the desired level of consumption on the indifference curve. The budget line, also presented in Figure 3.1, represents this constraint. It shows the various combinations of two goods that can be purchased with a given level of income at fixed commodity prices. An increase in the level of income shifts the budget constraint outwards, which means that at the new level of income the consumer can purchase a larger amount of the two goods.

The objective of a consumer is to maximize satisfaction subject to a budget constraint. Therefore, the best allocation of income occurs at point 1 where the indifference curve is tangent to the budget constraint. Any other allocation of the budget between goods X and Y will render an inferior level of consumer satisfaction.

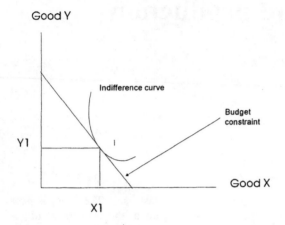

Figure 3.1

The allocation of inputs and production

To study production, we must understand first how the producers allocate inputs. The concept relating output to the factors of production is the **isoquant**, which shows the various combinations of two inputs that produce the same amount of output. A related concept is the **isocost**. In the final decision of how many units of each factor of production to employ, the firm must not only know the technical relationship between inputs and outputs, it must also consider the relative cost of those inputs. The concept that relates the relationship between the budget constraint and the relative cost of the factors of production is the isocost. It shows the various combinations of the factors of production that can be purchased with a given budget. Both the isoquant and the isocost are represented in Figure 3.2.

The best allocation of a budget, given a set of input prices, occurs at the intersection of the isoquant and the isocost line at point 1 in Figure 3.2. Any other combination will render a smaller amount of inputs with the same total cost.

22

Capital

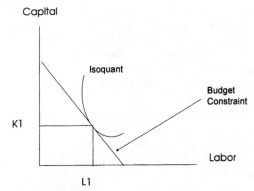

Figure 3.2

The production possibility frontier

Another useful theoretical tool that facilitates the analysis of international trade theory is the concept of the production possibility frontier, depicted in Figure 3.3. It shows all the combination of goods X (shoes) and Y (food) that can be produced with a given amount of inputs. The shape of the function demonstrates **increasing opportunity costs** when the production changes to increase the output of X (shoes) at the expense of the production of good Y (food).

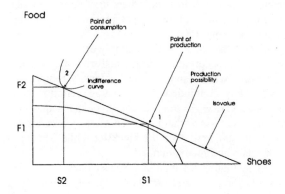

Figure 3.3

The standard trade model

The standard trade model, depicted in Figure 3.3, reflects the confluence of all the theoretical tools developed so far in this chapter. It facilitates the analysis of

23

international trade. For instance, it permits one to study the response of producers and consumers to price variations and technological change, and to explain the role played by trade in the allocation of domestic output and consumption.

In isolation, the availability of resources and the given level of technology limit the choices of domestic production and consumption to the feasible region, which is the area on or below the transformation curve. Given a set of prices, the optimum level of production and consumption in isolation is the combination of shoes (S1) and food (F1), depicted by point 1 in Figure 3.3.

The combination S1-F1, however, does not conform to the nation's preferences for the two goods since there are too many shoes and not enough food. A better mix of consumption of the two goods is the combination S2-F2 at point 2. This point, however, is in the unfeasible region and, as such, is unreachable in a closed economy. To correct this discrepancy between domestic production capabilities and desired consumption, the nation can trade its surplus of shoes (S1-S2) in exchange for food (F2-F1), which is the commodity in short supply. After this exchange, with the same mix of production as before, the nation has reached a higher level of consumption, and enjoys a superior level of satisfaction.

Other theories of international trade

Common sense suggests that different goods require different proportions of the various factors of production. Some goods are intensive in labor while others are either capital or land intensive.

Nature has endowed different countries with varying amounts of factors of production. While some countries are rich in land, others may be rich in labor or capital. This difference in the allocation of factors of production gives rise to differences in input prices between countries. In a nation rich in land, the price of this input is cheaper as compared to a country in short supply of it.

Two European economists, Hecksler and Ohlin, analyzed the relationship between a country's resource endowment and the input intensity required in the production of certain goods. They concluded that a nation benefits from the abundance of an input when it specializes in the production and subsequent export of commodities that require intensive use of that input. This theory is referred to as the "Modern Theory of International Trade" or the Hecksler-Ohlin Theory (H-O Theory) after the two economists who first expounded it.[1]

The H-O Theory depicted in Figure 3.4 includes isocost lines for the United States and China, and isoquants for shoes and bread. The visual inspection of the isocost curves reveals that capital is abundantly relative to labor in the US, whereas labor is abundantly relative to capital in China. This is explained by the fact that given a budget, a firm buys more capital than labor in the US.

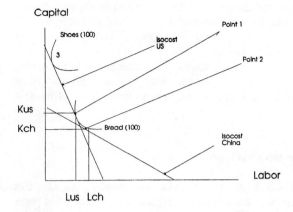

Figure 3.4

Given the relative endowments of labor and capital and a set of input prices, the US and China are equally efficient in the production of bread. Let us say that with the same budget of $100, they can produce the same 100 units of bread, even though the mix of inputs for production is different. In the US, bread is produced with a capital-intensive method, whereas China uses a more labor-intensive technique.

Its rich endowment of capital also permits the US to produce a certain amount of shoes with the same efficiency that it produces bread since the total cost of producing both commodities is the same. China, however, is in a weaker position to produce shoes. To produce the same amount of units as the US, China would need a larger budget. Overall, the United States and China are equally efficient in the production of bread, but the US is more efficient in producing shoes.

To make trade profitable, the countries have to specialize. Given their relative endowments of inputs, the US should specialize in the production and export of the capital-intensive good, shoes, while China should specialize in the production and export of the labor intensive good, bread.

Initially, the H-O Theory was quite popular. One of its benefits was that it provided a fairly simple set of readily testable predictions. Later, however, it fell into disrepute after it failed to hold empirically.[2] The Russian-born economist Wassily Leontieff used input-output tables for US patterns of trade that refuted this theory. The findings of his paper were labeled later as the "paradox of Leontieff."

Economies of scale and the role of demand-side factors in trade

The Hecksler-Ohlin Theory does not address the role of demand-side factors to determine trade. Stefan Linder, a former student of Ohlin, incorporated two improvements: affluence and the refinement of demand. He argued that factor endowment only plays a role in determining commodity trading, but is not relevant

25

in explaining the trade of manufactured goods which, in his opinion, was more a function of demand components. Linder presented as supporting evidence the fact that trading of manufactured goods is between countries with similar factor endowments and identical levels of income.

A prediction of Linder's model is that countries with similar levels of income per capita will exchange different varieties of the same product. This pattern of trade is known as **intra-trade**, which has become the dominant form of modern trade.

Economies of scale and international trade

Later, the concept of increasing economies of scale was incorporated into this model to explain new patterns of trade. In many industries, production takes place under conditions of increasing economies of scale (decreasing average cost). To develop a new product, firms often incur certain very large fixed costs, such as research and development, new plant and equipment, and so on. An important feature of a fixed cost is that its average cost falls with the expansion of output. This explains why only local firms operating in a highly protected industry produce a variety of differentiated products to satisfy the local taste. However, a multinational firm finds it unprofitable to produce many variations of one product because it prevents the firm from obtaining economies of scale. Rather than expanding the product offering, multinationals specialize in satisfying a portion of the local and world demand, while importing other varieties to please the increasing refinement of the local demand.

This approach permits the multinational firm to remain highly competitive by offering the consumers a larger variety of items at a lower price. This process of production and distribution is illustrated in Figure 3.5. The country's production possibility frontier, also known as the transformation curve, is depicted as a convex curve to reflect increasing returns to scale.

In a pre-trade situation, a ray represents domestic prices from the origin to point A. Initially, the firm in this country is producing a combination of jeeps and trucks. The opening of trade will force the firm to specialize by moving along the curve to either point B or C. If a firm in another country can produce trucks cheaper than this firm, the firm depicted in Figure 3.5 can still be competitive if it specializes in the production and export of jeeps. Production of trucks at home will cease, and the resources will be re-deployed in the production of jeeps. At the end of this process, jeeps and trucks can be produced in separate locations with greater economies of scale. Therefore, the price of the differentiated products will be below pre-trade levels.

Jeeps

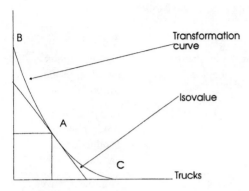

B

Transformation
curve

Isovalue

A

C

Trucks

Figure 3.5

The life cycle model

The deficiencies of Linder's theory became apparent with the emergence of new trade issues. Essentially it was a static theory built under the assumption that all countries have equal access to the same body of technological knowledge. Therefore, under its framework, technological changes have no relevance in explaining trade.

To amend Linder's approach, Raymond Vernon developed the Product Life Cycle Theory of trade in 1966, summarized in Chart 1. Vernon's model incorporates technological change and product innovation as engines of international trade. Also, it provides a rationale to explain the "paradox of Leontieff" and the pattern of US trade that eluded the H-O model.

Vernon casts his theory in terms of a product's life cycle. In the initial stage, latent but weaker demand for US products in other nations is satisfied through exports. At a later stage of the life cycle, the innovating firm establishes production facilities overseas to reduce shipping costs and to solidify localized preferences. In the latest stage of the life cycle, when demand in the US is vanishing, the firms cut production at home. To satisfy the residual US demand, imports take place.

One serious limitation of Vernon's approach is that it predicts a rather lopsided flow of trade from the advanced to the developing nations. This model does not, however, fit modern patterns of trade.

27

Chart 1
Phases of the Life Cycle Model

	Early	Growth	Mature
Demand Structure	Nature of demand is not understood	Competition begins	Competition is based on product differentiation
Production	Low capital intensity and changing production techniques	Mass production	Labor skills are not important. Production is capital-intensive
Industry	Small number of firms (Oligopoly)	Relatively large number of firms. Many casualties and mergers	Number of firms large but steadily declining
Implications			
Production	All in the US	Starts in other countries	Outside of the US
International Trade	US exports	Mixed	US imports

Imperfect competition and international trade theories

All the models described up to this point rely on the assumption of perfect competition. Recently, new models have begun to explain international trade assuming imperfect competition.

Models of trade based on imperfect competition began to converge on the specialized field of economics known as "industrial organization," which traditionally focused on national rather than international markets. However, as more adaptations were made to this field to fit the needs of international trade, a new theoretical synergy was created. Eventually, both areas shared methodologies and merged to form the **strategic trade theory**.

It was noted, in the early stages of the Life Cycle model, that sellers of differentiated products enjoy some degree of monopoly power, substantial economies of scale, and a price strategy aimed at maintaining the monopoly power achieved through technological or product innovation. All of these factors, in turn, contribute to the creation of imperfect market structures characterized by monopolistic competition, monopoly pricing, and collusive behavior between firms and their host governments aimed at international market dominance. This approach has provided fertile ground for high quality research, which has inspired the exploration of new international trade issues. The introduction of game theory was especially useful because it gave the new trade theory a great deal of flexibility. With some minor changes in assumptions, almost any behavioral outcome can now be generated. This advantage is also its greatest weakness because a theory that attempts to explain everything may not be able to deliver a coherent set of policy recommendations.

Intra-trade and strategic trade policy

One of the most important trends in postwar trade, especially in manufacturing, has been the growth of intra-trade. This has been defined as the simultaneous export and import of products belonging to the same industry. However, much of what is taught and written about international trade is still couched in terms of inter-industry specialization. To correct this bias, the remaining portion of this technical note will be directed toward developing a model to explain intra-trade.

Measurement of intra-trade

In a certain nation called "NAFTA" there are two industries. One is dedicated to producing cloth and the other to producing cars. The car industry is capable of producing either trucks or jeeps, or a combination of both. To achieve economies of scale in the production of automobiles, the management of NAFTA's auto industry decides to produce and export trucks and import jeeps from their trading partner, EC. EC has wine and auto industries. EC's auto industry can produce trucks or jeeps. However, in imitation of its competitor, the management of the auto industry in EC also decides to specialize in order to achieve economies of scale. They decide to produce and export only jeeps and import trucks from NAFTA. The trade flows of NAFTA and EC, which are described in Table 3.1, have an inter-trade and an intra-trade component. Inter-trade is determined by the exchange of cloth for wine. Intra-trade is conditioned by the exchange of trucks for jeeps. (Note: Intra-trade is the trade between similar but slightly differentiated products.)

Table 3.1
The trade balance of NAFTA

	Cloth	Trucks	Wine	Jeeps
Imports			500	1800
Exports	580	1620		

Inter-trade (IT) is measured as the sum of a nation's trade imbalance measured in absolute terms over the sum of the nation's trade flows.

$$IT = \sum |X\text{'s} - M\text{'s}|/(X\text{'s} + M\text{'s});$$

29

where Σ stands for the sum of X minus M, X stands for exports, and M stands for imports. The straight brackets denote that the sign of the trade balance is ignored. That is, only the absolute values are considered.

Intra-trade is measured as a residual trade or as the opposite of inter-industry trade. Therefore, it is measured as one minus inter-industry trade. An illustration of the application of these concepts is presented below.

$$\text{Inter-trade index (IT)} = \Sigma|Xi - Mi|/(X + M)$$

$$= \{\Sigma|(0-500) + (580-0) +(1620-1800)|/(2200+ 2300)\}$$

$$= \{ |500+580+180)|/4500 \} = (1260/4500) = \mathbf{0.28}$$

Since intra-trade (ITT) is the opposite of inter-industry trade then it is estimated as follows:

$$\text{ITT} = 1 - \Sigma|Xi - Mi|/(X+ M) = 1 - 0.28 = \mathbf{0.72}$$

To distinguish their products in the market, companies can resort to horizontal, vertical, and/or technological differentiation. These techniques are based on one or several dimensions of quality such as durability, performance, reliability, design, service, ease of use, and conformance.[3]

Horizontal differentiation occurs when a family of products share a set of basic "core" attributes that are combined in different proportions. For instance, tobacco can be used to produce cigarettes and cigars. Leather can be utilized to produce shoes or jackets. A certain type of fabric can be employed in the production of pants and jackets. This technique of distinguishing products, to a certain extent, is present in practically all industries, though it is more prevalent in industries like the ones mentioned above. Such differentiation is usually the firms' response to consumers' taste sophistication and rising levels of income. It may also be the result of the desire of the producers to increase their market share through product differentiation.

Vertical differentiation occurs where the products differ in quality from one another. For example, a Mercedes Benz is known to be a superior quality car to many other cars. Vertical differentiation is the result of competition and is aimed at allowing the consumer to rank products according to their quality. This form of product differentiation is very dominant in the automobile and watch industries.

Technological differentiation refers to product innovation resulting from technological change. This is prevalent in pharmaceutical and electronic industries where product innovation has moved at a very accelerated pace in recent years.

The model based on product differentiation predicts that the firms whose trade strategy is based on quality improvements will specialize in the exports of vertically differentiated products. The rationalization is that quality improvements require large expenditures. If these costs are spread over a large output, the unit cost will fall sharply. This will favor a geographically concentrated production that will be further supported by the fact that diversity of consumers' preference is not an overriding market concern in these industries. A second prediction of this model is that firms seeking product innovation will likely serve their foreign markets through exports rather than by transferring production facilities abroad.

A variation of this theme is the existence of economies of scale in science-based industries. It appears that such industries, which are typified by high levels of research and development expenditures relative to turnover, have to incur these costs before a product is actually produced and marketed. In these activities, firms recuperate research and development expenditures only years later, if the new product is a market success. However, such products may have a short life. In the pharmaceutical industry, for example, new patented products normally have market lives of only six to ten years. This is a very short time to recuperate large sums of research and development and earn a market return on these expenditures. An innovative firm must therefore sell as much as possible, as quickly as possible, and at the highest possible price that the market can bear. These considerations lead to the prediction that innovative firms will specialize in the worldwide production of a small range of products. Since the main cost is research and development, there are incentives for a fast paced, worldwide production and distribution system, rather than a centralized system of production.

Market structure and international trade

Oligopoly is a market structure characterized by the existence of market concentration in the hands of a reduced number of firms, each of which controls a significant share of the market. In this market, each firm has to take into consideration the reaction of its competitors to the firm's output, price, and profit strategies. Firms wanting to expand their market share by cutting prices are reluctant to implement this strategy in an oligopoly setting because they are afraid of retaliation. Oligopolistic firms are also averse to expanding in the domestic market because they are afraid of upsetting the existing market equilibrium. They know that a disturbance of this nature may result in "cutthroat" competition. As a result of these two aspects of oligopolistic competition, firms avoid open price competition and domestic market expansions. Rather, they seek improvements in market share through product differentiation or through expanding into foreign markets via exports.

Exporting confronts the firm with two different market structures: oligopolistic competition at home, and free or monopolistic competition in the world market. At home, the domestic demand is downward sloping while abroad the slope is perfectly or quasi-perfectly elastic.

To maximize profits in this context, the firm has to equate world marginal revenue (Pw) to its domestic marginal cost. This occurs at point 1 in Figure 3.6. The optimal allocation of output between the domestic and foreign markets occurs when the firm sells Qd at the price Pd at home (see point 2 of Figure 3.6), and the rest (Qt – Qd) in the foreign market at the price Pw. This allocation, while optimal from the micro perspective of the firm, is in violation of World Trade Organization rules. It leads to dumping because the price charged on sales abroad (Pw) is below the domestic price (Pd).

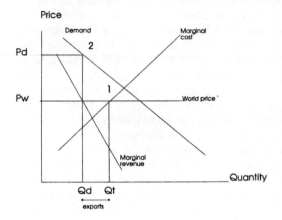

Pd = domestic price
Pw = world price
Qd = domestic demand
Qt = total demand
Qt – Qd = exports at world price, Pw

Figure 3.6

The best strategy for a firm operating with high fixed costs in an industry characterized by oligopolistic competition is to remain passive. Otherwise, expansion confronts it with choosing between cutthroat competition and anti-dumping duties. However, if expansion is a must, the model presented suggests that the manager of the oligopolistic firm choose dumping over cutthroat competition. This prediction conforms to reality and helps to explain the frequent occurrence of dumping among oligopolistic firms. It also explains the rise in dumping cases worldwide as being a direct consequence of the oligopolization of international trade and competition.[4]

Notes

1 Ohlin, Bertil, *Interregional and International Trade*, Cambridge, Harvard University Press, 1933.

2 Leontieff, W., "Domestic Production and Foreign Trade: The American Capital Position Re-examined," *Proceedings of the American Philosophical Society*, 97, 1953, pp. 331-349.

3 The degree of tolerance towards defectiveness as a dimension of quality was introduced by Wal-Mart as a cost savings device. The retailer reasoned that selling a product with a high defective rate is equivalent to selling a product with a higher operating cost.

4 According to the rules of the World Trade Organization, dumping occurs when the price of exports is less than the domestic price.

Problems

1. You are given the following information:

Product	Exports US$	Imports US$
Primary products	180	620
Manufactures	1000	600

What are the intra-industrial trade shares for exports and imports?

2. Consider the international trade information provided below:

	Exports of Spain to		Imports of Spain from	
	Canada	Mexico	Canada	Mexico
Primary products	75	50	60	55
Manufactures	70	65	150	20

What is the index of intra trade (ITT)?

3. Using the information provided in the graph, answer the following questions:

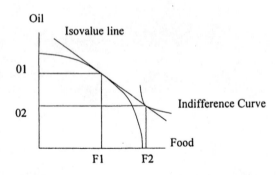

a. The domestic production of food and oil is represented by what coordinate?
b. The domestic consumption of food and oil is represented by what coordinate?
c. The amount of imports and exports of food and oil are represented by what coordinates?

4 The instruments of trade policy

Introduction

During the decade of the 1980s and the beginning of the 1990s, the world economy began to experience a drastic transformation that is expected to continue over the next century. Some trade barriers are being dismantled, while others—new and subtler—are being raised. Trading blocks are disintegrating in an unexpected way while new ones are being constructed. National systems, like China, are evolving from centrally planned economies into centrally directed market economies. Governments worldwide are changing from guardians of full employment and domestic economic stability to social reformers and advocates of trade liberalization. Multinational corporations are downsizing and restructuring. The nature of trade flows has shifted from commodities to manufactured goods, and the direction has shifted from North America-Europe to North America-Asia.

These changes in the world environment have prompted a refocusing on international trade theory and a reevaluation of the instruments used to fine-tune trade flows.

Purpose

This note is aimed at providing students of international business, managers, and government officials engaged in global affairs with the basic tools required to analyze the effect of trade policies on the well being of industrial activity.

The instruments of trade policy

Commercial policy, foreign direct investment incentive and restraints, foreign aid, and subsidies embody most of the instruments used by governments to promote balance of payment surpluses.

Commercial policies encompass tariffs, non-tariff trade barriers, and export promotion programs. Foreign direct investment policy tools include tax incentives designed to entice multinationals to transfer manufacturing facilities to territories under the control of the governments granting the fiscal stimulus. Foreign aid policies embrace private and public grants and loans provided by wealthy institutions to needy parties suffering from unusual hardship. A Subsidy is an incentive granted by government, usually in the form of cash or a tax break, to local producers to entice them to elevate their levels of production and or exports.

Tariffs

A tariff is a tax imposed by federal governments on physical good imports when they enter into the country. Tariffs may be imposed as ad-valorem, specific, or as a combination of the two.

An *ad-valorem* duty is imposed in terms of a percentage of the value of the imported good. These duties are widely used to control the flow of manufactured goods, which are very diverse in terms of quality and standardization.

A *specific* duty is imposed as a fixed amount of money per one unit of imports. This characteristic makes this surcharge very appropriate to control the flow of imports of fairly standardized products such as commodities and staple products.

Compound duties are a combination of an ad-valorem and specific duties. They are commonly applied to imports containing raw materials that are on the list of goods and services subject to a tariff under existing trade laws. The specific portion of the duty—known as the compensatory duty—is applied to protect the domestic production of raw materials, while the ad-valorem portion is used to protect the domestic industry processing raw materials. For instance, the US government imposes compound duties on the imports of textiles containing wool. The specific portion of the tariff is imposed to insulate the domestic wool producers against foreign competition, while the ad-valorem apportionment is aimed at protecting the clothing industry.

Reasons for tariffs

A country may want to impose a tariff to limit trade imports, to increase the treasury's revenues, or to improve the country's terms of trade. Normally, however, tariffs are imposed mostly to limit imports.

Tariffs fulfill their revenue role only when the price elasticity of the demand for imports is large—greater than one. Otherwise, the change in the tariff may end up lowering the revenues of the government imposing it. A tariff improves the well being of a country only when the nation imposing the tariff is large relative to the world economy—and when the tariff does not invite retaliation. If these two conditions are met, the expected benefit of the tariff may materialize.

To analyze the effects of a duty, it is necessary to understand how the laws of supply and demand operate in open and closed economy settings.

36

Supply and demand in a closed economy

One way to analyze the effect of a tariff on the welfare of different economic agents is by departing from a situation of market equilibrium in a close economy. A market is deemed to be in equilibrium when, at a given price level, the demand and supply are equal. A situation of equilibrium is depicted both in Figure 4.1 and by expression (c).

a) $Qs = \alpha + \beta Pd$

b) $Qd = \delta + \gamma Pd$

c) $Qs = Qd$

Qs and Qd are supply and demand, α and δ are the intercepts —which do not have a very important economic meaning. And β and γ are the slopes of supply and demand respectively. These last two symbols measure the simultaneous response of supply and demand to variations in the price level.

The application of these concepts is illustrated as follows.

1) Supply: $Qs = 10 + 0.12Pd$;

2) Demand: $Qd = 40 - 0.1Pd$;

3) Equilibrium condition: $Qd = Qs$

Using (1) and (2) in (3), solving by the domestic price level (Pd), and using the solution for Pd in either (1) or (2), we have that the equilibrium price is $136.36. At this price, supply and demand clear the market at 26 units. This numerical solution is also represented in Figure 4.1.

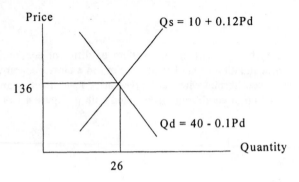

Figure 4.1

Supply and demand in an open economy

In an open economy the determination of market equilibrium is a more complex task since this is shaped by domestic and foreign supply and demand functions. To begin with, the price is set by both the world supply and demand functions and is given to the producers who are deemed under this setting to be price-takers.

To illustrate these concepts consider the closed economy depicted in Figure 4.1, to be fully open. Assuming a world price of $110 it is possible to estimate the quantities of local supply (which includes the offer of domestic and foreign producers) demand, and excess demand or domestic exporting surpluses.

Open Economy Scenario	Applying World Price	Solution
World price = Pw = $110		
Domestic supply = Qs = 10—0.12Pd	Qs = 10 + 0.12*110	23.2
Local demand = Qd = 40 - 0.1Pd	Qd = 40 – 0.1*110	29.0
Short supply = imports	Qs - Qd	-5.8

At the world price of $110, domestic producers are willing to supply only 23 units (rounded) of output. At this same price, consumers demand 29 units. The discrepancy between supply and demand results in a shortage of 6 units (rounded) satisfied by imports. This numerical solution is depicted in Figure 4.2.

Welfare effects of free trade

Comparing Figures 4.1 and 4.2, it can be conclude that under free trade, the consumers are better off. They may be able to consume a larger quantity of goods at a lower price. In contrast, the local producers are worse off. They sell a lesser amount of goods at a lower price.

The consequences of a tariff

In response to the hardship imposed on the producers by free trade, local management may file for protection. One possible avenue is to petition for an ad-valorem tariff.

If the drive for protectionism succeeds with the imposition of a 10 percent ad-valorem tariff on imports, then the domestic price of the relevant item increases from $110 to $121. This change in price is reflected in Figure 4.2, with an upward shift in the world price.

This price move motivates local producers to expand output, while encouraging domestic consumers to buy less of the taxed item. The net effect of this interplay of forces is an increase in local supply from 23 to 24 units (rounded), and a reduction of demand from 29 to 28 units (rounded). This change in price does not close the existing gap between supply and demand because, under the tariff scenario, there is still a local shortage of goods that is satisfied with imports, which drops from 6 to 4 units (rounded). The shaded area in Figure 4.2 shows the tariff revenue and the white and dark triangles show the producers and consumers distortion losses. A summary of the effect of the tariff on price and quantities is described in Chart 1.

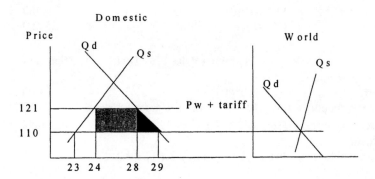

Figure 4.2

Chart 1

Scenario

World price = Pw = 110

Tariff = 10 percent

	Applying Price Plus Tariff	Solution
Domestic price = Pd = Pw*(1+ tariff)	Pd =110*(1.1)	121.0
Domestic supply = Qs = 10—0.12Pd	Qs = 10—0.12*121	24.5
Domestic demand = Qd = 40 - 0.1Pd	Qd = 40 - 0.1*121	27.9
Short supply = imports	Qs - Qd	-3.4

Welfare consequences of the ad-valorem tariff

The imposition of the tariff benefits the producers who petitioned for it ($407.77) and the government who imposed it ($37.18). These benefits are at the expense of a loss in consumer surplus ($312.95). Overall, however, the nation's welfare has improved since the gains of both the producers and the government is high enough to compensate the losers.

Chart 2

PRODUCERS

Scenario	Applying World Price	Solution
World price	Pw = 110	110.0
Domestic supply	Qs = 10 + 0.12*110	23.2
Gross revenue	GR = (Pw * Qs)	2,552.0
Production distortion loss	PDL =(ΔPw * ΔQs)/2	0.0
Net revenue	GR – PDL	2,552.0

	Applying Price Plus Tariff	Solution
World price plus tariff	Pd = 110*(1.1)	121.00
Domestic supply	Qs = 10—0.12*121	24.52
Gross revenue	GR = (Pd * Qs)	2,966.92
Production distortion loss	PDL =(ΔPd * ΔQs)/2 = (11 * 1.3)/2	7.15
Net revenue	GR – PDL	2,959.77
Net welfare gain	After net revenues—before net revenues	407.77

40

CONSUMERS

	Comparative Demand Conditions	Solution	
World price	Pw = 110	110.0	
Domestic demand under free trade	Qd = 40 - 0.1*110	29.0	
Price plus tariff	Pd = 110*(1.1)	121.0	
Domestic demand under tariff	Qd = 40 - 0.1*121	27.9	
Consumption distortion loss from tariff	CDL = (ΔP * ΔQd)/2 = (11*-1.1)/2	6.1	
Other loss in consumer surplus	OLCS = (ΔP * Qd under tariff) = (11*27.9)	306.9	
Total loss in consumer surplus	CDL + OLCS		-312.95
GOVERNMENT	GG = (imports after tariff) * tariff = (27.9 - 24.52)*11 =		37.18
NATION	(Net Producer Gain - Net Consumer Loss + Net Government Gain)		132.00

In the case previously described, the nation imposing the tariff benefits from it. However, the world as a whole is worse off. The systemic losses are represented by the production and consumption distortion losses. The **production distortion loss ($7.15)** is the marginal expense that is incurred by the world when the production shifts from the more to the less cost-effective producer. This marginal expense would not have occurred if the additional unit of output had been manufactured and supplied by the relatively more efficient producer. No one gains this loss of benefits. Therefore, it is a deadweight loss.

On the demand side, the $11 increase in price caused by the tariff persuades the consumer to reduce their purchases from 29 to 27.9 units. The change in price times the reduction in demand is a loss of consumer surplus ($6.1) or **consumption distortion loss** that is gained by no one. As such, it constitutes another deadweight loss for the world. The production distortion loss is the white triangle on the right hand side of the supply function in Figure 4.2. The consumer distortion loss is the dark triangle to the left of the demand function.

The effective rate of protection of a tariff

The degree of protection provided by a tariff depends on the tariff's effective rate of protection, and is measured by the percentage change in value added traced to the imposition of the tariff.

41

Effective rate of protection = {(VAa -VAb)/VAb}*100.

VAa is value added after the tariff and VAb is value added before the tariff.

Value added is the contribution of human beings to the final value of a product or service, and is estimated by taking away the cost of inputs from the final price of the product. The effective rate of protection depends on how the tariff is applied. Tariffs applied on imports of raw materials decrease the rate of protection, whereas the same application to a final product may increase it.[1]

The economic effect of a quota

As nations have progressively cut tariffs under the auspices the World Trade Organization, non-tariff trade barriers have become more prominent. The most visible forms of non-trade barriers are quantitative restrictions usually known as quotas. Quotas impose absolute limitations on international trade and inhibit market responses. This last characteristic turns quotas into a very effective weapon for restraining world trade when applied.

Quotas are used mainly to protect domestic industry or to allow a country in a serious economic crisis to adjust quickly to its balance of payment problems. For instance, at the height of the debt crisis in 1982, Mexico imposed severe cuts on imports by implementing a quota program.

Quantity restrictions may be unilateral, bilateral, or multilateral. Unilateral quotas are usually imposed on the exports of a nation by another country without prior consultation or negotiation with the trading partner. Accordingly, they invite retaliation. Bilateral or multilateral quotas are negotiated trade restrictions agreements between an importing country and its main suppliers. Voluntary export restraints (VER) belong to this type of quota.

Often, quotas are mixed with tariffs to afford a wider range of protection to local industries. A tariff-quota is a regulation that permits the imports of a product at a given rate of duty (tariff). Any additional quantity may be forbidden. They may be allowed only under a higher tariff. This restriction combines the features of both quotas and tariffs.

The economic consequences of a quota are represented in Figure 4.3 and by the relationship described in Chart 3.

The imposition of a quota limits the amount of imports and shifts the domestic supply downward. In comparison to free trade, the quota raises the price from $110 to $118. In response to the price variation, domestic supply is raised from 23 to 24 units, while demand is reduced from 29 to 28 units. Free trade leads to an excess demand of 6 units (29-23). The quota increases the price from 110 to 118. This lowers demand, but excess demand of 4 units still exists (28-24). These changes are illustrated in Figure 4.3.

42

Chart 3

	Scenario	Solution in equilibrium	Result
Quota	4 units		
Local supply	Qs = (10 + 0.12Pd)	Qs = 10 + 0.12*118	24
Total supply = quota plus local supply	Qs = 4 + (10 + 0.12Pd)	Qs = 4 + (10 0.12*118.18)	28
Demand	Qd = 40 - 0.1Pd	Qd = 40 – 0.1*118.18	28
Equilibrium condition	Qs = Qd		
Price in equilibrium	Pd =		
	(40 - 14)/(0.12 +0.1)	Pd =26/(0.22)	118

The welfare effect of a quota

The imposition of a quota has similar effects to a tariff. It reduces the consumer surplus and raises the revenue of local producers. However, in contrast to the tariff, the price benefits of the policy do not stay with the local government. Rather, they serve to promote the well being of the foreign producers who reap this benefit. The imposition of the quota helps overseas producers to export a lesser amount of goods at a higher price. The quota rent is the dark box in Figure 4.3.

This contumacious aspect of the quota is known as **quota rent,** which is measured by the variation in the price prompted by the quota multiplied by the numerical value of the quota. For instance, in the example previously discussed, the quota rent is equal to \$32.[2]

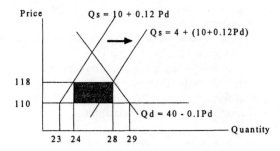

Figure 4.3

Local content

A local content rule is another form of quantitative restriction that permits a subsidiary of a multinational corporation to import, free of duty, parts and components in some specified proportion to purchases from domestic producers. Local content rules require that the subsidiary purchase a specified minimum proportion of their parts from domestic firms. Subsidiaries satisfying this requirement are granted a special rate of duty on their imports of components. This local government concession is normally a zero tariff. To assure that this agreement is not violated, governments impose heavy penalties on a subsidiary's imports if local content rules are violated.

Another way to specify local content rules is to set them in terms of volume rather than value. The final shape of the specification will depend largely on the nature of the products involved. If the final good and the parts and components are homogenous, a volume scheme is more likely to be used. However, if the products involved are heterogeneous, a value-based formula is deemed more appropriate from the government perspective.

Subsidies

Similarly to quotas, subsidies are strictly forbidden by the World Trade Organization. Nevertheless, like quotas, their use is widespread, particularly in markets for agricultural products, transfer of technology, acquisition of capital goods, and export financing.[3] Subsidies consist of financial packages provided to companies by local governments to promote a change in output. For example, local governments in emerging markets typically lack foreign exchange. To gain foreign exchange, they may provide subsidies to companies that will increase their exports. In the US and Japan, by contrast, agricultural subsidies are given to decrease output in order to preserve desired product prices.

To illustrate the effects of subsidization, an export subsidy on shoes is shown in Figure 4.4. Initially, the economy is closed. In this situation, the domestic price is Pd and demand is Q1. In world markets, the price of shoes is Pw, which is higher than the price clearing the domestic market (Pd). This discrepancy persuades the local producers to export all of their output.

Exports cause a local shortage of shoes that eventually raises the domestic price of shoes to Pw. At the export price, the firm supplies Q3. From this total, Q2 is the portion of output allocated to the domestic market. The remaining (Q3-Q2), are exports. This arrangement warrants internal and external equilibrium. However, an existing shortfall of foreign exchange coaxes the government to grant subsidies to exporting firms. Therefore, the shoe manufacturer is offered a subsidy of S for each pair of shoe exports.

The subsidy introduces a disturbance that alters the newly reached market equilibrium. In the eyes of the exporter, the price of exports is (Pw+S), even though it is only Pw in the market. This new *price* sways the exporting firm to expand output to Q4 and exports to (Q4 – Q2). Under this new arrangement, the gross revenue of the firm is broken down into three parts:

domestic sales = Pw*Q2;
export revenues = Pw*(Q4 – Q2); and
subsidies = S*(Q4 – Q2).

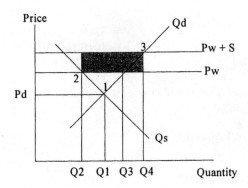

Figure 4.4

Notes

1   The appendix contains a detailed description of the different aspects of a tariff's rate of protection under different scenarios.
2   Quota rent = (Pq - Pw)*Import Quota = (118-110)*4 = 32.
3   Subsidies to domestic producers are permitted under the World Trade Organization rules, provided that the WTO is notified if the subsidies affect international trade.

Appendix

Comparative analysis of the economic effect of different trade policy instruments

Closed economy
* Quantity supplied   = 10+0.12Pd
* Quantity   = 40-0.1Pd
* Equilibrium condition: Qs = Qd
* Domestic price in equilibrium (Pd) = $136
* Quantity in equilibrium (Qd)   = 26

Open economy
* World price   = $110
* Quantity supplied   = 10+0.12(110)
* Quantity demanded   = 40-0.1(110)
* Quantity supplied at the world price = 23
* Domestic demanded at the world price = 29
* Excess demand (imports)   = 6

Ad-valorem tariff of 10percent
* World price   = $110
* Tariff   = 0.1 = 10percent
* Domestic price after the tariff   = $121
* Quantity demanded   = 40-0.1(121)
* Quantity demanded   = 28
* Quantity supplied   = 10+0.12(121)
* Quantity supplied   = 24
* Excess demand (imports)   = 4

Quota of 4 units
* Quantity supplied   = 10+0.12Pd
* Quantity supplied plus quota   = 4+(10+0.12Pd)
* Quantity demanded   = 40-0.1Pd
* Equilibrium condition: Qs = Qd
* Domestic price in equilibrium (Pd) = $118
* Quantity supplied under the quota = 28
* Quantity demanded under the quota = 28
* Domestic supply   = 24
* Excess demand (imports)   = 4

Effective rate of protection of a tariff imposed on manufactured products
Tariff is imposed on final good

Leather imports	$80.00
Domestic price of shoes	$100.00
Value added before the tariff	$20.00 (i.e., 100-80)
Tariff	10percent on imports of shoes
Price of the shoe after the tariff	$110.00
Value added after the tariff	$30.00 (i.e., 110-80)

Effective rate of protection (ERP)
ERP = (Value added after the tariff—value added before the tariff)/value
added before the tariff
ERP = (30-20)/20 = 10/20 = 0.5 = 50percent
The 10percent tariff increases the value added on shoes by 50percent.

Effective rate of protection of a tariff imposed on raw material imports
Tariff is imposed on imports of raw materials

Imported cotton	$80.00
Price of a suit	$100.00
Value added before the tariff	$20.00 (i.e., 100-80)
Tariff	10 percent on imported raw materials
Price of the suit after the tariff	$100.00
Value added after the tariff	$12.00 (i.e., 100-88)

ERP = (12-20)/20 = -8/20 = - 0.4 = -40percent
The 10 percent tariff on raw material or part imports reduces the value
added of the suit industry by 40percent.

Effective rate of protection of a tariff on manufactured products requiring
domestic and foreign raw materials

Tariff is imposed on final goods imports	
Domestic components	$40
Imported cotton	$80.00
Price of a suit	$140.00
Value added before the tariff	$20.00 (i.e., 140-120)
Tariff	10 percent on imported suits
Price of the suit after the tariff	$154.00 (i.e., 140-14)
Value added after the tariff	$34.00 (i.e., 154-120)

ERP = (34-20)/20 = 14/20 = 0.7 = 70 percent
The tariff on a product using domestic components provides a larger
degree of protection (70percent) than the tariff applied to a manufactured
product not using domestic parts or components (50percent effective rate
of protection).

Problems

1. Briefly explain the meaning of the terms *production distortion loss, consumption distortion loss*, and *quota rent*.

2. Nicaragua's domestic supply and demand are as follows:
   $$S = 20 + 2.8P \qquad D = 200 - 4P$$

   a. What is the price, supply, and demand in a closed economy equilibrium?

   b. What is the value of domestic supply and demand, and imports or exports, if the world price is $30?

   c. What is the value of domestic supply and demand, and imports or exports, if the world price is $20?

   d. Departing from the initial situation of free trade at a world price of $20, what is the value of domestic supply and demand, and imports or exports, if the government imposes a specific tariff of $2?

   e. What is the numerical value of the consumption distortion loss?

   f. What is the numerical value of the production distortion loss?

3. Uruguay, a small country, can import shoes at a world price of $10 per unit. The domestic supply and demand curves are as follows:
   $$S = 50 + 5P \qquad D = 400 - 10P$$

   a. If Uruguay imposes a $5 tariff on the imports of shoes, what is the level of domestic supply, demand, price, and the revenue of the domestic producers and the government?

   b. If Uruguay imposes a quota that limits imports to 100 pairs of shoes, what is the effect of the quota on domestic supply, demand, price, and the revenue of local producers and the government?

4. A small country can import a good at a world price of $16 per unit. The domestic supply and demand curves are as follows:
   $$S = 34 + 8P \qquad D = 340 - 9P$$

   Please round your figures.

   a. Find the price and quantity in equilibrium in the absence of international trade: Price = _____ ; Quantity = _____

48

b. Find the price and quantity in equilibrium if international trade is allowed: Price = _____ ; Quantity = _____

c. Calculate the effect of a $5 subsidy on the domestic price and quantity, assuming an international price of $16:
   Price = _____ ; Quantity = _____

   Note: The supply function shifts as a result of the subsidy, i.e. shifts from
   $S = 34 + 8P$ *to* $S = 74 + 8P$

5. A small country can import a good at a world price of 16 per unit. The domestic supply and demand curves are as follows:
   $$S = 34 + 8P \qquad D = 340 - 9P$$

   a. Indicate the price and quantities in equilibrium with free international trade: Price = _____ ; Quantity = _____

   b. Indicate the price and quantities in equilibrium if the country imposes a quota that limits imports to 20 units.

   c. Indicate the quota rent if the country imposes an import quota that limits imports to 20 units.

6. A small country can import a good at a world price of $16. The domestic supply and demand curves are as follows:
   $$S = 34 + 8P \qquad D = 340 - 9P$$

   a. Indicate the amount of imports under conditions of free trade.
      Quantity of imports = _____

   b. Indicate the price and quantities in equilibrium if the country imposes an ad-valorem tariff of 10 percent.
      P_____   S_____   D_____

   c. Indicate the effect of the ad-valorem tariff on:
      • domestic prices;
      • domestic production;
      • domestic consumption;
      • imports and;
      • government revenues.

7. The demand and supply functions for NAFTA and the EC countries are as follows:

	NAFTA	EC
Supply	25 + 1.25P	50 + 2P
Demand	250 - 5P	125 - 1.75P

a. What are the equilibrium prices and quantities in a closed economy?

b. Under conditions of free trade, what are the equilibrium quantities of supply and demand in the NAFTA countries?

c. Under conditions of free trade, the EC will _____ units to the United States.

8. You are given the following information on the demand (D) and supply (S) functions for beer in two countries: Uruguay and Paraguay.

	Uruguay	Paraguay
Supply	$8 + 4P$	$4 + 0.5P_f$
Demand	$24 - 6P$	$8 - 1.5P_f$

Note: P is the domestic price of Uruguay and Pf is the domestic price of Paraguay.

Allow Uruguay and Paraguay to trade with each other at zero transportation cost and find:
• the world supply and demands;
• the world price;
• supply and demand in each country at the world price;
• domestic imports and exports in each country.

9. During the "stock market crash of 1987," Mr. Gephard introduced a protectionist bill. However, as time passed by, it was "almost certain that congress would surely scrap the Gephard amendment, which would authorize presidential retaliation against countries reluctant to remove their trade barriers with the United States." Please comment.

10. You are given the following information pertaining to the cost and prices associated with the production of computers in Mexico which sell for MexP$5780.

Computer's cost of production

Domestic components		**Imports**	
Parts		*Parts*	
keyboard	MexP170	monitor	US$439
Labor		box	US$ 42
labor	MexP1067.6	mother board	US$ 84
		hard disk	US$420

The exchange rate is MexP3.4/$1

50

a. If Mexico imposes an 18 percent ad-valorem tariff on imported parts, indicate the numerical value of the effective rate of protection.
Effective rate of protection = _____

11. A wise policy for a developing country that wants to develop a manufacturing sector is to provide export subsidies to targeted industries and, at the same time, impose tariffs on imports having characteristics similar to the output of the industries targeted for protection. Please comment.

12. You are given the following information:

US production and international trade of shoes

Item	Situation With tariff	Without a tariff
World price	US$0.1	US$0.1
Tariff	US$0.02/ton	0/ton
Domestic price	US$0.12/ton	US$0.1
US consumption	20 bn tons/year	22 bn tons/year
US production	8 bn tons/year	6 bn tons/year
US imports	12 bn tons/year	16 bn tons/year

Calculate the following:

a. What are the US consumer gains from removing the tariff?

b. What are the US producer gains/losses from removing the tariff?

c. What are the US government tariff revenue gains/losses if the tariff is removed?

d. What is the net effect of the tariff removal on the welfare of the US?

13. A television sells in the world market for $200. In Mexico, the same product can be produced using $120 worth of foreign components and $40 of domestic components. To protect its relatively more inefficient TV industry from world competition, Mexico decided to impose the following nominal tariff rates:
On finished product: 40 percent
On imported parts Import: 20 percent
The Mexican domestic price of Televisions is MexP952 (world price measured in Mexican pesos at the exchange rate of MexP3.4/$1 times a 40percent tariff on the final product).

a. What is the numerical value of the effective rate of protection on TV production in Mexico?

51

b. What happens to the numerical value of the effective rate of protection if Mexico decides to eliminate the tariff on the imported parts?

Indicate which of the following actions are legal under WTO/GATT

14. A US tariff of 20 percent against any country that exports more than twice as much to the United States as it imports in return.
    Legal ( )   Illegal ( )

15. A subsidy to United States wheat exports, aimed at recapturing some of the market lost in the EEC.
    Legal ( )   Illegal ( )

16. A US tariff on Canadian lumber imports, not matched by an equivalent reduction in other tariffs.
    Legal ( )   Illegal ( )

17. A Canadian tax on lumber exports, agreed to at the demand of the United States, in order to placate US lumber producers.
    Legal ( )   Illegal ( )

18. A program of subsidy research and development in areas related to high technology, such as electronics and semiconductors.
    Legal ( )   Illegal ( )

19. Special government assistance to workers who lose their jobs because of import competition.
    Legal ( )   Illegal ( )

20. You are given the following information:

Item	BW footwear	Calzado Canada	Enzo
Factory Price charged for domestic sales	$10	$20	$30
Factory Price charged on exports, except US market	$10	$26	$30
Prices on exports to the US market	$13	$24	$28

a. Which one of the three shoe producers listed is guilty of dumping in the US market?

b. Under WTO/GATT, what specific action, which is legal under GATT, would you recommend to punish the dumping firms?

52

21. You are given the following information:

Price (Pesetas)	Domestic Supply	Demand	Japanese supply	German supply
10	0	40	0	0
12	4	36	horizontal*	0
16	12	28	horizontal*	
18	16	24		
20	20	20		

Note: Prices and quantities are in thousands.
"horizontal" describes a perfectly elastic supply curve

Given the information provided in the table and graph above, indicate the following:

a. In the absence of tariffs in Spain, what would be the revenue of the Japanese car producers? (in pesetas) Yj = _____

b. In the absence of tariffs in Spain, what would be the revenue of the German car producers? (in pesetas) Yg = _____

c. In the absence of tariffs, what would be the revenue of the domestic car producers in Spain? Ys = _____

22. If Spain decides to impose a 33percent ad-valorem tariff across the board on all imports:

Please round your figures

a. What is the revenue of the Japanese car producers after the imposition of the tariff? Yj = _____

b. What is the revenue of the German car producers after the imposition of the tariff? Yg = _____

c. What is the revenue of the domestic car producers in Spain? _____

d. What is the revenue of the government? Tx = _____

23. Spain decides to join the EC. As such, it has to impose a 50percent tariff across the board on all on non-EC members. The only non-EC member in this case is Japan. Therefore, the 50percent tariff applies to the products of this country.

53

Please round your figures

a. What is the revenue of the Japanese car producers after the imposition of the tariff? $Yj =$ _____

b. What is the revenue of the German car producers after the imposition of the tariff? $Yg =$ _____

c. What is the revenue of the domestic car producers in Spain? _____

d. What is the revenue of the Spanish government? $Tx =$ _____

5 Tendencies in global financing, some stylized facts

Introduction

Globalization has induced some identifiable finance innovations. The most visible aspects of this change are related to the way multinational corporations fund their operations, the manner in which they manage the finance function, and how they measure corporate performance.

Purpose

The aim of this note is to describe tendencies in financial innovation and provide a rationalization justifying these trends.

Greater reliance on New York and London

Non-US multinationals used to depend on local financial markets to finance their operations. In the era of globalization these corporations prefer to draw financial resources from the US and European financial markets, to take advantage of the high degree of liquidity existing in these centers.

The number of foreign companies listing their stock in European and US markets best describes this trend. For instance, by October of 1997, there were 385 foreign companies listed in the New York Stock Exchange.

The UK, (67), Canada (67), and Mexico (30) were the countries with the largest number of companies listed. In terms of shares, Canada (43 percent), Britain (14 percent), the Netherlands (6 percent), and Mexico (6 percent) were the top contributors of shares.

In terms of value, Canada was by far, the most important nation (35 percent). Britain (17 percent), the Netherlands (10 percent), and Mexico (5 percent) followed it. These four countries accounted for almost 68 percent of the total share values of non-US multinationals listing in New York.[1]

In contrast, for US multinationals, the rest of the world is not as compelling. However, they still find useful the additional liquidity provided by international financial listings. For instance, in 1992 when General Motors (GM) was in great need of financial resources, it embarked on a road show to Europe and Asia. There, GM raised plenty of cash.

Increasing complexity in global financing

The extensive use of derivatives is another important trend. A 1995 survey of major non-financial firms revealed that at least 70 percent of them are using some form of financial engineering to manage exchange rate, interest rate, or commodity price risks.[2]

Unexpectedly, the purchase and sell of financial derivatives and the speed at which the financial markets are changing increased the corporate exposure to exchange rate risk. To respond to this new challenge, the treasury divisions of many multinationals centralized the financial function and tightened up their guidelines on what is permitted to subsidiaries. These guidelines ranged from the establishment of ideal capital structures for each country to rules on foreign exchange risk hedging.

Centralization of the finance function

Centralization of the finance function goes beyond risk considerations. It has also en economic justification. For instance, financial executives, like Jan Haars, treasurer of Unilever, consider that the centralization of global finance at headquarters provides companies with economies of scale that help them to lower the operating expenses associated to the services provided by the Treasury.[3] This management philosophy is widely shared by many other finance executives.

Mark Greenquist, assistant treasurer of General Motors established a treasury center in Singapore in 1997 to serve GM's Asian operations. In his view, it was very inefficient having company executives in each Asian country doing foreign exchange hedging when it was possible to do it at the Singapore center for the entire region.[4]

There are variants to centralization. Many companies practice it with a certain degree of autonomy for their subsidiaries. At Hoechst, the local managers decide on their hedging strategies within the group's overall guidelines. However, they have to offer headquarters the right of first refusal in executing any financial deals.

Paying more attention to international debt ratings

Greater reliance on international financial markets has also forced companies to pay more attention to their international debt ratings and public opinion in the main financial centers of the world. Companies are eager to know the views held by US investors on the cutting edge of the shareholders value debate. They also value cross-cultural investing. For instance, US investors are focusing on whether companies are improving their balance sheets with cheap debt, rather than more expensive equity. In contrast, the investors in Europe and Japan favor companies having a cautious approach to financial leverage.

Performance measures

Another important tendency in cross-country finance is the application of new yardsticks to measure corporate performance. Many multinationals are still judging performance based on traditional measures such as profitability ratios and earnings per share growth. On the cutting edge, companies are paying more attention to economic value added (EVA), total shareholders return (TSR). Both of these yardsticks emphasize the creation of value for stockholders.

For example, in 1997, Unilever dropped earnings growth and adopted total shareholders return as its corporate objective. To implement this new measure, Unilever plams to match its overall performance against a peer group of 20 multinationals which broadly resemble its business spread across products and regions.

Ownership and financial reporting

The globalization of finance has also changed the way multinationals are owned and how they report their results. After the privatization of Deutsche Telekom's in Germany in November of 1996, it was found that 33 percent of the company's shares were held outside Germany. The largest proportion went to the United States (14 percent) and Britain (8 percent).[5] The privatization of the Mexican company Telmex in 1990 was even more dramatic since 85 percent of stock sold by this company is held outside Mexico.

To meet international listing standards, both Telmex and Telekom have changed the way they report their results. Both adopted US Generally Accepted Accounting Principles (GAAP).

Notes

1 For further details, see the statistical appendix.
2 For further details, see The Wharton School and The Chase Manhattan Bank, N. A., *Survey of Derivatives Usage Among Non-Financial Firms*, Philadelphia, PA, 1995.
3 *The Financial Times*, December 1, 1997.
4 Interview with Mark Greenquist, December 1, 1997.
5 Ralph Atkins and Leslie Crawford, "Case Study: Telefonos de México and Deutsche Telekom," *The Financial Times*, November 5, 1997.

Table 5.1
American Depository Receipts listed in the New York Stock Exchange

COUNTRY	COMPANIES	%	LISTED ADR'S/SHARES	%	MARKET VALUE	%	ACCUM %
Canada	67	17.4	4,873,405,876	43.49	119,823,609,598	35.48	35.48
UK	67	17.4	1,570,363,394	14.02	58,552,250,143	17.34	52.82
Netherlands	15	3.9	688,994,084	6.15	34,622,666,048	10.25	63.07
Mexico	30	7.79	620,869,079	5.54	16,217,733,191	4.8	67.87
France	13	3.38	289,726,519	2.59	12,721,076,344	3.77	71.64
Brazil	7	1.82	160,488,991	1.43	10,277,429,127	3.04	74.68
Argentina	12	3.12	386,012,232	3.45	9,823,101,141	2.91	77.59
Spain	15	3.9	272,071,465	2.43	9,678,733,501	2.87	80.46
Finland	3	0.78	97,096,206	0.87	8,407,041,002	2.49	82.95
Ireland	5	1.3	107,831,973	0.96	5,182,749,197	1.53	84.48
Chile	22	5.71	204,507,551	1.83	4,612,059,363	1.37	85.85
H K/China	9	2.34	182,123,823	1.63	4,285,836,655	1.27	87.12
Italy	15	3.9	118,590,717	1.06	3,615,430,666	1.07	88.19
Japan	11	2.86	74,206,806	0.66	3,611,716,393	1.07	89.26
Liberia	2	0.52	74,904,516	0.67	3,580,369,087	1.06	90.32
Panama	3	0.78	118,069,581	1.05	3,555,873,620	1.05	91.37
Peru	4	1.04	180,016,483	1.61	3,131,039,028	0.93	92.3
Australia	12	3.12	153,349,713	1.37	3,058,210,023	0.91	93.21
Germany	8	2.08	102,078,471	0.91	2,673,769,836	0.79	94
Norway	8	2.08	48,621,360	0.43	2,659,525,117	0.79	94.79
Bahamas	2	0.52	61,250,474	0.55	2,091,067,804	0.62	95.41
Venezuela	3	0.78	64,470,276	0.58	1,929,052,532	0.57	95.98
Denmark	3	0.78	48,777,842	0.44	1,674,723,684	0.5	96.48
Portugal	3	0.78	44,895,438	0.4	1,628,059,309	0.48	96.96
Sweden	5	1.3	96,081,362	0.86	1,608,546,357	0.48	97.44
China	8	2.08	80,360,003	0.72	1,298,969,763	0.38	97.82
Indonesia	4	1.04	59,738,075	0.53	1,139,211,233	0.34	98.16
Philippines	3	0.78	80,332,067	0.72	1,112,834,969	0.33	98.49
Russia	1	0.26	31,839,000	0.28	1,042,727,250	0.31	98.8
Israel	6	1.56	59,004,202	0.53	974,617,736	0.29	99.09
Korea	3	0.78	86,661,576	0.77	766,743,930	0.23	99.32
Total	385	100	11,204,610,901	100	337,706,166,765	100	

Source: New York Stock Exchange, International Listings, October 1997.

58

6 Interest rate parity and the foreign exchange market

Introduction

Modern financial markets offer the contemporary investor a large variety of investment and borrowing options. In the US money market, corporations can place debt at the prime, federal funds, or commercial paper rates. Financial institutions can issue finance paper, certificates of deposit, or bankers acceptances. Finally, government owned financial institutions can sell treasury bills (T-bills).

Money rates

Prime Rate	Base rate on corporate loans posted by at least 75% of the nation's 30 largest banks		7.25%
Federal Funds	Reserve traded among commercial banks in amounts of $1 million or more	Over-night	3.75%
Discount Rate	The charge on loans to depository institutions by the Federal Reserve banks		3.5%
Call Money	The charge on loans to brokers on stock exchange collateral		6%
Commercial Paper	Unsecured notes sold through dealers by major corporations	30-90 days	4.33%
Certificates of Deposit	Rates paid by major New York Banks on primary new issues of negotiable CDs, usually in amounts of $1 million and more	30-180 days	3.68%

Bankers Acceptances	Offered rates of negotiable bank-backed business credit instruments, typically financing an import order with a minimum amount of $100,000	30-180 days	4.36%
London Interbank Offered Rates (LIBOR)	The average of Interbank offered rates for dollar deposits in the London market based on quotations at five major banks	30-365 days	4.87%
Treasury Bills	Short-term government bills sold at a discount from face value in units of $10,000 to $1 million	13-26 weeks	4.15%
Foreign Prime Rates	These rates are not directly comparable; lending practices vary widely by location Canada 6.75% Germany 5.14% Japan 3% Switzerland 7.5% Britain 5.25%		

Source: *The Wall Street Journal*, June 7, 1997.

The international financial market is equally rich in borrowing and lending options. There are Eurodollar deposits taken at the London Interbank Offered Rate (LIBOR), and London Late Eurodollar loans at LIBOR plus a mark-up.

This extensive number of choices often complicates the decision of how to allocate wealth among the different investment opportunities. TIAA-CREF, one of the largest institutional investors in the United States, offered to its associates the opportunity to invest in a "New Global Account." The investment company allocated half of its assets to the "global account" of foreign stocks and close to 25 percent to domestic securities. In regard to the funds on the global account, CREF stated that

> (We) will at first go largely to countries with well-established markets. As opportunities emerge, however, the account may invest increasingly in the markets of economically developing nations...Initially, the assets will most likely be distributed along the lines of the Market Capitalization Weights of the Morgan Stanley Capital International (MSCI) World Index.[1]

At one point in time, the Morgan Stanley World Index suggested distributing available funds as follows:

Country	Weight
United States	38%
Japan	28%
United Kingdom	11%
Other Europe	16%
Developing countries	7%

Source: *The Participant*, Quarterly news for TIAA-CREF participants, May, 1997, p. 6.

The approach followed by the TIAA-CREF suggests that to maintain the profitability of a global fund depends of several factors. The institution managing the fund, must pay attention to the rate of return of each country fund, the strength of the currency in each of the target countries, and news regarding monetary and fiscal policies of the countries targeted for investment.

Purpose

The goal of this technical note is to provide the business executive with the analytical tools required to examine the relationship between monetary policy, interest rates, and the exchange rate. This note will also show how variations in the parity of the local currency, prompted by monetary policy, affect the rate of return on a foreign currency investment.

The exchange rates and the financial markets

The exchange rate is the price of one currency in terms of another currency. For instance, on June 5, 1997, a Japanese citizen required 115.85 yen to buy one dollar. In contrast, on the same day, a US citizen had to give up 1.6344 US dollars to buy one British pound. These two transactions implied that the yen's exchange rate against the US dollar was 115.85 yens per dollar, whereas the US dollar exchange rate against the pound was 1.6344 dollars per pound.

Since the exchange rate is the price of a country's money in terms of another currency, it is also an asset price.[2] An asset is simply a form of wealth, or a way of transferring purchasing power from the present to the future. Therefore, the current price of an asset is directly related to the future yield of goods and services that the asset will provide to its holder. Similarly to other price assets, the current dollar/pound exchange rate is closely related to people's expectations about the future level of this rate.

A Change in the exchange rate is described as a depreciation or an appreciation. A depreciation of the dollar against the pound is an increase in the dollar price of pounds. For example, a variation in the exchange rate from 1.8645 dollars per pound to 1.96 dollars per pound reflects a depreciation of the dollar because, under the new parity, a US citizen requires more dollars to buy one pound.[3] In contrast, a change in the exchange rate from 1.8645 dollars per pound to 1.6000 dollars per pound reflects a decrease in the dollar price of the pound, or an appreciation of the dollar.[4]

The foreign exchange market

The settlement of international liabilities stated in terms of foreign currencies often compels households, firms, and financial institutions to buy and sell currencies in the international market. This currency market is called the foreign exchange market. The major participants in this market are commercial banks, non-bank financial institutions, multinational corporations, and central banks.

Participants in the foreign exchange market have plenty of choices to satisfy their needs and wants. For instance, the treasurer of a multinational corporation who needs to purchase foreign exchange can buy the currency for immediate delivery or delivery in no more than 2 working days. On the other hand, the treasurer may want to purchase the currency today for delivery in 90 days or any other suitable date in the future. The first deal is called a *spot* transaction. The second purchase is usually labeled a *forward* transaction.

Other newly created instruments offer more flexibility and less risk than spot and forward transactions. These other instruments are the *futures* and *options* contracts. In the case of a *futures contract*, the buyer purchases a promise that a specified amount of foreign currency will be delivered to him at a specified date in the future. A *foreign exchange option contract* gives its owner the right to sell (*a put contract*) a specified amount of a foreign currency at a specified price (*the strike price*) at any time up to the specified expiration of the contract. The seller of the option contract, also known as the *writer*, is required to purchase the foreign currency at the discretion of the holder of the option contract, who is under no obligation to exercise his/her right. To give up the right to refusal, the seller of the options contract is compensated by the buyer with an up front fee called the *premium* of the option. A foreign exchange contract that gives its owner the right to purchase a specified amount of foreign currency at a specified price at any time up to the specified expiration of the contract is labeled a *call option contract*.

The demand for foreign currency assets

After reviewing how banks, corporations, central banks, and other institutions trade in the foreign exchange market, we now turn to explore the reasons and factors that determine the exchange rate. To understand how exchange rates are determined, it is necessary to first comprehend what determines demand for foreign currency deposits. The conventional view is that demand for foreign currency denominated deposits depends on the interest rate it offers—the return on the asset—and the expected change in the currency's exchange rate against other currencies.[5]

To rank the profitability of a foreign currency denominated deposit, the investors first look at the rate of return of the different foreign currency denominated bank accounts. This information, however, is not enough. To determine the profitability of the different investment opportunities in various countries, it is also necessary to ascertain the direction and magnitude of the change in the exchange rate over the investment period.

Ranking rates of return on foreign currency deposits

The following example illustrates how exchange rates are used, together with interest rates, to calculate and rank rates of return of different currency denominated bank accounts.

Suppose that the dollar interest rate is 14 percent per year while the British pound interest rate is 9 percent per year. This means that a one-dollar deposit pays $1.14 after a year, while a one pound deposit pays £1.09 over the same period. To determine which investment is more profitable, the investor must pose the following question to him/herself: if I use dollars to invest for one year in a pound-deposit, how many dollars will I get back at the end of the year?

This question can be answered with the following three-step calculation method.[6]The first step consists of using the spot rate to calculate the dollar price of one British pound. The second step incorporates the British interest rate on bank deposits to find out how many British pounds the investor will have at the maturity of the investment one year from now. The third step uses exchange rate expectations to estimate the dollar value of the British pound investment at maturity.

Step one

If we assume that the dollar price of a British pound in the spot market is 1.86 dollars, then the current dollar price of one British pound deposit is just 1.86 dollars.

Step two

We know that the interest rate on British pounds is 9 percent; therefore, at the end of one year the British deposit is worth £1.09.

Step three

If the dollar is expected to depreciate against the British pound to 1.96 dollars per British pound at the end of the investment period, then the dollar value of the British pound deposit is expected to be $[(£1.09)*(\$1.96/£1)] = \$2.14$.

Step one provides the dollar price of a one-pound deposit today ($1.86), while step three forecasts the dollar value of the British pound investment at maturity a year later ($2.14). These two pieces of information permit the calculation of the dollar rate of return on a one-pound deposit as follows:

Rate of return on the British pound deposit = [(2.14-1.86)/1.86]*100 = 15 percent per year

Despite the fact that the dollar interest rate exceeds the British interest rate by 5 percent per year—the dollar rate of return is 14 percent while the British rate is only 9 percent—the investor is still better off holding his deposit in pounds. The pound's expected appreciation against the dollar gives the pound deposit holders a prospective capital gain that is large enough to make pound deposits the best investment alternative as a result of their higher dollar yield (15 percent).

The calculations required to estimate the rate of return on a foreign currency deposit can be simplified if the following rule is used:

> The dollar rate of return on foreign deposits is approximately the foreign interest rate plus the depreciation of the dollar against that currency or the foreign interest rate minus the appreciation of the dollar against that currency.

If this rule is applied to the example presented, it can be shown that the dollar rate of return for a one-pound investment is 15 percent. This 15 percent return is derived by considering a 9 percent foreign rate of return in the British money market plus a 6 percent dollar depreciation against the pound. The dollar depreciation is calculated as follows:

Depreciation/Appreciation = [(1.96-1.86)/1.86]*100 = 5.4 percent

Supply and demand in the foreign exchange market

An intuitive explanation on how supply and demand are determined in the foreign exchange market can be constructed. If a person is offered the option of investing in a dollar denominated account or in a yen denominated account, that person probably would invest in the most profitable alternative. To appraise the profitability of an international investment, one must consider the rate of return of the foreign currency investment and the currency's expected depreciation or appreciation. If the interest rate paid on a yen deposit is four percent and *the dollar is expected to depreciate* 11 percent, then the dollar return on the yen account is 15 percent. If the rate of return of a similar investment in the United States is only 9 percent, no one will be willing to continue holding dollar deposits; therefore, holders of dollar deposits will try to sell them to "buy" yen denominated deposits. Thus, there will be an excess supply of dollar denominated deposits and an excess demand for yen denominated deposits in the foreign exchange market.

As a contrasting example, suppose that *the dollar is expected to appreciate against the yen* by three percent, while the interest rate on dollar and yen deposits is 9 and 11 percent respectively. If the three-step method is applied to this case, it will be found that the return on the yen deposit is only 8 percent per year—11 percent interest paid on yen deposits *minus* a three percent dollar appreciation. This result suggests that the return on dollar deposits is one percent higher. In this case, we should expect an excess supply of yen denominated deposits and an excess demand for dollar deposits.

From these two examples, it can be concluded that there is a relationship between the rate of return and the variation in the exchange rate. If a currency—in this case the dollar—offers a higher return than a foreign currency denominated deposit, then that currency should appreciate as investors try to switch their funds into local currency deposits. In contrast, a depreciation of the local currency should be expected when the rate of return on foreign currency deposits is higher than the return on domestic deposits.

The shift of funds between countries will cease only when all expected returns are equal. At that point, the foreign exchange market is in equilibrium, since the different foreign currency deposits offer the same expected rate of return.

The condition where the expected returns on deposits of any two currencies (or more) are equal is called the *interest parity condition* or the "Fisher Effect."

Interest rate parity between dollar and yen deposits

1) $R_\$ = R_¥ + [E^e_{\$/¥} - E_{\$/¥}]/E_{\$/¥}$

where $R_\$$ = today's interest rate on one-year dollar deposits;

   $R_¥$ = today's interest rate on one-year yen deposits;

   $E^e_{\$/¥}$ = dollar/yen exchange rate expected to prevail a year later;

   $E_{\$/¥}$ = today's price of a yen in terms of dollars—dollars per yen.

To understand how the mechanism of interest parity works, it is necessary to describe how variations in the exchange rate help to maintain equilibrium in the foreign exchange market.

Variations in exchange rates and expected returns

To explain how changes in the exchange rate affect the expected return on a foreign currency deposit, some new assumptions must be introduced: 1) the spot rate a year from now is expected to be \$1/¥100 and 2) current yields on yen and dollar deposits are four and nine percent respectively. These assumptions are incorporated into Table 6.1 below.

65

Table 6.1
Dollar-returns on a yen savings account

Today's dollar/ yen spot rate	Rate of return on yen deposits	Expected rate of change of the yen ($1/¥100-E)/E	Total return on a yen deposit
$1.10/¥100	0.04	- 0.09	- 0.05
$1.05/¥100	0.04	- 0.05	- 0.01
$1.00/¥100	0.04	0	0.04
$0.95/¥100	0.04	0.05	0.09
$0.90/¥100	0.04	0.11	0.15

Note: **E** stands for today's dollar/yen exchange rate and **$1/¥100-E)/E** is a measure of the expected appreciation or depreciation of the dollar over the one-year period.

The results presented in the last column of Table 6.1 *(Total return on a yen deposit)* were estimated using the interest parity principle. They show that a rise in today's dollar/yen exchange rate—a dollar depreciation—*always lowers* the expected dollar return on yen deposits. For instance, in Table 6.1, a depreciation of the dollar from $0.9/¥100 to $1.1/¥100 lowers the dollar return from 15 percent to minus 5 percent. In contrast, a fall in today's dollar/yen exchange rate—a dollar appreciation—*always raises* this return.

In short, the numerical information presented in Table 6.1, shows that a *current dollar depreciation* that affects neither exchange rate expectations—$1/¥100—nor interest rates, leaves the expected future dollar reward of a yen denominated deposit the same, but raises the yen denominated deposit's current dollar cost. This change in dollar cost makes yen denominated deposits less attractive relative to dollar denominated deposits.[7]

The determination of exchange rate equilibrium

Exchange rate equilibrium is determined in Figure 6.1 by the intersection of the downward sloping function, describing the alternative dollar returns of an investment in a yen denominated deposit, and the horizontal line, describing the interest paid on a dollar investment (9 percent). At this point, both returns— measured in dollars—are equal. That is, the interest parity condition is satisfied.

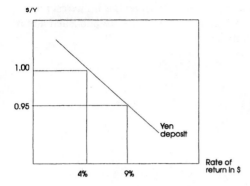

Figure 6.1

To see why the exchange will settle at this point, let us suppose that the dollar/yen exchange rate today is $1/¥100. At this rate, the expected dollar return of the yen investment is only four percent as compared with nine percent in dollar deposits. In this situation, the holders of yen deposits will try to "sell" them to acquire the more profitable dollar deposits. These two actions lead to an excess demand for dollar deposits and an excess supply of yen deposits; at this juncture, the foreign exchange market is out of equilibrium.

In this situation, the unsatisfied owners of yen deposits attempt to sell their deposits to buy dollar deposits, but because the return on dollar deposits is higher than that on yen deposits, no holder of dollar deposits is willing to switch to yen deposits at the current exchange rate of $1/¥100.

As yen deposit owners try to induce dollar holders to trade by offering them a better price for dollars, the dollar/yen rate falls toward $0.95/¥100. That is, the yen becomes cheaper in dollar terms—the yen depreciates. Once the exchange rate reaches the level of $0.95/¥100, the incentive to switch yen deposits for dollar deposits ceases to exist, since the dollar deposits offer the same return as the yen denominated deposits. The same process works in reverse. The main conclusion that can be drawn from this exercise is that *exchange rates always adjust to maintain interest rate parity.*

Effects of a rise in the dollar interest rate on the exchange rate

In an article published by The Wall Street Journal, it was stated that:

The yen continues to weaken on speculations that the Bank of Japan may ease (interest) rates ... "

67

The implication of this remark is that the yen may depreciate if interest rates in Japan fall relative to the US interest rate. Similar statements are published almost every day for the dollar and other currencies.

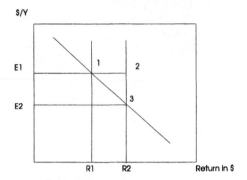

Figure 6.2

Figure 6.2 helps to explain the relationship between interest rates and exchange rates. It shows a rise in the interest rate on dollar deposits from R1 to R2. This rise in the dollar interest rate shifts the vertical schedule. At the initial exchange rate E1, the expected return on dollar deposits is now higher than that on yen deposits by an amount equal to the horizontal distance between points 1 and 2. In this situation, the market is in disequilibrium. The earning differential between dollar and yen deposits causes the dollar to appreciate to E2 (point 3). This appreciation of the dollar in the spot market also raises the expected dollar return on yen deposits by increasing the rate at which the dollar is expected to depreciate in the future.

In other words, since there has been no change in the yen interest rate or in the expected future exchange rate between the dollar and the yen, *the increase in the dollar interest rate today simultaneously causes an appreciation of the dollar in the spot market and expectations of a dollar depreciation in the forward* markets.

Another way of looking at the interest parity condition is by restating Equation 1 as follows:

2) $R_\$ - R_¥ = [Ee_{\$/¥} - E_{\$/¥}]/E_{\$/¥}$

For this example, Equation 2 stipulates that the interest rate differential between the dollar and yen markets should be equal to the forward premium or discount of the dollar relative to the Japanese yen. If this condition does not hold, then it is possible to engage in international arbitrage. A possible discrepancy between interest rate differentials and forward premium or discount may lead to locational, triangular, or covered interest arbitrage.[8]

68

Notes

1 *The Participant,* quarterly news for TIAA-CREF participants, May 1992, p. 4.
2 P. Krugman and M. Obstfeld, *International Economics,* second edition, Harper-Collins Pub., 1991, p. 315.
3 A depreciation of the local currency, in this case the US dollar, makes US goods cheaper in foreign markets.
4 Appreciation of the US dollar makes US goods more expensive to a British citizen.
5 P. Krugman and M. Obstfeld, *International Economics,* Harper-Collins, 1991, p. 327.
6 Ibid., p. 331.
7 Ibid., p. 337.
8 A discussion of how to implement these transactions is discussed in my technical note: "International Arbitrage," which is included in this volume.

Problems

1. If the spot rate in Germany is DM1.9/$1 and the 90-day forward rate is DM1.98/$1, is the German Mark selling at a forward premium or discount against the dollar?

2. A one-year forward rate is $0.48/DM1 and the spot rate is $0.462/ DM1.
   a. What is the net forward premium or discount on the mark, assuming a 10 percent tax on foreign exchange capital gains?
   b. If interest rate parity holds, what is the difference between the interest rate on one-year dollar deposits and that on one-year DM deposits?

3. Considering the information below, indicate whether the Canadian dollar is at a premium or discount against the French franc.

Country	Spot	90-day forward
Canada	$0.8010/Can$1	$0.7976/Can$1
France	$0.1736/FF1	$0.1730/FF1

   a. What is the numerical value of the Canadian dollar's premium or discount?
   b. If interest parity holds, which country should be exhibiting the higher interest rate?

4. Assume that US and Swiss investors require a real rate of return of 3 percent and that the US and Swiss interest rates are 6 percent and 4 percent (annually) respectively. If interest parity holds, what is the numerical value of the Swiss franc premium or discount against the dollar?

5. Given the French franc below, what is the numerical value of the annual premium or discount for the French franc against the dollar?

Rates	
spot	$0.18/FF1
90-d forward	$0.178/FF1

6. The spot rate of the German mark is $0.31/DM1 and the one-year forward rate is $0.33/DM1. What is the forward premium or discount for the German mark?

7. If interest rate parity holds, the rule is that the larger the degree by which the US interest rate exceeds the foreign exchange rate, the smaller will be the forward premium of the foreign currency. Please comment.

7 Purchasing power parity and the foreign exchange market

Introduction

Theories of exchange rate determination have relied on the idea that currency parities are greatly affected by nations' price levels, especially in the long run. This idea is known as the *purchasing power parity theory* (PPP).

Purpose

The aim of this note is to explain how anticipations about the future relationship between domestic and foreign prices, *or* the ratio of domestic to foreign inflation, create expectations regarding the future of the exchange rate. In the first instance, adjustments in the exchange rate are explained by the theoretical approach identified as *absolute purchasing power parity*. If the variations in the exchange rate are explained by inflation differentials, then the performance of the exchange rate is explained by *relative purchasing power parity*.

Absolute purchasing power parity

This concept is based on the *law of one price*. This law states that in a competitive market, identical goods sold in different countries must sell for the same price when the price of the two or more goods are expressed in terms of the same currency. Obviously, this equality holds only if there are no trade barriers and transportation costs, and the goods are identical. For instance, given an exchange rate of 124 yen per one dollar, and a price of shoes of $100 in the US, absolute purchasing power parity only holds if the price of shoes in Japan is $100 (¥12,400). That is, the equivalent price in yen adjusted by the exchange rate.

$$\$100 = ¥12,400*(\$1/¥124)$$

In practice, we do not use the price of two goods to estimate the exchange rate, but the prices of two baskets of goods. For example if the price of the basket of good in the United States is $67 and in Germany is DM100, then, the exchange rate that maintains parity between the currencies is $67/DM100 = $0.67/DM1. Therefore, absolute purchasing power parity can be expressed as ($/DM) = (P$/PDM). This expression indicates that the exchange rate between two currencies, in this case between the dollar and the German mark, is equal to the ratio of the US and German price levels. P$ and PDM represent the price of the US and German baskets of goods respectively.

Relative purchasing power parity

To provide an intuitive explanation for this relationship, imagine that a US resident living in Nogales, Arizona —which is right on the US - Mexico border— wants to buy a chair. This person has the option of walking to stores located in both the US and Mexico. If he finds that the price of the chair in the Mexican and US stores is three Mexican pesos and one dollar respectively. And that the exchange rate between the two currencies is three Mexican pesos in exchange for one dollar, then the buyer is indifferent between buying the chair in a Mexican or US store. The reason is obvious. The customer can purchase the chair in a US shopping center for one dollar or he can trade the dollar in a local bank for three pesos, cross the border, and buy the chair in a Mexican store for three pesos. Under this scenario, the exchange rate of MxP3/$1 is properly reflecting the purchasing power parity of the two currencies.

Over time, the domestic and foreign prices of the chair may be changed due to inflation. For instance, if the rates of inflation in the United States and Mexico are five and ten percent respectively, then the price of the chair should rise to $1.05 in the US and to MxP3.3 in Mexico. Under this new scenario, the exchange rate of MxP3/$1 will no longer reflect the same purchasing power parity for the dollar and the peso in the two markets. For the US resident to be indifferent between buying the chair in the US or Mexican stores, the exchange rate must adjust to MxP3.1428/$1.[1]

The reason for the dollar to be traded in the foreign exchange market for a larger number of pesos reflects the fact that, over the year period, the peso's purchasing power in Mexico has been undermined by a relatively higher Mexican rate of inflation.

The relationship previously described suggests that equivalent assets in different markets sell for the same price. This means that in the absence of market imperfections, transaction costs, or other barriers to trade, identical assets must have the same price regardless of where they are bought or sold. If purchasing power parity does not hold, then there is an arbitrage opportunity, which consists of simultaneously buying an asset at a low price and selling it at a higher price to secure an arbitrage profit. Relative purchasing power can be expressed as $\Delta E/E_0 = [(1 + i_d)/(1 + i_f)] - 1$, where ΔE is the expected change in the exchange rate, E_0 is the current spot rate, and i_d and i_f are the anticipated domestic and foreign rates of inflation.

Example

Suppose that the inflation rate in Germany is 4 percent, while it is 7 percent in the United States. According to the purchasing power parity theory just expounded, the dollar must depreciate by 2.88 percent to maintain the initial purchasing power parity of the two countries in both markets. To justify this assertion, consider that changes in the exchange rate ($\Delta E/E_0$) are a function of the inflation differential. That is:

$$\Delta E/E_0 = [(1 + i_d)/(1 + i_f)] - 1 = [(1.07/1.04) - 1] = 1.0288 - 1 = 0.0288 = 2.88\ \%.$$

Implications

If the exchange rate in period zero was \$0.6/DM1, the exchange rate that maintains purchasing power parity a year later is \$0.6173/DM1. That is:

$$E_1 = E_0(1 + 0.0288) = (\$0.6) * (1.0288) = \$0.6173/DM1$$

The exchange rate E_1 is an equilibrium rate only if the initial exchange rate E_0 was an equilibrium rate and if the inflation rates used to perform the calculations are the appropriate measure of the two countries' inflation rates. Otherwise, E_1 will not represent the equilibrium- exchange rate at the end of period one.

Purchasing power parity in practice

When using PPP as a measure of the long-term relationship between two currencies, it is worth keeping in mind the following considerations. First, it is necessary to carefully select the base period. While the selection of an appropriate base-period equilibrium exchange rate is always somewhat arbitrary, it is not necessarily impossible. To select a base-period, one can explore intervals in which a parity is either relatively stable or close to a long-run moving average. Second, it is important to select the appropriate price indices. In practice, one can choose between several indices. There is the consumer price index (CPI), the wholesale price index (WSI), the gross domestic product deflector (GDP deflector), and the basket price of tradable and non-tradable goods. The tradable index reflects what part of a nation's output can compete against imports or be exported at existing exchange rates. The basket price of non-tradable refers to that group of commodities that are not part of international trade due to high transportation costs, perishability, and other factors.

The ideal price to estimate the exchange rate based on purchasing power parity is the index on tradable goods. However, this is not always available and it is not easy to construct one. A second choice is to resort to the wholesale price index. This index has several advantages. The basket on which it is based contains a large tradable component, it is easy to find, and it reflects long-term price relations.

Many important international institutions, such as the International Monetary Fund (IMF), use PPP extensively to calculate real exchange rates for many countries.

While popular in the classroom, PPP has several major practical problems and shortcomings. Contrary to the assumption of the law of one price, transport costs and restrictions on trade do exist. These barriers often prevent the free trade of goods and services. Another problem is that the consumption basket may be different for each country. There is no reason to expect each basket from each country to have the same price across countries even in the absence of barriers to trading. Finally, the existence of market distortions such as monopolistic practices may further weaken PPP.

Note

1   Adjusted exchange rate in period one is approximately,
$E_1 = E_0 * (1 + \text{inflation}_{MxP} / 1 + \text{inflation}_\$) = 3*(1.1/1.05) = \text{MexP}3.1428/\$1$.

Problems

1. For the same basket of goods at time zero, price indices in Japan and the United States are 100 and 1 respectively. The spot rate is $1/¥100. The inflation rates are expected to be two percent for Japan and 4.5 percent for the US over the foreseeable future. What are the price index levels and the expected currency parity after a year?

2. If the rate of inflation in France becomes high relative to the German inflation rate, what should the trader in the foreign exchange mark expect? In your answer consider the demand and supply of German marks and French francs, and any change in the price of the German mark in terms of the franc. Please comment.

3. Perform the following tasks.

Step One: Choose any country of interest, for example, Thailand.

Step Two: For a five-year period, obtain the following:

a. Gross domestic product per year in terms of the local currency.
b. Producer or consumer prices per year.
c. Inflation based on either producer or consumer prices. If inflation data is not available use a spreadsheet and the price information to calculate inflation.
d. Yearly exports, imports, and the trade balance.

Step Three: Use the trade balance information to find exchange rate equilibrium. It may happen when the trade balance is the closest to zero.

Step Four: Use the year in equilibrium as your base year and estimate the exchange rate based on purchasing power parity.

Step Five: Use the exchange rate forecast —based on PPP— to estimate GDP in dollar terms.

Step Six: Find the actual exchange rate at the end of each year.

Step Seven: Compare your estimates of the exchange rate versus the actual exchange rate, and determine the years where the local currency is undervalued or overvalued.

Step Eight: Calculate the amount of exchange rate correction required in percentage terms to eliminate accumulated under or overvaluation.

Note: The information required to carry out this exercise can be found in the International Financial Statistics published by the International Monetary Fund (IMF).

8 The foreign exchange market

The functions of money and the foreign exchange market

Within the boundaries of a domestic market, the local currency of a country may function as a medium of exchange, a unit of account, a store of value, and a standard to defer payments. In the US, this is the role played by a dollar. A local currency may perform these same functions in global currency markets. In this instance, the local currency is identified in the foreign exchange market as a unit of *foreign exchange*.

Purpose

The aim of this note is to provide the reader with an integrated vision of how the foreign exchange market works. It lists the most important players, describes the components of this institution, and offers an explanation of why and how traders buy and sell currencies.

The benefits of having a market for trading currencies

The availability of a foreign exchange market inside a country enables the residents of a nation to exchange the local currency for foreign currencies which, in turn, allow them to purchase foreign goods and services. For instance, a resident of the United States can trade dollars for German marks in the foreign exchange market and use the marks to import a German made car. In this instance, the local currency—the dollar—is indirectly performing the function of a medium of exchange.

The existence of both internationally traded currencies and exchange rate quotations allows residents to compare the value of a variety of raw materials and finished goods produced in different locations under a variety of circumstances. If a pair of Japanese produced shoes are worth 1000 yen in Tokyo and the exchange rate quoted in the international currency market is US$1/Y100, then the dollar price of the Japanese shoes is 10 dollars. Given the dollar price of the Japanese shoes, a U. S. resident can compare the price of Japanese shoes with American made shoes of similar quality and determine, based on this price comparison, which pair of shoes is cheaper in terms of dollars. In this example, the local currency—the dollar—has played the role of an international unit of account. Mexican residents fearful of a peso devaluation often trade their peso-savings for dollars in existing spot markets and stash them in dollar-denominated accounts in US banks. In this instance, the local currency—the peso—has played, indirectly, the role of store of value.

The foreign exchange market also lets firms and individuals issue and settle foreign currency denominated payables and accept receivables to be settled in terms of foreign exchange. For example, a Spanish resident living in Madrid can purchase French francs at the train station in Chamartin, take the RENFE train from Madrid to Paris at night, arrive the next day in Paris, and settle a French franc payable owed to a Parisian bank. In this instance, the local currency—the peseta—has acted as a means to settle an international payable denominated in French francs.

Participants in the foreign exchange market

Central and commercial banks, multinational corporations, and individual speculators and arbitrageurs are the most active players in the foreign exchange market. The central banks are considered to be the dominant players in this market as a result of their ability to issue or restrict the supply of currencies. An additional reason is that they possess large amounts of foreign exchange reserves that they frequently trade in order to manage the parity of their currencies or those of their trading partners. It is well known that in recent years the central banks of Japan and Germany have often intervened in the foreign exchange market by selling considerable amounts of their dollar reserve. The purpose of this intent was to flood the markets with US dollars to force a depreciation of this currency, hoping that the depreciation would ease the US trade balance deficit. Central banks also influence the foreign exchange market through their balance of payment operations. Often, central banks have to sell part of their foreign exchange holdings to finance a balance of payments deficit or buy foreign exchange to neutralize or "sterilize" a nation's balance of payments surplus.

The importance of the commercial banks in the foreign exchange market is explained basically by their active trading on their own behalf or on the interest of their customers. Banks trade foreign exchange with each other directly or through brokers. Foreign exchange dealings can be a considerable source of profits for a commercial bank. The size of these profits, however, varies considerably since they are heavily dependent on the swings of the market and the position taken by the bank.

Firms participate in the foreign exchange market to settle foreign currency payables, to turn foreign exchange receivables into local currency, to arbitrage, to hedge, to speculate, or simply to repatriate profits. Most of the time their intervention is channeled through commercial banks or brokers who act on behalf of their corporate customers. Individuals partake in the currency markets either as traders or brokers. A trader purchases or sells currencies to facilitate international traveling, to purchase foreign goods, to arbitrage, to speculate, or to switch savings from one currency to another. In contrast, the broker is an "order filler" who is paid a fee to execute orders for customers on the trading floors of the exchange. In essence, a broker takes a position only at the request, and on the behalf of a customer.

The international currency markets can be classified according to their pricing rules, the time to maturity of the contracts, the degree of freedom allowed to market participants, the marketability and convertibility of the currencies swapped, and by how they quote the currency and the contracts. In general, there are five basic currency markets: the eurocurrency, the spot, the forward, the futures, and the options markets.

The Eurocurrency market or Eurodollar market

The Eurocurrency market originated in London during the Cold War period of the 1950s. At that time, the Soviet Union held a substantial amount of dollar denominated deposit in US banks. These deposits were held to finance the soviet trade with the US. The soviet government, fearful of the US government's ability to freeze or seize these deposits, asked their London banks to hold dollar deposits in London. The British bankers were more than delighted to have this opportunity. A holding of dollar-denominated deposits allowed them to accept new dollar deposits and to issue dollar-denominated loans to their European customers.

From the previous explanation, it is reasonable to depict the **Eurocurrency** market as an international money market where commercial banks accept variable-interest bearing deposits in a variety of currencies that include the US dollar, the pound, the German mark, and other currencies. In the Eurocurrency market, the commercial banks, which are also known as **Eurobanks**, are able to accept foreign currency deposits that are known as **Eurodeposits**. These markets are fairly unregulated, therefore, on the Eurodeposits there are neither reserve nor insurance requirements.[1]

The incorporation of the Eurodollar market into the international financial system has turned out to be a great success. Today, this market is considered the most competitive and efficient credit market in the world. Daily volumes—in the hundreds of millions of dollars—traded in this market are quoted at the **bid** or **offer** rate. The bid rate is the quotation at which the Eurobanks take deposits from other Eurocurrency banks. The offer rate is that at which these banks make loans. The difference between offer and bid rates is called the **interbank spread**, which is in fact the gross bank profit resulting from a Eurotransaction.[2]

The spot market

The spot market is an interbank market where the participants trade currencies for immediate delivery or release in a period which is not to exceed 48 hours at a pre-agreed price known as the spot rate. Spot quotations may be stated directly or indirectly. A direct quotation, or **"American,"** is given when the rates are quoted in terms of the number of units of the local currency required to purchase one unit of foreign exchange. The logic behind a direct quotation is that it allows the residents to understand foreign exchange quotations; i. e., US$0.64/DM1 indicates that it takes only 64 cents of a dollar to purchase one German mark. An indirect quotation, or **"European,"** is stated in terms of the number of units of foreign exchange required to purchase one unit of the local currency. For instance, Ff5/US$1 indicates that five French francs are required to purchase one dollar in the spot market.

Very often, traders cannot find spot quotations on "exotic currencies." It is not easy to find printed spot quotations either for Indian rupee in terms of the Mexican peso (rupee/Mexican peso) or the spot rate between the Guatemalan currency, the quetzal and the Polish currency, the zloty. To overcome this problem, the traders can resort to the use of the "chain rule" to estimate the required "cross rate". To estimate the cross rate, let us say, between the Indian rupee and the Mexican peso, there has to be a third currency linking them. For instance the dollar, the pound, or the yen. The most commonly used linking currency is the dollar. Then, to get the required cross rate, it is necessary to have both the number of rupees required to purchase a dollar, an indirect quotation, and the amount of dollars required to purchase a Mexican peso —a direct quote.

Quotations:	Indirect	Direct
	Rp33/$1	US$0.3/MexP$1

Estimation of the Cross Rate
Cross rate = (Rp33/$1)*($0.3/MexP$1) = Rp 9.9/MexP$1

In addition to facilitating trade, cross currency quotations can also be utilized to identify triangular arbitrage opportunities. This transaction consists of simultaneously buying a currency in a location where it is "cheap" and selling it in another where it is "expensive".

The forward market

The forward market is another interbank market where the participants make the commitment to purchase or sell foreign exchange at a quotation known as the forward rate for delivery at a specified future date (beyond the two days required for settlement on a spot transaction). Forward contracts are usually stated in 30, 90, and 180 days, even though other arrangements are possible. Normally, the size and maturity of the forward contracts are negotiated to satisfy the particular needs of the traders. Forward quotations are restricted to a selected number of currencies which include, but are not limited to the U. S. and Canadian dollars, the British pound, the Swiss franc, the Italian lira, the Japanese yen, and the German mark. Forward rates can also be quoted at a premium or discount in relation to the current spot rate. A foreign currency is quoted at a premium when the number of units of the local currency required to purchase a unit of foreign exchange is less in the spot than in the forward market. In contrast, the foreign currency is selling at a discount when the resident pays more in the spot than in the forward market. For instance, if the spot and forward quotations of the British pound in term of US dollars are $1.54/£1 and $1.56/£1 respectively, then the British pound is selling at a forward premium against the dollar. Annualized premiums or discounts are estimated by using the following expression:

1) *Premium or Discount = {[forward rate - spot rate)/spot rate]*100}*(12/n);*
   where *n* is the number of months to maturity.

For instance, if the spot and 180-day forward rates are known to be $0.18/Ffl and $0.2/Ffl respectively, then the French franc is selling at a premium. The numerical value of this premium can be estimated by applying the spot and forward quotations to expression 1.

$$P/D = [(0.2 - 0.18)/0.18]*100*(12/6) = 22.22\%$$

The result indicates that the French franc is selling at a 22 percent annualized premium against the dollar. Also, it can be said that the dollar is selling in the European markets at a 22.22 percent annual discount against the franc.[3] Over the 180-day period, the dollar discount is only 11.11 percent. This means that it takes 11.11 percent more dollars to buy a franc in the 180-day forward market than in the spot.

The futures market

The first futures market in the United States was established in Chicago in 1919 to serve the needs of the American farming community in the Midwest region. In May of 1972, the Chicago Mercantile Exchange (CME) established an international money market division, the International Monetary Market (IMM)), to trade currencies and securities in the futures market. Trading with futures is subject to strict regulations established by both the Commodities Futures Trading Commission and the Exchange.

The futures contract is a commitment made on the trading floor to buy or to sell foreign currencies. Each contract specifies the quantity of the item and the time of delivery or payment. The buyers and the sellers agree on a price today—the futures price—for a currency to be delivered and paid in the future. Delivery dates are the third Wednesday of the month of the contract month. Delivery months are March, June, September and December. The last day of trading is two

81

business days before the third Wednesday of the contract month. The price quotations are in US$ per unit of foreign exchange.

Table 8.1
CME futures,
currency contract highlights

Currency	Trading Units	Minimum Price	Fluctuations Tick	Daily Price Limit
Australian dollar	100,000	0001 (1 pt.)	10/pt. = $10.00	150 points
British pound	62,500	0002 (2 pt.)	6.25/pt=$12.50	400 points
Canadian dollar	100,000	0001 (1 pt.)	10/pt. = $10.00	100 points
Deutsche mark	125,000	0001 (1 pt.)	12.5/pt=$12.50	150 points
Japanese yen	12,500,000	000001 (1 pt.)	12.5/pt=$12.50	150 points
Swiss franc	125,000	0001 (1 pt.)	12.5/pt=$12.50	150 points
French franc	250,000	00005 (1 pt.)	2.5/pt.=$12.50	500 points

Source: *CME, Futures and Facts,* Chicago Mercantile Exchange. The contract size specifications are from the Chicago Mercantile Exchange (CME). Other exchanges may have different contract sizes.

Since exchange rates fluctuate, international investors use futures contracts both to protect an investment and to profit from it. A futures contract is an impersonal agreement between two parties unknown to each other. Yet, there is virtually no chance for failure because the contracts are guaranteed by the Exchange. To guarantee the contracts, the Exchange imposes a deposit or margin requirement to cover the fluctuations in the value of the contract. **The margin has** two parts: the initial margin and the maintenance margin. The exact amount of the initial margin depends on the daily price movement limit set forth in the contract and by the broker. Any gains or losses are added to or subtracted from the margin. If continuous losses occur and the margin declines below 80 percent of its required level, then a transfer of margin takes place. This additional margin, which is equivalent to the change in the value of the contract, is called the **variation margin**.

Futures pricing

A currency futures contract's total value is determined by multiplying the contract amount times the price of the contract. Future prices are closely related to the spot exchange rates, but there is a variance, which is due to the difference in delivery dates. This difference—the futures price minus the spot price—is called the **swap**. The swap tends to zero as the delivery date for future contracts is near. As a result, the futures delivery ultimately becomes a spot delivery. In theory, as a result of arbitrage, spot and futures contracts become perfect substitutes for each other as time passes by; therefore, they should have the same value. This principle is crucial in a futures market because it is the essence of futures pricing.[4]

Table 8.2
Futures quotations
DEUTSCHE MARK (CME)—125,000 marks, $ per mark

	Open	High	Low	Settle	Change	Lifetime High	Lifetime Low	Open Interest
Mar	.5545	.5452	.5401	.5436	-0.0011	.5520	.4370	56,576
June	.5435	.5472	.5422	.5459	-0.0011	.5538	.4850	1,839
Sept	.5460	.5494	.5460	.5483	-0.0010	.5525	.4868	270

Est. vol. 24,426; vol. Thur. 35,278; open int 58,685—1,399.

Source: Using Currency and Futures, Chicago Mercantile Exchange.

The swap is an application of the interest parity principle where the swap is the interest rate differential between countries.[5] For example, if interest rates are three percent higher in Germany than in the US, the futures price for the German mark should be at a three percent discount on an annual basis in terms of the US dollar.

The swap can be calculated using the expression in (1) or by using the following expression:

2) *Swap= (Spot exchange rate)*(Eurodollar interest rate - Eurocurrency interest rate)*(Days to delivery/360)*

Example of How to Calculate a Swap and a Futures Price

Assumptions

Trading date	March 19
Delivery date for June British pound futures	June 18
Three-month Eurodollar interest rates	7.6875%
Three-month Europound interest rate	13.9375%
Spot value of the British pound	$1.9098/£1

Swap = $1.9098*(0.076875-0.139375)*(91/360) = -$ 0.0298

Once the swap value is calculated, the next step is to add the swap to the spot rate to determine the futures price.[6]

Futures price = ($1.9098 - $0.0298) = $1.8800/£1

The swap provides useful information to a trader. If the actual futures price is less than $1.8800/£1, then the trader should sell spot British pounds and buy futures. If the actual price is higher than $1.8800 then the trader should buy pounds

83

in the spot and sell futures. In any one of the two previous instances, the trader, likely, will end up with a profit equivalent to the difference between the current futures price and $1.8800.

Futures pricing and market strategies

A trader confronted with the futures market faces a host of futures-price quotations—which are always expressed as the dollar price of foreign exchange or the number of dollars to one unit of foreign exchange. These quotations include the opening price for each one of the different maturity periods for each day, the high, the low, and the settlement prices for the entire life of the contract, the open interest, and the volume traded.

The **opening price** is the quotation at which the currency is offered at the beginning of the trading day. Traders have the choice to purchase or sell currencies at this price prior to the opening of the exchange.

The **settlement price** denotes the price at which the futures contracts are settled at the end of the day. If the market is very active, the settlement price may be the last price of the day. Otherwise, the Exchange's Settlement Committee may estimate it as the weighted average of the last 30 minutes of trading. Ultimately, the Settlement Committee decides the settlement price based on what they consider to be reasonable and fair. This determination is very crucial for the traders because it will resolve who has profits and losses as well as determine the value of the margin since futures contracts settle daily.

The **open interest** refers to the number of contracts still standing at the end of the previous day's trading session. Each unit represents *a buyer and a seller* who still have a contract position. The open interest fluctuates during the life of the contract and is used to assess whether the market is "robust" or "thin." Ordinarily, open interest is low in the early stages of the contract, increases to a maximum of four to six weeks before maturity, and then declines as the contract is close to expiration.

At the bottom of the table of the futures quotes, **the estimated volume** represents the number of trades transacted in the previous two trading sessions prior to the last one. **The open interest** shows first, the total of the last column, *(56,576 + 1,839 + 270) = 58,685,* and the change from the prior trading day *(1,399).*

The most active participants in the futures markets are businesses who take a position to hedge or speculate. A hedging transaction is aimed at protecting an international business transaction from changes in the exchange rate or to limit the exchange rate risk on the transaction. Traders may take long or short positions, even though combined positions are also feasible.

A **long position** is taken when the investor buys a futures contract, accepting delivery of a specified amount of currency at the maturity of the contract, or when someone has a contract to purchase a currency and still owns it. A **short position** is taken when the trader has sold currency and has an obligation to deliver. The positions taken by the traders usually reveal their market expectations. When the

84

traders are "bullish," it is because they expect the price to go up and as such, they normally take long positions; in contrast, when the traders expect price declines, they are in a "bear mood" and act upon it by taking a short position.

The options market

Trading currencies in the options market is based on the same principles governing the futures markets. Trading takes place in a specific site, under fixed rules, with standard size contracts, standard delivery dates, and with open auction outcry. Options are usually entered into through registered brokers who charge a fee for the service rendered.

Table 8.3
CME options,
currency contract highlights

Currency	Trading Units	Minimum Price Change	Value of 1 point	Strike Price Interval
Australian dollar	100,000	0001	$10.00	US 1¢
British pound	62,500	0002	$12.50	US 2.5¢
Canadian dollar	100,000	0001	$10.00	US 5¢
Deutsche mark	125,000	0001	$12.50	US 1¢
Japanese yen	12,500,000	000001	$12.50	US 0.01¢
Swiss franc	125,000	0001	$12.50	US 1¢

Source: *CME, Futures and Facts,* Chicago Mercantile Exchange. The contract size specifications are from the Chicago Mercantile Exchange (CME). Other exchanges may have different contract sizes.

Nature of the options contracts

An options contract gives its holder the right to buy or sell—depending on the type of contract—foreign exchange prior to the expiration of the contract at an explicit quotation called the **strike price.** To have this right, the holder of the contract has to pay a fee known as the **premium,** or price of the option.

Strike prices

When a new contract is listed for trading in the Deutsche mark, Japanese yen, Swiss franc, or British pound, there will be thirteen put and call strike prices arranged systematically. At the center is located the nearest strike to the underlying futures price. Above this price there are six strike price quotations higher than the center price. Below the center price, there are six more strike quotations. For the

Canadian and Australian dollars, there are only nine put and call strike prices. One of them is the nearest strike to the underlying futures. From the remaining, four are higher and four are lower than the center strike. For example, if the March DM futures price closes at $0.5651 on the previous day, the strikes listed for March puts and calls will be 51¢, 52¢, 53¢, 54¢, 55¢, 56¢, 57¢....,63¢; where 57¢ will be the closest to the underlying futures price. A new strike price will be listed for both puts and calls when the underlying price—bid or offer price—touches within half a strike price interval of either the fourth highest or the fourth lowest strike prices.

Contracts

In the options market, there are two types of options contracts available: *put* and *call*. **Put contracts** confer to their **"holder"** the right to sell foreign exchange at the **"strike price."** In turn, the seller of the contract, **"the writer,"** is obligated to buy the foreign exchange at the request of the holder if the holder wants to exercise the option. **Call contracts** grant to their holder the right to purchase from "the writer" foreign exchange at the strike price. In this contractual arrangement, the "writer" is obligated to furnish the foreign exchange at the holder's request if he or she wants to exercise the option.

Interpreting currency options information

The first column of the option quotes shows the strike price. Normally, there is a choice of strike prices. The other columns show the expiration months and the premia attached to the different periods listed.

Table 8.4
Option quotations
DEUTSCHE MARK (IMM)—125,000 marks, $ per mark

Strike Price	Calls—Settle			Puts—Settle		
	Feb-c	Mar-c	Apr-c	Feb-p	Mar-p	Apr-p 52
	2.46	2.63	....	0.11	0.29	....
53	1.63	1.87	2.21	0.28	0.52	0.65
54	0.96	1.27	1.60	0.60	0.91	....
55	0.50	0.80	....	1.14	1.44	....
56	0.25	0.50	....	....	2.13	....
57	....	0.30	....	....	....	....

Est. vol. 8,145, Thur.; vol. 9,077 calls, 9024 puts. Open interest Thur.; 47855 calls, 47,767 puts.

Source: Using Currency and Options, Chicago Mercantile Exchange.

86

The estimated volume shows the volume of options traded in the previous two trading sessions. Each unit represents both the buyer and the seller. The open interest shows the number of option contracts that was still open at the end of the previous day's trading session.

A premium, either on call or put contracts, is the price, on a per unit basis, of the option. For example, a quote of 0.50 for a 55 call represents a dollar premium equivalent to $625.[7] The premium associated with a contract varies. The reasons for this variation are due to the existing discrepancy between the spot price relative to the strike price, the life span of the contract and the variability of the currency traded.

The level of existing spot price relative to the strike price

The higher the current spot price relative to the strike price, the higher the call price. This is due to the high risk incurred by the seller of the contract who may have to deliver foreign exchange at the maturity of the contract at a price well below the future spot price.

Time left in the contract before the expiration date

It is generally accepted that the longer the maturity of the contract, the higher the variance between the spot rate and strike price. Therefore, the "writer" charges a higher premium in compensation for the time-risk implicit in longer contract life spans.

Potential variability of the currency

The greater the variability associated with a currency, the higher the probability that the spot rate will differ from the strike price.

Notes

1   Commercial bank deposits in the United States are insured up to $100,000 through the Federal Deposit Insurance Corporation (FDIC).
2   Interest rates and currencies also trade in other markets at bid and offer rates. The difference between a bid and an offer price is the spread, which is gross profit resulting from the transaction.
3   Premium or discounts are annualized to compare either one of them with interest rates, which are usually quoted on a yearly basis.
4   For further details on this point, see Currency Futures and Options, Chicago Mercantile Exchange, p. 3.
5   For further details see chapter 6, "Interest Rate Parity and the Foreign Exchange Market."

6 Since the swap is negative in this case, it is taken away from the spot rate. The result is a reduction of the dollar price of the pound due to the fact that the dollar interest rate is less than the pound rate.

7 [\$625 = 0.50¢ *DM 125,000].

Problems

1. If the exchange rates are 84 yens per dollar, and $0.64 cents per German mark, what is the yen/mark rate?

2. If a German corporation desires to avoid exchange rate risk on a 90-day payable, ¥100,000, would you recommend the corporation sell its yen in the forward market?

3. Bank of America is quoting French francs at Ff5.22/$ Bid and Ff 5.44/$ Offer. What are the bid and offer prices in "direct" or dollar terms?

4. An exporter in Canada must sell foreign currency received from exports to Switzerland, the United States, and Singapore. She received the quotes listed below:

Spot Quotes from Canadian Banks	Spot Quotes from Foreign Banks
$58.53/Swf100	Swf1.7/$1
$86.95/Can$100	Can$1.15/$1
$48.62/S$100	S$2.1/$1

   Should the exporter sell her currency to the Canadian or the foreign banks? Explain.

5. The following information is provided:

	Spot rate Quotations	
	Boston	Geneva
Finland (markka)	$0.2461/Fmk1	Fmk4.0805/US$1
Greece (drachma)	$0.0073/Dr1	Dr134.55/US$1
Venezuela (bolivar)	$0.03425/B1	B32.85/US$1

   An importer in Switzerland must settle his payables to Finland, Greece, and Venezuela. For each currency, he receives two quotes: one from his local bank in Geneva and one from his bank in Boston. What is the lowest cost alternative to settle the payables?

6. The French franc and the German mark are worth $0.22 and $0.68 respectively. Indicate what the French franc/German mark cross rate is.

7. Dai-Kal is a US based multinational corporation that has net inflows DM200 million and net outflows of Ff50 million. The spot rate of the DM is US$0.4/DM1, while the spot rate of the Ff is US$0.1/Ff1. The mark (DM) and the franc (Ff) are highly correlated in their movements against the dollar, and Dai-Kal has not hedged these positions. If the dollar weakens, what will

happen to Dai-Kal's foreign exchange rate position: will it improve or deteriorate in dollar terms?

8. If a US firm's cost of goods sold exposure is much greater than its sales exposure in francs, what will be the effect of a depreciation of the franc on the profit position of this firm?

9. The Dai-Kal Corporation is a US exporter invoicing its exports to Italy in Liras. If the company expects with a great deal of certainty an appreciation of the Lira against the dollar, what is the firm's best strategy to hedge, assuming that there are only spot and forward markets?

10. If a currency is expected to appreciate, what is the best strategy for a speculator operating in the futures market?

11. The US subsidiary of the Mexican Corporation FEMSA invoices its exports to Italy in Liras. If the company expects an appreciation of the Lira against the dollar, what is the firm's best strategy to hedge, assuming that it is limited to hedge in the futures market?

12. Briefly explain under what exchange rate conditions a speculator should purchase a put option on German marks.

13. The Dai-Kal Corporation is a US exporter invoicing its exports to Italy in Liras. If he company expects with a great deal of certainty an appreciation of the Lira against the dollar, what is the firm's best strategy to hedge, assuming that it is limited to operate in the options markets?

14. Your affiliate in Mexico declared a dividend of 50,000,000 pesos, which is transferable in six months to the parent company in the United States. You are worried about adverse conditions in Mexico that could trigger a sharp depreciation of the peso during the next six months. Your attempts to hedge in the forward market were unsuccessful, as your bankers were not able to quote a forward rate for the peso. You are looking at two options:

- Invest in the Bolsa de Valores in Mexico's government securities yielding 18 percent per annum and take the six-month exchange rate risk.

- A US firm operating in Mexico that needs local funds approaches you. They expressed their willingness to borrow 50,000,000 pesos from your affiliate against a payment of $16,000,000 to your bank in the United States in six months.

You asked your staff to research the prospects of the peso/dollar exchange rate in the next six months. They compiled the following data:

Information	Spot Rate	Probability
Current	MxP2.850/US$1	
Six months best scenario	MxP3/US$1	35%
Six months worst scenario	MxP3.4/US$1	65%

a. Indicate the most likely dollar amount of the company's investment in La Bolsa de Valores in Mexico.

b. What is the most profitable option?

Hint: To solve this problem you have to estimate the expected spot rate six months from today. This is a weighted average of the worst and best scenario cases.

9 SKF in Poland: Foreign exchange rate corporate reporting

Tore Bertilsson, Finance Director of the Swedish manufacturing firm SKF, was thinking about all the changes that he had introduced into the company's finance reporting over the last five years. From being mostly a local manufacturer with some experience in other European countries such as Italy, the company had turned into a global player by expanding heavily into Asia, America, and Eastern Europe.

To cope with problems posed by globalization of the company's activities, Tore introduced a financial reporting structure which closely scrutinizes costs and investments worldwide without hampering operational management or strangling local plant innovation. He called the new system the *Twin Track Approach*. It was aimed at providing production managers in different parts of the world—whether Sweden, Malaysia, Brazil, or Mexico—with relative freedom to make capital investment expenditure decisions.

What prompted the implementation of the *Twin Track Approach* were the difficulties initially faced by country managers in getting approval of small and large capital expenses. In the initial phase of expansion, the old approval system created terrible bottlenecks around the world because every capital expenditure had to be referred to headquarters in Gothenburg for approval. Moreover, headquarters had little or no knowledge of the reasons for the request.

Under the *Twin Track Approach*, the only spending subject to headquarters approval are large investment expenditures where the final approval has to come from the office of Mr. Bertilsson. Before these proposals reach his desk, however, they have to have the approval of both the Country Manager and the Regional Treasurer. Both of these executive officers, as a rule, consider only carefully crafted proposals showing a positive net present value.

The role of a Regional Treasurer, which may be based in any one of the largest company markets, such as Germany, France, Italy, Singapore, or North America, is to calculate likely returns on the proposed investment and to find the most suitable sources of capital funding in a particular territory. There are two exceptions, however. The treasury functions in Asia and South America are centrally administrated from Gothenburg.

At the regional offices of the treasury, the analysis of how and where to fund a project starts with an analysis of the relationship between spot, forward, and local and foreign interest rates. This exercise leads to the identification of possible foreign exchange market distortions which may help the company identify relatively low interest rate costs and find exchange rate instabilities. This analysis of both interest rates and currency parities is also useful in relocating the capital surplus of different subsidiaries to countries offering better returns.

Currently, there is tremendous pressure at SKF to expand in the emerging markets because the firm wants to reduce its dependence on slow growing Western Europe, which accounts for 65 percent of the firm's manufacturing base. One of the countries targeted for expansion is Poland, where the demand for the company's products grew by 40 percent in 1996. To tap the potential of this market, SKF is considering a six month, $10 million dollar investment to lay down the financial groundwork for the operation of a new Polish plant.

To obtain these funds, the company is considering borrowing from foreign markets. To do so, the company has to adjust its financial reporting to meet GAAP, (Generally Accepted Accounting Principles,) that provide the investors with more and better quality information about the company in which they are investing. Also, SKF is considering geographic subtleties. The US investors, for instance, are not very concerned about operational matters. They look at the strategy of the company and its approach to the US market. The British and other European investors look closer at whether the company is cutting costs and the size of the advertising budget.

Andreas Erickson, a financial manager for SKF in Gothenburg, is reviewing the financial information to figure out the most convenient way to finance the $10 million dollar loan and the potential foreign exchange risk involved with that loan over the six-month period.

Interest and exchange rate information

Country	Currency		$ equivalence	1-month interest rates	3-month interest rates	6-month interest rates
Argentina	Peso		1.0014			
Australia	Dollar		0.7036			
Bahrain	Dinar		2.6525			
Brazil	Real		0.9101			
Britain	Pound		1.6847	7.28125	7.34375	7.5
		1- month forward	1.6824			
		3-month forward	1.6779			
		6-month forward	1.6718			
Canada	Dollar		0.7136	3.9375	4.125	4.21875
		1- month forward	0.7146			
		3-month forward	0.7167			
		6-month forward	0.7193			
China	Renminb		0.1203			
France	Franc		0.1732	3.4375	3.78125	3.78125
		1- month forward	0.1736			
		3-month forward	0.1742			
		6-month forward	0.1749			
Germany	Mark		0.5802	3.65625	3.875	3.8125
		1- month forward	0.5813			
		3-month forward	0.5833			
		6-month forward	0.5859			
Hong Kong	Dollar		0.1293			
India	Rupee		0.02753			
Japan	Yen		0.008192	0.50	0.50	0.53125
		1- month forward	0.008228			
		3-month forward	0.008305			
		6-month forward	0.008411			
Mexico	Peso		0.1225			
Poland	Zloty		0.2908			
Sweden	Krona		0.1319			
Switzerland	Franc		0.7123	1.84375	2.09375	2.125
		1- month forward	0.7142			
		3-month forward	0.7191			
		6-month forward	0.7256			
Taiwan	Dollar		0.03254			
United States	Dollar			5.625	5.6875	5.75

Source: Taken from *The Wall Street Journal* and *The Financial Times*, November 5, 1997.

94

Key cross-currency rates (London)

	Dollar	Pound	SFranc	Peso	Yen	D-Mark	Ffranc	CndDllr
Canada	1.4014	2.3609	0.99815	0.17164	0.01148	0.81311	0.24277	
France	5.7725	9.7249	4.1115	0.70698	0.04729	3.3493		
Germany	1.7235	2.9036	1.2276	0.2108	0.01412			
Japan	122.07	205.65	86.944	14.95				
Mexico	8.165	13.756	5.8155					
Switzerland	1.414	2.3653						
U.K.	0.59358							
U.S.								

Source: Taken from *The Wall Street Journal* and *The Financial Times*, November 5, 1997.

Options

JAPANESE YEN (CME)
12,500,000 yen; cents per 100 yens

		Calls Settle			Puts-Settle	
Strike price	Nov	Dec	Jan	Nov	Dec	Jan
8150				0.17	0.84	
8200	0.62	1.36		0.3	1.04	1.11
8250	0.36	1.1		0.54	1.28	1.3
8300	0.2	0.89		0.88	1.57	1.5
8350	0.1	0.71	1.67	1.28	1.88	1.74
8400	0.06	0.56		1.74	2.23	2.01

BRITISH POUND (CME)
62,500 pounds; cents per pound

		Calls Settle			Puts-Settle	
Strike Price	Nov	Dec	Jan	Nov	Dec	Jan
16600	2.42	3.3	3.8	0.16	1.04	
16700	1.56	2.68	3.26	0.3	1.42	
16800	0.86	2.14	2.78	0.6	1.88	
16900	0.42	1.66	2.36			
1700	0.2	1.28	1.98			
17100		0.96				

DEUTSCHE MARK (CME)
62,500 marks; cents per mark

		Calls Settle			Puts-Settle	
Strike Price	Nov	Dec	Jan	Nov	Dec	Jan
5700	1.27	1.54	2.02	0.05	0.33	
5750	0.81	1.21	1.68	0.08	0.49	0.69
5800	0.44	0.9		0.22	0.68	0.88
5850	0.21	0.67		0.49	0.95	
5900	0.09	0.5	0.89	0.87	1.28	1.38
5950	0.04	0.36	0.7			

Futures

12,500,000 yens; $ per 100 yens

Yen	Open	High	Low	Settle	Change	Life time High	Life time Low	Open Interest
Dec	0.829	0.8297	0.8225	0.8232	-0.0046	0.932	0.8135	104,782
Mar-98	0.8377	0.8385	0.834	0.8343	-0.0046	0.9375	0.8269	1,124
Jun-98								

125,000 marks; $ per mark

Mark	Open	High	Low	Settle	Change	Life time High	Life time Low	Open Interest
Dec	0.5778	0.5833	0.5762	0.5822	0.005	0.661	0.5343	62,119
Mar-98	0.5852	0.586	0.5843	0.585	0.005	0.616	0.5383	2,782
Jun-98	0.589	0.589	0.5875	0.5875	0.005	0.5876	0.5687	113

Source: Taken from *The Wall Street Journal* and *The Financial Times*, November 5, 1997.

10 The fundamentals of the time value of money

Introduction

The time value of money is a concept used to explain present and future value calculations, as well as the rate of return and the cost of capital. All of these concepts are extremely important tools that are vital for comprehending the subject matter of international finance.

Purpose

The aim of this note is to develop, in a gradual fashion, an understanding of the present value concepts and techniques. These tools can be applied to estimate: 1) cash flows, 2) the cost of capital, 3) present values, 4) net present values and, 5) the role of uncertainty in the evaluation of new capital investments.

The present value concept

If a person is given the option between having a dollar today or a dollar a year later, this individual most likely will choose the first option, since a dollar at hand is worth more than a dollar to be received next year. A dollar today can be invested and earn some interest. To illustrate this process known as **compounding**, suppose that you have $1 and you deposit it in a savings account that pays ten percent interest compounded annually. If the dollar is left in that account for the entire year, the investor will collect $1.10 at year's end. This dollar amount is the one-year future value of one dollar held today. This one-year future value can be expressed as follows:

$$FV = PV + K$$

where FV is the future value of money, PV is the principal and K is the dollar value of one year's interest paid on the one dollar deposit. The future value of the deposit left in the savings account for one year, can also be represented by the following expression:

$$FV = PV + PV(k) = PV(1 + k).$$

If the one-dollar deposit is left in the savings account for several years, the future value is:

$$FV = PV + PV(1 + k) + PV(1 + k)*(1 + k) + ...+ = PV(1 + k)^i*(1 + k) \text{ or}$$

1) $FV = PV(1 + k)^n$

where FV and PV are as before, k is the interest earned on the deposit, and n is the number of periods the money is left in the account earning interest.

Present value

The present value is the inverse of the future value. It is a *principal* that if held today grows to match a future payment or stream of payments due over n periods. Alternatively, it can be viewed as the value today of a stream of payments discounted at rate of k. Since the present value is the mirror image of the future value, then equation 1 can be transformed into a present value expression. Solving equation 1 for PV we have that:

2) $PV = FV/(1 + k)^n$

where PV and FV hold the same meaning as before except that k now plays the role of a discount rate used to estimate the discount factor $1/(1 + k)$.

Illustrations of present and future value concepts

A $100 investment in a two-year savings deposit that earns a fixed ten percent yearly interest can be used to illustrate the future and present value concepts previously developed. In this example, the principal or present value is $100, the discount rate k is 0.1 or ten percent, and the number of investment periods n is two. Applying this information to equation 1), we have that:

$$FV = \$100*(1.1)*(1.1) = 100*(1.1)^2 = \$121$$

This result implies that $100 today will be worth $121 two years later. This can also be interpreted to mean that an investor is indifferent between having $100 today or $121 two years from now.

As a second example, suppose that a firm is holding a $500 payable due in three years to be discounted at 0.12 or 12 percent. Applying all this information to 2), we have that:

$$PV = \$500*[1/(1.12)*(1/1.12)*(1/1.12)] = 500/(1.12)^3 = \$355.89$$

This result implies that with the 12 percent discount rate, $355.89 today is equivalent to $500 three years from now. It also means that the holder of the $500 payable is indifferent between waiting three years to collect $500 or trading the payable today for $355.89.

The rate of return and the opportunity cost of capital

Suppose that a US trader purchases a container loaded with Brazilian shoes at a price of $5.5 million for delivery in six months. To finance this transaction, the trader can borrow dollars from a bank in New York at an interest cost of 8 percent per year. Upon delivery of the container, the trader expects to sell the cargo to a large US retailing firm for $6 million. Using the present value concept, it is possible to estimate 1) the present value, 2) the profits associated with this transaction, and 3) the rate of return:

Present value = (selling price six months from today)/(1+0.08/2) = ($6 million)/(1.04) = $5.77 million.

The profit on this transaction = (selling price - purchase price) = (5.77-5.5) = $0.27 million.

The rate of return on the transaction is as follows:

Rate of return = (profit/purchase price) = (0.27 /5.5) = 0.049 = 4.9%.

The 4.9% return over the six-month period is a return above the cost of borrowing.

This example suggests a very important investment decision rule: *accept an investment when the rate of return of the transaction exceeds the opportunity cost of capital. This is known as the rate of return rule.*

Net present value

Normally, an investor is confronted with an infinite number of possibilities when deciding how to allocate his or her wealth. A common instance is the purchase of a future stream of benefits in exchange for a payment today. For example, an investor may consider purchasing a bond today for $9,500 which promises three $1,000 coupon payments at the end of each year, plus a repayment of the bond's original $10,000 principal at the end of the third year, when the investor's cost of capital is ten percent.

Considering all this information, it is possible to determine whether this transaction makes a net contribution to wealth by estimating its net present value. To do so, the following factors have to be considered: 1) the initial investment ($-I_o$ = $9,500$), and 2) the present value of future benefits ($1,000 each year plus repayment of the principal at the end of the third year) discounted at $k = 0.1$.

	Period	0	1	2	3	3
Stream of benefits			$1,000	$1,000	$1,000	$10,000
Discount factor @ 10%			0.90909	0.8264	0.75131	0.75131
Present value of each benefit			909.091	826.45	751.315	7513.15
Present value of stream of benefits	$10,000					

3) $\text{NPV} = -I_o + C1/(1 + k)^1 + C2/(1 + k)^2 + C3/(1 + k)^3 + \text{Principal}/(1 + k)^3$
    $= -\$9,500 + \$10,000 = \$500$

In this specific instance, the results indicate that the investment in the bond is worth $500.00 more than it costs. Therefore, this investment will increase the investor's wealth by $500 if the transaction is executed. This example also suggests that the investors should always accept investment opportunities having positive net present values. This rule is known as *the net present value rule.*

Net present value of an uneven series of payments

In practice, the sequential payments of a stream of benefits are not always evenly distributed. To estimate the present value of an uneven series of payments, the financial analyst has to add up the present values of each individual cash flow, that is:

4) $\text{NPV} = -I_0 + [R1/(1+k) + R2/(1+k)^2 + ... + Rn/(1+k)^n] = -I_0 + \sum R_i/(1+k)^i$

where *NPV* is the net present value of the uneven series of payments, I_0 is the initial investment, R_i is the benefit in period i, k is the discount rate, and $(1+k)^i$ is the discount factor over n periods.

100

To illustrate this concept, assume a firm considering whether to invest $100, in a three-year project offering a stream of benefits of $20, $20, and $70 at the end of years one, two, and three respectively. The discount rate is ten percent. To assess the viability of this capital investment, the firm has to estimate the net present value of the project to determine whether it makes a net positive contribution. The evaluation of the net present value of this uneven stream of benefits is shown below.

Table 10.1
The present value of a changing cash flow

Period	Cash Flow R_i	PV factor $1/(1 + 0.1)^i$	Present Value $R_i/(1 + 0.1)^i$	Cumulative Present Value $-I_0 + \sum R_i/(1 + 0.1)^3$
0	-100	1.00	-100.00	-100.00
1	20	0.9091	18.18	-81.82
2	20	0.8264	16.52	-65.30
3	70	0.7513	52.59	-12.71

The estimate presented in Table 10.1 indicates that the $100 investment yields a negative net present value. To avoid the loss of wealth, the firm must reject this project.

Risk and return

Until now, the returns on new investment opportunities have been considered as certain. In reality, investment decisions are often based on *expected* rather than *secured* payoffs. For instance, consider the case of a US merchant who pays $100,000 for a load of grain that may be sold for $132,000 if the conditions of the economy are good. However, if the state of the economy is fair, the selling price is only $107,000. A third possibility is a bad state of economy, where the expected selling price drops to only $88,000. If all states of the economy are equally likely, the payoff for this transaction is estimated and summarized below.

State of Nature	Probability	Selling Price	Expected price (Probability * selling price)
Good	0.33	$132,000	$44,000
Fair	0.33	$107,000	$35,666
Bad	0.33	$88,000	$29,333
Expected payoff			*$108,999*

The expected profit on this transaction is (108,999 - 100,000) = $8,999. The expected return is = 8,999/100,000 = 0.089 = 8.9 percent.

101

If the cost of capital is less than 8.9 percent, then the project is worth undertaking, since the expected rate of return (8.9 percent) will be higher than the cost of capital. Otherwise, the project should be rejected.

Problems

1. What is the present value of $500 to be received three years from now if the discount rate is nine percent per year?

2. What is the future value of $300 compounded semi-annually at an interest rate of 12 percent over a two-year period?

3. Over what period of time will the amount of $100 turn out to be $153.90, assuming that it is compounded at a rate of nine percent?

4. Mr. Hosing is selling his house for $95,000. He bought it for $78,000 three years ago. What is the annual return on this investment?

5. Banca Confía offers a 12 percent interest rate compounded every six months on its savings accounts. If you make a two-year deposit of 8,000 pesos today, how much money will you have at the end of the two-year period?

6. Consider the following information:

Period	0	1	2	3
Cash Flow	-100	0	78	75

   If the discount rate is 18 percent, what is the net present value of the stream of payments?

7. You can purchase a container of computer parts in Taiwan for $8 million to be delivered to you six months later. The net cash flows from selling this product are very sensitive to technological change. The discount rate is 8 percent.

State of Technological Change	Probability	Net Cash Flow
No change	0.2	$16 million
Mild change	0.6	$10 million
Drastic change	0.2	$5 million

   a. What is the return on this transaction?

8. What is the present value of a $1,000,000, 180-day certificate of deposit when the discount rate is 6 percent?

9. What is the present value of a 30-day, Ff500,000 receivable when the French discount rate is 6.5 percent (annual)?

10. What is the present value of £2,000,000, 60-day British pound receivable when the British discount rate is 4.5 percent (annual)?

103

11 The present value of annuities and perpetuities

One common circumstance in international investment is the consideration of replacing old equipment. To pick up the surrogate machine, the international executive often has to choose from a variety of options offering different replacement costs and distinct life spans. Also, it is part of the responsibilities of the financial officer of a multinational corporation to assess the market value of subsidiaries, mergers, and the cost of different investment alternatives having dissimilar dates to maturity.

Purpose

The aim of this technical note is to provide the executive of a multinational corporation with the conceptual tools required to rank the replacement cost of new equipment, new investment opportunities, alternative financing schemes, and the market value of a group of subsidiaries.

The first step in the accomplishment of the proposed goal is to introduce the perpetuity and annuity concepts.

Perpetuities

In theory, perpetuity refers to a financial instrument that offers to pay to its holder a fixed income each year, forever. The market value of this financial instrument is the present value of the perpetuity. The logic behind this association is that the maximum price an investor is willing to pay to purchase a stream of benefits is the present value of the benefits. A shortcut to estimate perpetuity's value is described as:

1) $PV = CF/k_d$

where PV is the present value of the perpetuity, CF is the fixed annual payment, and k_d is the discount rate.

To illustrate the application of this concept, consider the case of a bond issue stating an annual coupon payment of $100 forever. If the discount rate is ten percent, the present value of this perpetual stream of benefits is $1,000.

$$PV = \$100/0.1 = \$1,000.$$

This conceptual approach can be also applied to determine the market value of preferred stock, which is equal to the present value of the dividends. To depict the calculation of the market value of preferred equity using the perpetuity approach, consider the case of a stock offering an annual dividend of $500 a year for perpetuity, when the cost of equity is 16 percent. In this case, the present value of the stream of benefits, which is also the price of the stock, is $3,125.

$$PV = Dividend/Cost \text{ of equity}$$

$$PV = D/k_e$$

$$PV = \$500/.16 = \$3,125$$

The perpetuity concept can be also applied to estimate the market value of a firm, since a business is an entity that provides its shareholders with a perpetual stream of dividends. To depict this case, consider the case of a business reporting annual dividends of $600,000. If the cost of equity is 15 percent, the market value of the firm's equity is $4 million.

$$PV = Dividend/k_e$$

$$PV = \$600,000/.15 = 4,000,000.$$

However, this conceptualization of the value of the firm does not work very well in practice, due to the fact that firms often display growing or declining dividends. To take into consideration this important feature of the business world, it is necessary to incorporate the notions of growth and decay into the perpetuity formula.

Valuing growing perpetuities

Due to innovation and technological improvements, many firms exhibit growing dividends. To estimate the market value of firms experiencing growth, the perpetuity formula can be restated as follows:

105

PV = Dividend/(cost of equity - the growth rate of dividends) = D/(k$_e$ - g).

To apply this model, reflect on the case of a firm offering, at some initial point in time, a dividend of $100,000 when the cost of equity is 14 percent. If the firm is expected to maintain a steady growth of 12 percent per year, the market value of the firm's equity is $5 million.

PV = $100,000/(.14 - .12) = 100,000/.02 = $5,000,000.

To apply this model to a business situation encompassing growth and decay, consider a firm planning to invest in a new oil field in Venezuela. The oil well is expected to produce oil forever. Initially, production stands at 250,000 barrels per day. Oil production, however, is foreseen to decline steadily by five percent per year. In contrast to production, oil prices, which are initially at $16 per barrel, are expected to increase by three percent per year. To estimate the market value of this venture, it is necessary to assess sales revenue and the growth or decline of this item over time.

Sales revenue = price * volume of sales = P*Q

To estimate the sales revenue for each year, the volume and the price from the previous year are multiplied by .95 and 1.03 respectively. In other words, the factor to be used each year is .9785 (1.03*.95). Thus revenues decline every year by 2.15% (1-.9785).

If the discount rate is 12 percent, the present value or market value of the Venezuelan oil field is $28,268,551.

PV = 250,000*16/[.12 - (-.0215)] = $28,268,551

Projects with different times to maturity

In corporate practice, the officer of a multinational corporation is often confronted with the task of ranking different streams of payments with varying dates to maturity. A relatively simply procedure to accomplish this task is to apply the annuity concept. An annuity is an asset that pays a fixed amount of money each time period for a specified number of terms. Car loans are a typical example of an annuity. The holder of this loan is entitled to an equal payment each month for a specific number of months.

The Present value of an annuity

To estimate the present value of an annuity, consider the case of two payment streams. In the first case, the fixed payment starts in period zero and lasts forever. In the second instance, the first payment starts in period "i" and extends to perpetuity. The difference between these two perpetuities is the present value of an annuity, that is:

2)   Present value of an annuity $= A*\{1/k - [1/(k*(1 + k)^i)]\}$

In expression 2, A is the fixed or annuity payment, k is the discount rate, and i is the annuity's time horizon.

To apply this concept, think of a consumer who is undecided between leasing a Honda Accord or a Toyota Camry. In the scale of preferences of the consumer, the two vehicles are perfect substitutes for each other. The key consideration in choosing one over the other is the cost of the lease. The consumer wants to enter into the cheapest lease contract. There are two choices: Autofair, from New Hampshire and Cambridge Honda.

The Toyota dealer offers a 36-month lease contract on the Camry in exchange for a $631 down payment and 36 equal payments of $270 each. The discount rate is 12 percent per year. The present value of this lease, which is the down payment plus the present value of the annuity payments, is $8,760. (12 percent is the annual interest, implying 1percent per month.)

$$PV = \text{Down payment} + \{A*[1/k - (1/k(1 + k)^i]\}$$

$$PV = 631 + \{270[1/.01 - 1/[.01(1 + .01)^{36}] = \$8,760.03$$

Cambridge Honda offers the same 36-month lease on the Accord in exchange for a down payment of $1,100 and 36 equal monthly payments of $241 each. The discount rate is also 12 percent per year. The present value of the annuity on this lease, is $8,355.91.

$$PV = \$1100 + \$241[1/.01 - 1/[.01(1 + .01)^{36}] = \$8,355.91$$

Given these estimates, the consumer's best option is to lease the Accord, for it offers the cheapest lease contract.

Ranking of international business projects with different times to maturity

Annuities can also be applied to rank payment streams with differing times to maturity. To explain by example, consider the Belgian company, Van Damme. It plans to replace its old equipment. The suppliers are offering two substitutes. Under the first proposal, the acquisition cost of a new machine is 150,000 Belgian francs (BF). The machine lasts for three years and can be operated with an annual budget of BF40,000. Under a second proposal, the acquisition cost of the new machine is only BF100,000. The shortcoming of this surrogate is that it will last only two years and will have a higher operating cost of BF60,000 per year. Either one of the two alternatives produces the same amount of output, and the discount cost for either project is ten percent.

Since the two machines yield the same output per year, a way to rank the two proposals is by choosing the equipment that provides the lowest production cost per year. To calculate the cost per year associated to each one of the proposals, the financial manager can assume that the company can rent, rather than purchase the machines. The rental payment or *equivalent annual cost* is an annuity.

To estimate the yearly rental payment for Machine One, the financial analyst needs to take two steps. First, he calculates the net present vale of the cost associated to running Machine One for three years. This is shown in the last row of Table 11.1.

Table 11.1
Present value of the cost of running machine one
(BF'000)

	0	1	2	3
Acquisition cost	150.00			
Operating cost		40.00	40.00	40.00
Discount factor @ 10%		1.00	.91	.83	.75
Present Value of the cost of running Machine One	150.00	36.36	33.06	30.05
Accumulated present value	249.47			

In a second phase, the financial analyst has to set the present value of a three-year annuity equal to the present value cost of running Machine One. At this stage, the analyst knows the present value of running the machine and the discount rate. Finding the yearly rental cost is only a matter of solving the equality by the present value of the annuity as shown below.

$$BF249.47 = A*\{(1/0.1) - [(1/0.1)*(1/(1.1)^3)]\}$$

$$A = BF249.47/2.49 = BF100.32$$

This annuity equivalence cost is the amount of money that the company has to pay to run Machine One, since the accumulation of the three annuities is equivalent to the accumulated present value of running Machine One.

Applying the same procedure to the second proposal, the annual cost equivalence is BF117.62, which is shown in the last row of Table 11.2. Again, the addition of the two annuities is equal to the accumulated present value of running Machine Two for two years. Considering the two results, the Belgian corporation should purchase the machine offered in the first proposal.

Table 11.2
Annual cost equivalence of machine two
(BF'000)

	0	1	2
Acquisition cost	100.00		
Operating cost		60.00	60.00
Discount factor @ 10%	1.00	.91	.83
Present Value of the cost of running Machine One	100.00	54.55	49.59
Accumulated present value	204.13		
Present Value of the Annuity payment A1 = 204.13/1.74 =	117.62	117.62	117.62

These results could also be interpreted to mean that Machine One, while performing the same task with the same level of efficiency, is the best alternative because, if rented, it would cost less than Machine Two.

Ranking investment expenditures

This same technique can be applied to rank investment expenditure projects or financing options having different dates to maturity. For example, consider the hypothetical case of Sherman Inc., a South African subsidiary of General Motors. Given the social changes experienced by this country, General Motors has decided to increase its presence in this nation. It can expand its production facilities by investing in either one of three locations: Johannesburg, Pretoria, or Cape Town. The cash flows associated with each location are shown in Table 11.3.

The comparative analysis of the results presented in Table 11.3 indicates that General Motors will be better off investing in the Cape Town project for a year. At the end of the year, the company should re-invest again, and so on. By following this investment strategy, GM gets the highest possible annual return on its South African investment, since the annual equivalent revenue on this option is the highest.

Table 11.3
Annual equivalence revenues of the South African projects
(Rand, million)

Johannesburg, flows	-300.00	350.00	320.00
Discount factor, 13%	1.00	.87	.76
Present value	-300.00	304.35	241.97
Net present value	246.31		
A1 = 246.31/1.62		152.05	152.05
Pretoria, flows	-1,000.00	750.00	760.00
Discount factor, 13%	1.00	.87	.76
Present value	-1,000.00	652.17	574.67
Net present value	739.71		
A2 = 739.7/2.28		324.43	324.43
Cape Town, flows	-600.00	1,100.00	
Discount factor, 13%	1.00	.87	
Present value	-600.00	956.52	
Net present value	356.52		
A2 = 356/0.86		409.80	

Problems

1. The British affiliate of the US multinational Rice Co. is contemplating raising $12 million with a bond issue denominated either in dollars or pounds. The coupon on the dollar issue is ten percent. On pounds, it is 13 percent. In either one of the alternatives, the date to maturity is five years with semi-annual interest payments. The principal repayment is at maturity. The US and British tax rates are 30 and 35 percent respectively. All the interest payments, including exchange rate losses on interest payments, are deductible. If the spot rate is $1.94/£1, what is the best financing alternative?

2. Plumrose, a Venezuelan company, is in the meat packaging business. It produces 3,000 tons of meat per month. The price in terms of the local currency is 250 bolivars per ton. Eighty percent of the output (2,400 tons per month) is for domestic sales and the remaining 20 percent (600 tons per month) is for export to Japan.

   Domestic sales have been increasing at a rate of 2 percent per year and they are expected to keep this pace in the foreseeable future. Exports have been growing at 10 percent per year. This pattern of exports is expected to continue for the next three years. Afterwards, exports in Japan will grow only 4 percent per year. Export prices are expected to increase by 1 percent over the next three years; thereafter, they will not grow. In contrast, the domestic price is expected to grow at a steady 1 percent per year in the predictable future.

   Plumrose has $10 million to promote exports or domestic sales through the acquisition of new outlets and more equipment. The discount rate for Plumrose is 17 percent.

   Which is the best use of resources: promoting domestic sales or elevating exports?

3. Cervecería Modelo, a Mexican brewery, is offered a five-year contract providing $3 million each year to allow an Australian company to market the company's products in Australia and the Pacific Rim. Alternatively, a competing firm from Indonesia is offering Modelo $14 million for a five-year contract to distribute the Modelo products within the same region. This contract provides $4 million down and $2 million a year for five years. The discount rate in both cases is 10 percent.

   What is the net present value of each option, and what is the best choice?

   Note: The present value of the two options are not directly comparable since they have different maturity periods.

12 Wendy's franchising in Argentina

Introduction

While waiting for the flight that was going to take him from Miami to Columbus, Paul Vandelen, Wendy's International Franchise Manager for South America, began to ponder the prospects of Wendy's expansion in Argentina. He had to present a long-term business plan to the Board soon, stating the full market potential for the South American country and the financial resources required to implement the program. In the short-term, the most pressing task faced by Mr. Vandelen was to fine-tune the joint venture with Pumper Nic, a well-established Argentinean fast food chain. Wendy's had already purchased eleven Pumper Nic's outlets, located in the Greater Buenos Aires metropolitan area, and had turned them into Wendy's restaurants. By comparison, McDonald's already had one hundred restaurants in 1996, up from only ten in 1991.

The number of restaurants

To estimate the extent of Wendy's expansion in Argentina, Mr. Vandelen was considering a host of factors that are summarized in the following formula:[1]

Restaurants =
[(TPCarg/CNRus)*(HCPCarg/HCPCus)*(IPCarg/IPCus)*(PSHarg/PSHus)]

where:
- TPCarg is the population of largest cities in Argentina;
- CNRus refers to the number of customers needed to support an average Wendy's restaurant in the US;
- HCPCarg is the estimate of hamburger consumption per capita in Argentina;
- HCPCus represents the estimate of hamburger consumption per capita in the US;
- IPCarg is income per capita abroad;

- IPCus is meant to describe income per capita in the US;
- PSHarg is the proportion of income per capita spent on hamburgers in Argentina; and
- PSHus refers to the percentage of income per capita spent on hamburgers in the US.

Naturally, the financial plan depends to a large extent on the number of outlets required to serve the Argentinean market, as well as on the expansion mix between company-owned restaurant and franchises. Another factor playing a role is the ratio of independent restaurants to mall-type stores.

The cost of the building and land for an independent unit is $800,00. The average of a mall-type store ranges from $200,000 to 400,000. Mall-type stores in Argentina, however, are rare. In the Greater Buenos Aires there are only six of them. In the rest of the country, on average, there is only one major mall per city of more than one million inhabitants.

The restaurants are normally located in heavily populated urban areas and are built according to the company's specifications concerning exterior style and interior décor. The majority are free-standing, one-story brick buildings, substantially uniform in design and appearance, constructed on sites of approximately 40,000 square feet, with parking for approximately forty five cars. Restaurants have a preparation area, a dining room capacity for ninety persons, and double pick up windows for drive-through service.

Depreciation is straight line for buildings, kitchen equipment, and restaurant furniture. For the former, depreciation is over forty years and for the second and third items depreciation is over an average of seven years.

The company

With no real intention to be a national chain, Wendy's began in 1969 as a single unit in downtown Columbus, Ohio. A second unit quickly followed on the other side of the city. The next step, after three years of operations, was the first franchise opening in Indianapolis, Indiana. This first franchise sparked the beginning of yet another American fast food sensation.

Wendy's success appears to be the result of focusing on old-fashioned quality. It is the only fast food chain still serving freshly prepared hamburgers, one at a time, made to order. Wendy's philosophy is not about being number one in terms of size, but about being number one in terms of quality. The company's founder, Mr. Thomas, has expressed his philosophy on many occasions:

> I opened the first Wendy's restaurant because I felt there was a place for fresh hamburgers made just the way the customer wants...This philosophy sets us apart from other chains and helped us to grow to 5,000 restaurants worldwide.[2]

This quality approach is reflected in the company's pricing policy. Wendy's hamburgers are more expensive. By the end of 1997, Wendy's had 4,993 restaurants, from which 481 were located outside the United States. By the year 2002, the company plans to open a total of 8,000. This expansion program foresees an opening of 150 restaurants per year internationally.[3]

In 1997, Wendy's market intensity in the US was estimated at 61,055 people per unit. Comparatively, McDonald's has one restaurant for every 22,000 persons. Another interesting comparison between the two companies is that McDonald's has the third most recognized brand name in the world, whereas Wendy's is barely known outside the US.

Another intriguing aspect of the hamburger war is advertising. Wendy's has the second highest advertising awareness among the US fast food service restaurants in spite of the fact that McDonald's, which is in the number one position, outspends Wendy's by a proportion of five to one.[4]

Wendy's financial position

Total assets increased to $272.3 million or 18 percent during 1995.Common shareholder's equity rose to 29.1 percent in 1996 and amounted to more than one billion, by the first time in the history of the company. On per share basis, equity increased to $8.16 per share in 1996, from only 14.5 percent in 1995.

The company manages its portfolio debt in response to changes in interest rates and foreign exchange by periodically retiring, redeeming, and repurchasing debt. For instance, in 1996, debt was reduced by more than $100 million. In the same fashion, convertible debentures, previously outstanding, were all converted to common share. These two adjustments helped Wendy's to reduce the ratio of debt to equity from 41 percent in 1995 to only 33 percent in 1996. The weighted annual interest rate stood at 7.1 percent in 1996. This financial performance has helped the company to earn high ratings. Standard and Poor and Moody's have placed Wendy's debt ratings at BBB and Baa-1, respectively. By comparison, McDonald's has better ratings at Aa2 and AA+.

McDonald's expansion strategies

The strategy of McDonald's has focused on global dominance through a rapid expansion of additional restaurants to penetrate new markets and establish a brand name ahead of its competitors.[5] For instance, by the end of the first half of 1997, McDonald's had opened 677 new restaurants outside the US.

The leading fast food company in the world has a strong presence in Latin America. It has more than 1,000 restaurants in 27 countries. These outlets provide the company with four percent of total operating income. McDonald's presence in the region began in 1979 and in Argentina in1986. To further its presence in this region, McDonald's is planning to invest one billion there through the year 2000. Half of this money will be allocated to Brazil.

114

McDonald's success in world markets has been attributed to its tradition of adapting to the conditions of local demand. For instance, it serves non-beef hamburgers in India, while offering a teriyaki burger in Japan. In Switzerland, it cancelled its breakfast service to avoid conflicting with "cultural nuances."[6] Another important aspect of McDonald's strategy in world markets is its program to develop local suppliers. In Brazil, for instance, it has invested a significant amount of resources into helping farmers master the cultivation of potatoes.[7]

Wendy's expansion strategy

Unlike McDonald's, which expands one store at a time, Wendy's preferred to unfold in blocks. In 1995, for instance, it entered into a strategic alliance with Tim Horton, a Canadian fast food retailer. This alliance gave Wendy's access to more than 1,323 restaurants in Canada.[8] In the future, however, the firm is planning to grant new franchises both in the United States and foreign countries on a unit-by-unit basis.[9]

Promotional marketing abroad has been absent from Wendy's strategy, due to lack of economies of scale in advertising. The minimum scale required to launch an advertising program is 25 stores per country. So far, only Canada, Japan, and the Philippines are meeting this standard.

A comparative analysis of performance in the fast food industry suggests an overwhelming dominance by McDonald's, both in the US and abroad. This perception is somewhat misleading, however. In 1996 and 1997, McDonald's has been well behind Wendy's in terms of US growth in the number of restaurants, sales and profitability.

The profile of Argentina

Argentina is the eighth largest country in the world in terms of area. As a member of Mercosur, Argentina enjoys free access to a combined market of over 200 million people. Its infrastructure is modern, featuring highly developed railroad links, good quality international airports, and well designed seaports.

Of its more than 34 million inhabitants, 87 percent of them live in urban areas. The largest of all is the Greater Buenos Aires Metropolitan area, hosting more than 18 million residents. Other major cities with populations over one million include Córdoba, Santa Fe, Mendoza, Tucumán, and Entre Rios.[10]

Natural resources

Argentina is a country well endowed with natural resources. The climate ranges from sub-tropical to sub-arctic and supports a large variety of crops. The pampas, the agricultural heartland of Argentina, are among the most fertile lands in the world, boasting abundant annual harvests of grains and oilseeds. Although the yield per unit of land in the production of grains is similar to that of Australia and Canada, the use of fertilizers is considerably less intensive. Therefore, agricultural output contains fewer chemicals. Livestock and meat production also play an important role in the Argentinean economy. Over 73 percent of country's land is devoted to cattle raising and breeding.

The labor market

The Argentines are highly educated, with a literacy rate of 95 percent. However, the skills are highly concentrated in traditional activities. This aspect of the educational system has led to an oversupply of lawyers, sociologists, and psychologists and a shortage of engineers, agronomists, and other technicians.

The normal workload is eight hours per day, 48 hours per week. Overtime is compensated with a 50 percent premium. Workers with less than two-thirds of the normal load are considered part-timers. The minimum wage rate is Ps1 per hour, though the average salary is Ps 3.25. This wage, while low in terms of US standards, is relatively high for Latin America.

The relatively high cost of Argentinean labor has led to a sharp increase in the unemployment rate, up from 12 percent in October of 1994 to 17 percent in May of 1997. Also, it has induced a large increase in the cost of living. The Greater Buenos Aires metropolitan area is considered one of the most expensive cities in the world. Between 1991 and 1997, the cost of living in Argentina rose 58 percent.[11]

Gross domestic product and the Argentinean markets

Argentina's gross domestic product in 1996 amounted to $295 billion. On a per capita basis it was equivalent to $8,900. This was the highest GDP per capita in Latin America. This is an important index for the fast food industry, since it is well known that the consumption of hamburgers, and of beef in general, is positively correlated with the GDP per capita. In Argentina, the use of GDP per capita as a measure of consumption of red meat may be misleading, since per capita consumption of beef in Argentina is twice as high as the US.[12]

While the Argentinean consumers eat a lot more beef than their American counterparts, they do not consume as many hamburgers. It is estimated that consumption of hamburgers per capita in Argentina is only one third of the US consumption. The average price of a hamburger in Argentina is Ps25, or $2.5. In the US, Germany, Japan, and Switzerland is $2.56, $2.69, $2.08, and $3.87 respectively.[13]

Foreign direct investment

Since 1990, Argentina has been modifying its foreign direct investment laws. These changes have given foreign firms an unprecedented access to local markets. Foreign investors are not required to seek prior approval of their investment expenditures from the Argentine government. Another advantage is that they can repatriate, tax free, the full amount of their capital investments and earnings at any time. More importantly, foreign and domestic companies are treated equally. Foreign firms have open and equal access to all economic sectors. Taxation of earnings is also very even. Corporate taxes on wholly owned subsidiaries are similar to those paid by the local companies. It amounts to 33 percent, which is very similar to US tax rates.

The franchising industry in Argentina

Prior to 1990, the franchising industry did not exist in Argentina. With the process of privatization implemented by President Menem, many public employees lost their jobs, for which they were compensated with generous severance payments. Many of these individuals used their severance payments to purchase franchises. The franchising industry had grown from practically zero in 1990 to $620 million in sales by the end of 1994.

However, as more and more companies entered into the franchise market, several unpleasant trends began to unfold. To begin with, quality of the products sold by the franchises faded. The franchise products did not seem to match the quality featured by the items sold by the parent company in the home market. Naturally, dwindling quality led to a decline in sales and profit margins. These trends led to a collapse of the franchise industry in 1995. The pervasive effects of the Tequila Crisis on the economy of Argentina deepened the maladies of the industry even further. The conditions prevailing in the industry were so harsh that companies like Kentucky Fried Chicken and Domino's Pizza folded after operating in Argentina for less than one year. However, companies like McDonald's and Burger King appeared to have been spared by the crisis. They lead the fast food industry with 55 and 26 percent market shares respectively.

By 1997, while the Argentinean economy had fully recovered from the 1995 recession, the franchising industry had not. A study conducted at the end of 1996 revealed that the franchise industry in Argentina was still facing the same problems that it had in 1995. Lack of quality (38 percent), limited financial resources and know-how (26 percent), poor labor training (20 percent), and a small demand for franchise products (16 percent). [14]

Wendy's franchising system

The Restaurant Franchise Document details the conditions that rule a franchise. It gives this fast food chain the right to construct and own, or lease, restaurants only on sites it approves. After submitting an approved application and financial materials, an individual becomes an accepted applicant upon the execution of a Preliminary Letter of Agreement. This document does not guarantee acceptance as a franchise owner. It only entitles the applicant to commence a training program intended to allow both parties the opportunity to assess the prospects for a long-term relationship.

Upon the execution of a Preliminary Letter of Agreement, which gives the applicant only the right to be considered, the prospective franchisee is required to pay a non-refundable fee of $5,000. If the application is accepted, the franchisee pays a technical assistance fee of $30,000. Once this is met, the franchisee can purchase the franchise at a price of $350,000.[15] At the acquisition of the franchise, the franchisee is assigned a restaurant that it leases from Wendy's. For the use of this facility, the franchiser is entitled to receive rent and royalties, which are, respectively, 12.5 percent and 4 percent of gross sales.

In addition to paying all the fees previously discussed, the franchisee has to supply kitchen equipment and restaurant furniture. These two items cost $400,000. A franchise is also required to spend four percent of its gross receipts in advertising and promotion. This can be increased at Wendy's request to five percent. Two percent of the advertising fee is allocated to local and regional advertising and the other two percent goes to Wendy's Advertising Program. The franchise agreement is for an initial term of twenty years or the term of the lease, whichever is shorter.

Notes

1 Rocío Alcazar developed this formula with the assistance of Keri Bittner, Gerhard Huttel, Gabriella Nicolau, and Markus Winter under the direction of Professor Francisco Carrada-Bravo. The formula was developed originally for America's Favorite Chicken Company.
2 www.investquest.com/InvestQuest/w/wen/ne/news/wenrest.htm.
3 www.hoover.com/premium/profiles/11621.html.
4 www.investquest.com/InvestQuest/w/wen/main/wencp.htm, Wendy's International, Inc., Corporate Profile, July 27, 1997, p. 2.
5 www.mcdonald.com/a_system/investinfo.
6 Gray, Steve, and Burns, Melanie, McDonald's Corporation. Personal interview, fall 1996.
7 Willman, John, "Perspective: Managing Global Brands," in *The Global Company*, The Financial Times, London, UK, October 22, 1997.
8 Tim Horton is a baked goods and coffee retailer.
9 www.wendy's. com/10k95.txt., Securities and Exchange Commission, Form 10-K, July 27, 1997, p. 11.
10 See Table 1 in the Statistical Appendix.
11 US Department of Labor, *Foreign Labor Trends: Argentina*. Bureau of International Labor Affairs, 1993-1994. Consumer Latin America 1996, Euro

Monitor, PLC, p. 96. Also, Tran, Hoai, Huong, *Official Guide to Household Spending*, New Strategist, 3rd edition, 1995, p. 176.

12 *The Economist*, "Big MacCurrencies," April 11, 1998, p. 58.
13 www.exporthotline.com, "Argentina Industry Report—Franchising."
14 The franchise price is reassessed periodically.
15 This varies.

Technical Appendix
Formula to Estimate the Number of Outlets per Country

To estimate the number of restaurants in a country, several steps are required.

Number of Customers Needed

The number of customers required to support a Wendy's Restaurant in Argentina is based on the number of customers that support a restaurant in the US (CNRus) adjusted by the relative scale of preferences between US and Argentinean consumers for hamburgers. That is,

$$CNRadjusted = CNRus*[HCPCus/HCPCarg]$$

where CNRus is as before, and HCPCus and HCPCarg are hamburger consumption per capita in the US and Argentina respectively.

CNRadjusted reflects the number of customers required to operate a restaurant in Argentina, given different levels of hamburger consumption per capita between the US and Argentinean consumers.

To find out the number of customers required to operate a restaurant in Argentina, it is also necessary to incorporate into the formula differences in the levels of income per capita between Argentina and the US.

$$CNRarg = CNRadjusted*[IPCus/IPCarg]*[PSHus/PSHarg]$$

where IPCus and IPCarg are income per capita in the US and Argentina respectively, and PSHus and PSHarg are proportions of income per capita spent on hamburgers in each country. As income rises, people do not always allocate the same proportion of the new level of income to food consumption. For instance, if income rises by ten percent, the consumers may change their consumption of food by more or less than ten percent.

Number of Restaurants in Argentina

Since the number of customers is already known, the next step is to estimate the number restaurants in Argentina by dividing the population target by the number of customers per restaurant. That is

$$Number\ of\ restaurants\ in\ Argentina = TCParg/CNRarg$$

where TCParg is the target population in Argentina and CNRarg is as before. Substituting CNRarg for its expression in point 3, the following is obtained:

Number of Restaurants =

TCParg/[CNRus*(HCPCus/HCPCarg)*(IPCus/IPCarg)*(PSHus/PSHarg)]

The substitution of terms provides a one-step formula to estimate the number of restaurants as follows:

Number of Restaurants =

[(TPCarg/CNRus)*(HCPCarg/HCPCus)*(IPCarg/IPCus)*(PSHarg/PSHus)]

STATISTICAL APPENDIX

Table 12.1
Population of major cities of Argentina, 1996
(millions)

City	Population
Greater Buenos Aires	18.66
Santa Fe	3.35
Córdoba	3.29
Mendoza	1.71
Tucumán	1.34
Entre Ríos	1.22

Source: *Instituto Nacional de Estadísticas y Censos*, INDEC, Censo Nacional de Vivienda, 1991.

Table 12.2
Wendy's average net dollar sales per domestic restaurant, 1993 - 96
(net sales are in dollars, thousand)

	1996	Growth	1995	Growth	1994	Growth	1993	Growth
Company	1,049	3.45%	1,014	1.30%	1,001	2.35%	978	2.35%
Franchise	978	0.41%	974	-0.81%	982	2.29%	960	2.29%
Total Domestic	998	1.22%	986	-0.20%	988	2.28%	966	2.28%

Source: Securities and Exchange Commission, Form 10 – K, July 27, 1997.

Table 12.3
Wendy's cost of sales and its distribution, 1995
(Percentage of sales)

ITEM	1996	1995
Cost of sales	60.1	58.7
Distribution of cost of sales		
Food cost	30	29.1
Labor cost	26	25.6
Other	4.1	4.0
Total	60.1	58.7

Source: Wendy's International, Corporate Profile, July 27, 1997, p. 20.

Table 12.4
Operating profit margin, 1994-1996
(Percentage of retail sales)

ITEM	1996	1995	1994
Retail Sales	100	100	100
From which:			
Cost of sales	60.1	58.7	58
Operating cost	26.6	26.2	26.3
Operating Margin	13.3	15.1	15.7
Income tax	38.8	33.3	35.2

Source: Wendy's International, Corporate Profile, July 27, 1997, p. 22.

Table 12.5
International Wendy's, 1996

Country/Territory	Company Owned	Franchise
Argentina	11	
Bahamas		4
Canada	105	98
Dominican Republic		4
El Salvador		5
Greece		8
Guatemala		3
Honduras		5
Hong Kong		7
Indonesia		18
Italy		2
Japan		54
Mexico		8
New Zealand		6
Philippines		31
Puerto Rico		19
Saudi Arabia		14
South Korea		6
Switzerland		3
Taiwan		12
Thailand		3
Turkey		4
UK	6	1
Virgin Islands		3
Other		41
Total	**122**	**359**

Source: Securities and Exchange Commission, Form 10-K, July 27, 1997.

Table 12.6
Wendy's domestic and international restaurants

	1996	1995	1994
Open at the beginning of year	4,667	4,411	4,168
Opened	343	333	298
Closed	77	77	55
Acquisitions within the system	283	203	82
Dispositions within the system	283	203	82
Open at the end of the year	4,993	4,667	4,411

Source: Wendy's International, Corporate Profile, July 27, 1997, p. 24.

Table 12.7
Fast food restaurants financial statistics, 1996
(Percentage of retail sales)

(Percentage of sales)	%
Food sales	96.4
Beverage sales	3.6
Cost of food	31.2
Cost of beverages	0.9
Salaries	24.4
Employee benefits	2.7
Direct operating expenses	7.4
Marketing	5.3
Utility services	7.7
Occupancy costs	6.4
Repairs	1.6
Depreciation	1.7
Other	2.1
General and administrative	5.7
Corporate overhead	1.9
Interest	1
Other	0.1
Income before taxes	9

Source: National Restaurant Association, Restaurant Industry Operation, Report - 1996.

Table 12.8
Exchange rate, 1991-1996
(Pesos/$)

1996	1995	1994	1993	1992	1991
1.0	1.0	0.999	0.999	0.994	0.99

Table 12.9
Country statistics, 1996

Key Statistics	US	Argentina
Area (square kilometers)	9,372,610	2,766,890
Population (million, 1995)	266.4	34.7
Population growth (%)	0.91	1.1
Labor force (million)	132.2	10.9
GDP ($, billion)	7,240	295
GDP growth (%)	2.1	4.4
GDP per capita ($)	27,500	8,900
Inflation (%)	2.5	1.7
Unemployment rate (%)	5.6	16
Hourly wages ($)	13.22	3.25

Source: Central Intelligence Agency, CIA, *The World Fact Book*, 1998.

Table 12.10
Wendy's international consolidated income statement
(dollars, million)

	9/29/96	10/1/95
REVENUES		
Retail sales	1,170	1092
Franchise revenues	238	194
Total	1,408	1,286
COST AND EXPENSES		
Cost of sales	729	662
Company restaurants		
operating cost	284	260
operating cost	39	42
General and Administrative	96.7	96.1
Amortization of property	66.1	59.3
Special charges	0	27
Interest net	5.1	8.1
Total	1,220	1,155
INCOME BEFORE TAXES	188	132
Income taxes	72.4	40.125
Net income	116	91
Earnings per share	0.9	0.76
SYSTEM-WIDE SALES		
Wendy's International	3,568	3,382
Tim Horton	469	393

Source: Wendy's International, Corporate Profile, 1997.

Table 12.11
Average sales per restaurant and number of restaurants
(sales in dollar, million)

Company	0.784	0.766
Franchise	0.734	0.739
Total domestic	0.748	0.747

Number of Wendy's Restaurants

Company	1,296	1,290
Franchise	3,545	3,297
Total	4,841	4,587
Tim Horton	1,323	1,117

Source: Wendy's International, Corporate Profile, 1997.

13 Transnational investment

Introduction

Expanding opportunities in world markets have provided incentives for a large increase in cross-border capital expenditures. Similar to local expenditure projects, international investment projects need to be assessed to determine their contribution to the value of the firms implementing them. To evaluate transnational investment, the financial manager is required to understand the factors shaping the cross-cultural appreciation of the firm's products in foreign markets, the tax complexities involved in overseas investments, and the degree of the firm's exposure to country and exchange rate risks.

Purpose

The purpose of this note is to provide the student of International Finance with the financial tools required to incorporate country and exchange rate risk exposure in the evaluation of an international investment project. To illustrate the application of these tools, this note will use examples associated with US corporate investments overseas.

Analytical framework to evaluate capital expenditures

To evaluate capital expenditures, one can resort to applying the net present value, internal rate of return, or discounted benefit cost ratio techniques. Given these choices, this note will rely on the use of the net present value concept because of the theoretical advantages offered by this approach in comparison to the other competing techniques.[1]

The meaning of net present value (NPV)

The net present value is the present value of future cash flows after deduction of the initial cash outlay required to meet the capital expenditure. The first step in the application of this method is to discount both outflows and inflows by an appropriate rate of return or cost of capital; the second step is to subtract the capital expenditure outflow from the inflows.
If the net present value is positive, the project is deemed to be acceptable. It can be estimated using expression 1,

1) $NPV = -I_0 + CF_1/(1 + k) + CF_2/(1 + k)^2 + ... + CF_n/(1 + k)^n = -I_0 + \Sigma CF_i/(1 + k)^i$

where I_o is the initial capital expenditure; CF_i is the cash flow in period i; k is the discount rate, and i is the investment horizon going from 1 to n (years, months, etc.). To estimate the net present value of an overseas capital expenditure, it is necessary to have information on sales revenue, operating expenses, depreciation, interest expenses, taxes, and the life expectancy of the project, as well as a discount rate.

Revenues

To estimate the revenues related to a foreign project, the firm has to forecast - usually for a five-year period prices, volume of sales, and inflation trends in the host country. Other factors affecting revenues are price control mechanisms, import duties, export subsidies, the availability of foreign substitutes for the firm's products, cross-cultural differences regarding taste, and the income policies of the host country.

Operating expenses

Operating expenses are composed of manufacturing and administrative expenses. Manufacturing or direct expenses refer to the variable cost incurred by the firm to manufacture the company's output. Administrative expenses are the costs of running the company.

Depreciation

Depreciation refers to the wear and tear of the capital equipment resulting from the manufacturing of the company's output. It is a non-cash expense that can be estimated using either a straight-line or an accelerated depreciation method. Under straight line, annual depreciation equals a constant proportion of the initial investment less salvage value. Accelerated depreciation can be estimated using the rules set by different countries to allow firms an accelerated cost recovery system. In the United States, there are at least six depreciation schedules. Depreciation is a very important item to consider in the evaluation of the net present value of the cash flows of a subsidiary for the following reason: *it reduces taxable income through the annual tax shield equivalent to the value of the depreciation times the marginal tax rate.*

Interest expenses

Interest expense refers to the procedure used by the firm to finance capital expenditures and working capital. To fund these expenses, the firm may resort to issuing short-term or long-term debt. Otherwise, it may consider equity funding.

If long-term debt is the preferred funding alternative, the firm has a choice between bonds with fixed coupon rates or convertible bonds to be exchanged into equity at some point of time in the future. If the firm desires to use equity to finance its capital expenditures, it may choose between issuing preferred or common stock. Preferred stock imposes on the firm the obligation to meet a pre-agreed fixed coupon payment at the end of each fiscal year. In contrast, common stock liberates the firm from this responsibility, since common stock holders are entitled only to a claim on the net income left after the company has met its preferred stock liability.

Taxation

Understanding the implications of the host and home country fiscal laws regarding foreign direct investment is paramount in determining the net present value of cash flows. Carrying out this task is not easy because international projects are subject to numerous taxing jurisdictions, multiple tax regimes, and complex credit provisions.

Estimation of foreign-currency cash flows

In corporate finance, there are two widely accepted methods for estimating cash flows: the *equity* approach and, the *free cash flow* (FCF) technique. The basic difference between the two approaches is the treatment of interest expenses. However, the FCF approach is more widely quoted and used. Under the FCF approach, net income (NI) is restated by eliminating the interest expense.

Depreciation is then added back to arrive at the FCF as shown in the hypothetical example in Table 13.1.

Table 13.1
Estimating cash flows

Free Cash Flow Approach

Revenue	140
- Operating expenses	100
- Depreciation	10
Operating income (EBIT)	30
- Interest expense	0
Earnings before taxes (EBT)	30
- Taxes @ 50%	15
Net income	15
Depreciation	10
Foreign currency cash flow	25

To get the net present value (NPV), the cash flows from different periods should be discounted using the weighted average cost of capital (WACC), which is discussed in the following section. Then the NPV stated in foreign currency is converted into home currency terms.

A second way to get the NPV in home currency is: 1) project exchange rates for each period, 2) convert the free cash flows from foreign into home currency, and 3) discount the cash flows at the home country WACC. The choice of technique to estimate the NPV depends on where the project is financed. If it is financed in the host country, the first method should be used; when financed in the home country, then the second technique is more appropriate.

Risk and return

To estimate the rate of return that compensates an investor for the risk implicit in a specific business activity, it is customary to use the *Capital Asset Pricing Model* (CAPM).

2) $k = k_f + \beta(k_m - k_f)$

Under the basic tenets of this model in a competitive market, the return associated with an investment in a specific business activity depends on:

1   The numerical value of the risk free rate (k_f)
2   The beta index (β), a measure of the degree of risk associated with a business activity relative to the market.

131

3   The risk premium (k_m), measured by the difference between the risk free rate and the market return.

The higher the value of beta, the higher the business risk. Consequently, a business activity showing a higher beta has to offer a higher return to compensate the investor for the added risk. The beta of a well-diversified portfolio is known as the market beta, and is equal to one. This is interpreted to mean that the risk associated with a well-diversified portfolio is equal to the market risk.

Funding and risk

If a new project is fully financed with equity, the appropriate return on equity is measured as follows:

3) $k_e = k_f + \beta_e(k_m - k_f)$

where k_e is the expected rate of return on the firm's equity. However, if the capital expenditure is fully financed by issuing debt, then the return on the firm's debt is measured by the following expression:[2]

4) $k_d = k_f + \beta_d(k_m - k_f)$

where k_d is the expected return on the firm's debt.

Another alternative for financing a capital expenditure is to resort to a mixture of debt and equity. To measure the rate of return on projects financed both by debt and equity, it is customary to apply the weighted average cost of capital (WACC). The numerical value of this index depends on the proportion of debt and equity to the market value of the firm. That is,

5) $WACC = k_w = (D/V)k_d (1 - tx) + (S/V)k_e$

where k_w is the weighted average return on a capital expenditure financed by a mixture of debt (D) and equity (S). (D/V) is the ratio of debt to the total value of the firm, k_d is the cost of debt, tx is the corporate tax rate, (S/V) is the ratio of equity to the total market value of the firm, and k_e is the cost of equity.

Example

To apply the concepts previously discussed, consider the hypothetical case of the Spanish company, Laboratorios Alfa, which is assumed to be a subsidiary of the US multinational Merck. To estimate the cost of capital of this subsidiary, it is further assumed that the capital expenditures of this ancillary were financed with a mixture of debt and equity in pesetas. If the Spanish risk-free interest rate (k_f) is 10 percent, Alfa's equity beta (β_e) is 1.5, and the expected return on the Spanish market portfolio (k_m) is 18 percent, the cost of equity of Alfa is 22 percent.

$$k_e = k_f + \beta_e(k_m - k_f)$$

$$k_e = .1 + 1.5*(.18 - .1)$$

$$k_e = .1 + .12 = .22 = 22\%$$

If Alfa's return on debt (k_d) is known to be 12 percent, the beta[3] of debt (β_d) is 0.25. This results obtains using expression 4 and solving by β_d, we have that

$$\beta_d = (k_d - k_f)/(k_m - k_f)$$

$$\beta_d = (.12 - .1)/(.18 - .1) = .02/.08 = 0.25.$$

If Alfa's ratio of debt to the market value of the firm, (D/S) is 0.5, and the Spanish tax rate is 40 percent, the average cost of capital (WACC) of Alfa is 14.6 percent.

$$k_w = (D/V)k_d (1 - tx) + (S/V)k_e$$

$$k_w = (0.5)*.12*(1 - 0.4) + (0.5)*.22$$

$$k_w = .036 + .11 = .146 = 14.6\%$$

Exchange rate forecast

A widely used approach to forecast long-term future exchange rates is the purchasing power parity approach (PPP) presented in expression 6. Under this version of PPP, the anticipate spot rate (Et), is a function of the current equilibrium spot rate (Eo) and the ratio of the expected price indexes of both the country hosting the subsidiary and the US.

6) $Et = Eo*[(1 + i_h)/(1 + i_{us})]$

To apply this concept, consider the case of Alfa again. If the Spanish peseta is currently trading at 100 pesetas per one dollar (Ps100/$1), and if the inflation in both Spain and the US are expected to be two and four percent respectively, then the peseta/dollar parity a year from now (E1)is expected to be approximately, Ps98.08/$1.

133

$$E1 = Eo*[(1 + i_h)/(1 + i_{us})]$$

$$E1 = (Ps100/\$1)*(1.02/1.04)$$

$$E1 = (Ps100/\$1)*(.9808)$$

$$E1 = Ps98.08/\$1$$

To provide a second example, consider the relationship between the French franc and the dollar. If the spot rate is FF5/$1 and the rates of inflation are seven percent in France and four percent in the US, then the franc/dollar spot rate expected a year later is FF5.144/$1.

$$E1 = Eo*[(1 + i_h)/(1 + i_{us})]$$

$$E1 = (FF5/\$1)*(1.07/1.04)$$

$$E1 = (FF5/\$1)*1.0288$$

$$E1 = FF5.144/\$1$$

Evaluation of transnational investment

To apply the entire salient points covered in this note, consider the hypothetical case of the US multinational corporation Virtual Office, Inc. This company is planning to establish a $10 million subsidiary in Malaysia to manufacture, distribute, and service all the company's products in this country. The policy of the company is to accept projects showing positive net present values.

To fund the $10 million capital expenditure, there are two proposals. The first one is based on a 100 percent equity contribution from Virtual Office. The US dollar cost of equity is eight percent. The second proposal considers a partnership with a Malaysian firm. In this instance, the partner makes a 40 percent equity contribution in Malaysian dollars. The cost of equity in Malaysia is estimated at 18 percent. The remaining 60 percent can be financed with a debt issue in Malaysian dollars by Virtual Office in Malaysia. Virtual's cost of borrowing in Malaysia is 14 percent. The staff of Virtual Office has prepared the cash flows and exchange rate forecast over a 5-year period shown in Table 13.2.

Table 13.2
Cash flows and exchange rate forecast

(1) Year	1997	1998	1999	2000	2001	2002
(2) Investment (million $)	-10.0					
(3) Cash flow (million M$)		6.24	7.09	8.65	10.52	13.08
(4) Exchange Rate (M$/$1)	2.9	2.95	3.02	3.00	3.02	3.05
(5) Cash flow (million $)		2.12	2.35	2.87	3.48	4.29

Net present value of option one

To compute the net present value of this option, which is based on a 100 percent dollar equity financing and a US dollar cost of equity of 8 percent, it is necessary to undertake two steps. Bring the dollar cash flows shown in row five of Table 13.2 to present value. Estimate the net present value. Under the assumptions specified in Option One, the net present value—which is equal to the initial $10 million cash outflow plus the accumulated present value of the free cash flows—is positive $1.75 million, as detailed in Table 13.3.

Table 13.3
Net present value of the Malaysian project under option one

Year	1997	1998	1999	2000	2001	2002
Investment (million $)	-10.00					
Cash flow (million $)		2.12	2.35	2.87	3.48	4.29
Discount factor, $(1/1.08)^i$	1.00	.93	.86	.79	.74	.68
Present value of cash flows ($ million)	-10.00	1.97	2.02	2.27	2.58	2.92
NPV ($ million)	1.75					

Net present value of option two

Under this alternative, all the funding mixture of 60 percent debt and 40 percent equity, originates in Malaysia. Therefore, to compute the net present value of this choice, it is necessary to take several steps. First, to estimate the weighted average cost of capital. Second, to use the WACC to bring the Malaysian dollar cash flows (row 3 of Table 13.2) to present value. Third, to turn the accumulated present value of the Malaysian dollar cash flows into dollar terms by multiplying them by the spot rate. Forth and last, to estimate the net present value.

135

The WACC for the project is 0.1224 or 12.24 percent.

$$k_w = (D/V)k_d (1 - tx) + (S/V)k_e$$

$$k_w = .6*.14*(1 - .4) + .4*.18$$

$$k_w = .0504 + .072 = .1224 = 12.24 \%.$$

This rate (WACC), is used to discount the Malaysian cash flows in Table 13.4. The net present value under this alternative yields a positive net present value of $0.77 million.

Table 13.4
Net present value of the Malaysian project under option two
(million)

Period	1997	1998	1999	2000	2001	2002
Investment ($)	-10.0					
Cash flow (M$)		6.24	7.09	8.65	10.52	13.08
Discount factor, $1/(1.122)^i$	1.00	.89	.79	.71	.63	.56
PV of cash flows (M$)	0	5.55	5.6	6.14	6.63	7.32
Accumulated present value of cash flows (M$)	31.24					
Exchange Rate (M$/$1)	2.9					
Accumulated present value of cash flows ($)	10.77					
Net present value ($)	0.77					

Comparative analysis

The results obtained for the two financing alternatives studied indicate that under either one of the two options available, the Malaysian project yields a positive net present value measured in dollar terms, after the project has been adjusted for business and exchange rate risks. Therefore, this project should be accepted because it helps increase the wealth of Virtual Office, Inc. In addition, if the company wishes to obtain the highest net percent value on this project, it should finance the project with equity, since this option yields a higher net present value. However, if the company wants to minimize risk, it should choose option two, which offers a natural hedge against exchange rate risk.

136

Problems

1. An Indian manufacturing company currently imports 200,000 units that are used as electrical parts in cars assembled in India. The Indian producer buys the parts from a US supplier at a price of 2 rupees per unit. The Indian plant manager believes that it is cheaper to manufacture these parts in India since direct production costs per unit are 1.5 rupees. The equipment required to manufacture the parts in India costs 150,000 rupees. This investment could be written off for Indian tax purposes using a four-year depreciation schedule that permits a 33.3, 44.45, 14.81, and 7.41 percent depreciation over years one through four.

   The Indian plant manager supporting this proposal believes that the Indian operation will require working capital equivalent to Rp30,000. He argues, however, that working capital could be ignored since it is recovered at the end of the fourth year.

   The tax rate in India is 35 percent and the cost of capital is 15 percent.

   To solve this problem you should estimate:

   - The rupee value of savings each year;
   - The rupee value of depreciation each year;
   - Savings after depreciation (EBT), which are equal to total savings minus depreciation;
   - Net savings (NI), which is equal to savings after depreciation minus taxes;
   - The free cash flow associated to the investment, which is equal to net savings plus depreciation;
   - The present value of the cash flows discounted at the Indian cost of capital;
   - The net present value of the project.

2. The Kino Corporation is a US multinational producing and distributing copy machines worldwide. At the present moment, the company considers establishing a subsidiary in Ecuador to produce and market copy machines in this country. Initial capital expenditures are estimated at $9 million. The life expectancy of this project is 3 years.

   To finance the project, the company may issue new shares of common stock. The company's dollar cost of equity is 18 percent. The company, however, could borrow pesos in Ecuador to finance the project. Kino's cost of borrowing in Ecuador is 20 percent.

   The pricing policy of Kino is to adjust the price of its products by inflation. The price for copy machines in Ecuador has been set at 525 Ecuadorian pesos. The company expects to sell 60,000 machines in Ecuador and export 6,000 during the first year of operation. A forecast of subsequent volume of domestic sales and exports is presented in the table below.

137

The cost to produce the goods and administrative expenses are 40 and 15 percent respectively of total revenue. Plant and equipment are depreciated over 5 years using a straight-line depreciation method. The income tax rate in Ecuador is 30 percent; in addition, there is a withholding tax of 10 percent on remitted earnings. The US government allows tax credits on remitted earnings and does not impose additional taxes.

Information

ITEMS	1994	1995	1996	1997
Spot rate ($/Peso)	0.47			
Price per unit (pesos)	500.00	525.00	551.25	584.33
Inflation forecast, Ecuador (%)		5.00	5.00	6.00
Inflation forecast, US (%)		4.00	3.75	3.00
Volume of domestic sales (units)		60,000	65,000	68,750
Subsidiary's exports (units)		6,000	6,500	6,875

The policy of the company is to accept projects yielding positive net present values. Is this project worth taking?

To resolve this problem, you should:
- Forecast the price over the three year period (already given in table above);
- Estimate the volume of total sales, which is equal to domestic sales plus exports;
- Estimate the value of sales (price times quantity);
- Estimate earnings before taxes (EBT) by taking away from sales, the cost of goods sold (COGS), administrative expenses, and depreciation;
- Estimate net income (NI) by taking away taxes from earnings before taxes;
- Subtract the 10 percent withholding from net income, under the assumption that 100 percent of net income will be repatriated;
- Estimate the Ecuadorian peso free cash flows by adding depreciation back to net income;

If the funds are borrowed in Ecuador, you should continue as follows:
- Estimate the discount factor using a 20 percent discount rate, which is the cost of borrowing in Ecuador;
- Estimate the peso present value of the project by discounting the free cash flow at each period by the appropriate discount factor;
- Estimate the peso net present value by subtracting the initial investment from the accumulated net present value;

138

- Estimate the net present value in dollars by multiplying the net present value of the flows in Ecuadorian pesos times the spot rate.

If the funds are from the US, you continue as follows:
- Forecast the exchange rate using PPP, departing from the initial spot rate of $0.47 per Ecuadorian peso;
- Estimate the dollar value of the cash flows by adjusting the cash flow in Ecuadorian pesos times the spot rate at each point in time;
- Discount the dollar cash flows by using the US cost of equity of 18 percent;
- Estimate the dollar net present value of the investment in Ecuador.

Finally, determine the viability of the project and the source of funds to finance the project.

3. Solo, a US corporation engaged in the production and distribution of plastic products, is planning to invest MxP5,000,000 in a new plant in Mexico. The Mexican rate of inflation is currently at 28 percent and is expected to decline to 22.7, 17.3 and 12 percent over the next three years. The spot rate is MxP9/$1= $0.111/MxP$1. The US rate of inflation is 3 percent, and is expected to remain at this level for the foreseeable future. During the first year of operations, Solo expects to sell 124,000 cases of the plastic products in Mexico. Thereafter, the volume of sales is forecasted to grow at 4 percent per year.

The current price of Solo's products is MxP35. The pricing policy of Solo is to adjust the price of its products by local inflation. Labor, material, and parts are estimated at 30 percent of sales. Administrative expenses are 6 percent of sales. Depreciation of plant and equipment is based on straight-line depreciation over 3 years.

Corporate income taxes in Mexico are at 30 percent. The tax credit granted in the US on the taxes paid in Mexico fully offset corporate income taxes in the US. That is, the repatriation of Mexican profits is exempt from US corporate taxes. The cost of equity in both Mexico and the US is 25 and 9 percent respectively. The Mexican and US costs of debt are 22 and 8 percent respectively. The company wants to finance the project with 40 percent equity and 60 percent debt.

4. Thornton, Inc., a Houston based manufacturer of disc drive controls, is switching to offshore production in Taiwan. Projected yearly net income from the Taiwanese plant is Tai$18 million. Thereafter, revenues are expected to grow at 8 percent annually. The rate on Taiwanese treasury bills is four percent. The Taiwanese market return is 9 percent. The Taiwanese beta for the industry is 1.8. The spot rate is Tai$129/$1.

What is the market value of the Taiwanese subsidiary in terms of US dollars?

To solve this problem you should estimate:

- The discount rate using the capital asset pricing model;
- The Taiwanese dollar value of the firm using the perpetuity growth model;
- The dollar value of the subsidiary using the Taiwanese dollar value.

Notes

1 For further details on this point, see Bierman, H. and Smidt, S., *The Capital Budgeting Decision*, 8th ed., MacMillan Company, New York, 1992.
2 In fact, the cost of debt is calculated by using the yield to maturity adjusted for taxes. If the company borrows from a bank and gets the face value of the debt, the yield to maturity is equal to the coupon rate.
3 This is the implied beta of debt (indicated by the market).

14 Cuetara in Morocco

Introduction

In 1951, the brothers Juan and Florencio Gómez Cuetara founded a firm in Reinosa, a province of Santander, Spain. The firm, Cuetara, started selling biscuits – crackers, wafers, cookies – baked according to a formula that the brothers originally developed. The uniqueness of their products and the lack of competition in this industry at that time paved the way to turn their business into the leading producer of biscuits in Spain. Until 1990, the company had remained financially sound both in Spain and abroad. It had exports to Germany, France, Britain, Italy, Russia, the United States, Morocco, Eastern Europe, and had created lucrative subsidiaries in Mexico and Portugal.

Management issues

After 1990, the company's expansion came to a halt. For the first time since its inception, due to increasing imports and the aging of some of the key Cuetara products in the Spanish market, the corporation had a string of market share losses that reduced its participation from 26 percent in 1989 to 16.8 percent in 1993. These events forced the management team to reassess the firm's strategy.

The industrial evolution of the Spanish biscuit industry

This biscuit industry is integrated by more than 2,325 firms employing 33,000 workers. It reached its peak – in terms of both output and sales – in 1990. The next four years it declined at an average rate of 3 percent per year. The decay was attributed to a Spanish recession, new trends in consumer preferences, and the gradual substitution of domestic products by imports.

Competition in the Spanish market

The local firms, Cuetara and Fontaneda dominated the different segments of the Spanish biscuit industry. Their rise in prominence was due to sound management practices and the protectionism provided by the Spanish government. Minority ownership status was imposed on foreign direct investment, and high tariffs were levied on the import of biscuits. In addition, in order to secure their profitability, local companies were granted subsidies and guaranteed prices for the purchase of raw materials.

The accession of Spain to the EC forced a change in the government's industrial policies. The Spanish market was opened up to powerful multinationals from the EC and other countries, which quickly established local subsidiaries. Soon, competition from within and from abroad intensified to a point that threatened the leading position of the two Spanish firms in this market. In spite of all these changes, however, Cuetara and Fontaneda were still in command of the market in 1992. A list of the most important competitors in the biscuit industry and their key products is given in Table 14.2.

Demand trends

Foreign competition was not the only challenge faced by the local producers of biscuits in Spain. Adverse trends in consumption and the aging of some of their key products further eroded the position of Cuetara and Fontaneda. The younger Spaniards, contrary to their parents, want a healthier diet based more on cereals and fruit pastries and less of the traditional "María" cookie and the "Magdalena" muffin, which constitute the stronghold of the local biscuit producers. The spectacular decline in the demand for Fontaneda's "María" cookie, from 14 to 11 percent in one year, is an example of how changes in the market conditions are affecting the local Spanish producers. A final trend observed in the bread industry was the increased demand for frozen food products, inspired by the more active participation of Spanish women in the labor market.

The regional markets in Spain

In terms of regions, the per capita consumption of biscuits, bread, and pastries is higher in the central and south-central regions of Spain, and is much lower in the Canary Islands. This fact is simply the result of two factors: lifestyles and the prevailing density of population.

The business structure of Cuetara

The firm has four factories and 17 warehouses strategically located throughout Spain, with a potential to produce and distribute 75,294 metric tons of biscuits. In 1993, however, its production was only 55,400 tons, down from 57,700 tons a year before. The largest processing plant is located in Villarejo de Salvanes (Madrid), where it has 15 production lines operating 24 hours a day, all year round. Two other processing plants, with six and three lines working two shifts each, are located in Jaen and Museros (Valencia). A fourth and smaller plant, with only three lines working two shifts, is in Reinosa (Cantabria).

Product portfolio and distribution channels

Sales of 17 billion pesetas in 1993 furnished Cuetara with an 18 percent market share – down from 26 percent in 1990. To distribute this vast array of brands that is has, more than one hundred, the company has its own fleet to serve more than 17,000 distributors, most of which are small "mom and pop" Spanish outlets.

The issue

Recently, Cuetara has been approached by its Moroccan distributor – Distribuidora General Alimentaria (DGA) – which is interested in entering into a joint venture with Cuetara to start up a subsidiary in Morocco. However, Miguel Angel Cuetara, the CEO, is not absolutely convinced that the joint venture is the best option. He has asked Isabel Alvarez and Julio Guijarro, two of the company's executives, to look into this matter and provide him with a recommendation on this request He has asked them to compare the benefits of a new plant to a more structured direct export strategy. He also asked them if one of these two options would be better than maintaining the status quo: to continue exporting and selling through its distributorship.

Cuetara products are already well-known and highly regarded in Morocco, especially its "María," "Surtido," and "Frescoso" brands. The potential partner, Distribuidora General Alimentaria (DGA), sells these items in this foreign market. This company imports the Cuetara products directly from the Jaen plant on a wholesale basis, which carries a 20 percent discount. Imports are also carried by a large number of independent distributors, who purchase the Cuetara products at retail prices in Ceuta and Melilla – the Spanish territory in Africa bordering Morocco. The products are then smuggled into the country for distribution in small villages and rural communities by small shops and "little street markets." The "white" or direct exports through the distributor are subject to an 80 percent tariff and amount to 3,500 metric tons of biscuits. The "gray" or indirect exports through Ceuta and Melilla are smuggled by bribing customs officers, and amount to 900 metric tons.

143

Smuggling biscuits into Morocco is not unusual since the local products are very expensive and of poor quality in spite of the favorable labor and raw material costs faced by the local producers. Barring technological and know-how considerations, a producer in Morocco enjoys a good deal of comparative advantage in the production of biscuits, as illustrated in Table 14.6.

There is a small Moroccan company producing and distributing biscuits under the patented brand mark of "Cuetara." The "real" Cuetara is trying to buy this Moroccan company to rescue its brand name.

New operation in Morocco

Some of the executives of Cuetara, sympathetic toward the new plant project, favor siting the new plant inside zone IV, which is 90 km from Casablanca. It offers the highest tax exemption – 50 percent over the first five years of operation.[1] The investment required to purchase three lines of production, which is the minimum scale production required to meet fixed cost operations, amounts to Dh190 million. Other expenditures related to the project are the 1,500 square meters of land, which can be leased at a monthly rate of Dh200 per square meter, or purchased at the present value equivalent of the lease.

The remaining initial expenditures consist mostly of start up costs, such as salaries for the first three months of operation, legal fees amounting to ten percent of total investment expenditures, and other miscellaneous expenses. The sales forecast is based on the volume of current exports plus a growth rate of three percent per year. The structure of sales follows the Spanish pattern, given the relatively close cultural association between Morocco and Spain. The sales price for the first year of operation is estimated considering the peseta price of the products per ton and the exchanger rate. In subsequent years, the price is expected to fully adjust to local inflation.

Considering the sanitary conditions required to operate a bakery plant, 80 percent of the workers are required to have a certain degree of specialization. The remaining 20 percent may be unskilled workers. Administrative expenses are estimated at 20 percent of total sales. Salaries have to be estimated at the Moroccan guaranteed inter-professional minimum salary (SIMG) of Dh6.60 an hour. A description of professional salary ranges in Morocco is given in Table 14.7.

Lines of production are normally depreciated using straight-line depreciation over their life, which is estimated at five years. Salvage value is 130 pesetas. The gross tax rate for zone IV is 20 percent. Also, Morocco has a withholding tax of ten percent.

It is a policy of Cuetara to assess its domestic and international cash flows in terms of pesetas. Cuetara's good ratings permit the company to obtain credit at 15 percent in pesetas. The Spanish inflation rate in 1994 was 14 percent. It was expected to steadily decline to six percent by the year 2000. Moroccan inflation was at 22 percent in 1994. However, with the assistance of the IMF, it is expected to gradually decline to 12 percent by the year 2000. By 1994, the interest rate in

Morocco was 24 percent for short-term loans. Long-term borrowing was expected to steadily adjust to inflationary expectations. At the time that the investment was under consideration, the following exchange spot rates were quoted: Ps114.5/$1 and /Dh9.2/$1.

The potential Moroccan partners want to have the plant located in Casablanca for carrying cost and delivery considerations. Transportation costs – which are estimated at ten percent of gross sales – and timely delivery of goods can be major problems during the monsoon season.

Morocco: Country profile

Morocco gained its independence from both France and Spain in 1956. Since then it has been a constitutional monarchy ruled by the Alawi dynasty. It has a territory of 710,850 square kilometers, of which almost one-third – 252,120 square kilometers – is part of the Saharan desert. The most important city is Casablanca, the capital, with 2.9 million inhabitants. Other important metropolitan areas are listed in the statistical appendix.

The population was estimated at 28.1 million in 1993. Of the total, more than 15 million speak Arabic, which is considered the first, though not official language, followed by Berber, which is spoken by one fifth of the population. The use of Spanish and French is widespread. The Berbers inhabit the mountainous regions of the Rif, the Middle and High Atlas, and the Anti-Atlas.

The other ethnic groups are concentrated in the fertile plains and coastal areas of the Northwest region. Similar to many developing countries, Morocco is experiencing a migration from the rural to the urban areas. In 1961, only 3.2 million people were in areas considered urban. By 1993, the number of people in the cities and metropolitan areas had grown to 49 percent of the country's population.

Morocco is experiencing a very high rate of population growth – 2.16 percent per year, which is one of the highest in the world. This has been reflected in a high rate of unemployment, estimated at 17.5 percent of the economically active population in 1994, that has been palliated by emigration to the EC countries.[2] This labor surplus has been reflected in limited opportunities for social advancement that has led to escalating social tensions. In the 1990s, Casablanca was often shaken by massive demonstrations of popular dissatisfaction and strikes called by the three major labor unions: the Confederation Democratique du Travail (CDT), the Union General Marocaine du Travail (UGMT), and the Union Marocaine du Travail (UMT).

The economy of Morocco

In a normal year, exports finance two-thirds of the country's imports. However, due to shortages of food supplies, rising import bills, and increased agricultural imports, the trade gap reached an alarming level in 1994.[3] To regain some international liquidity, the Moroccan government approached the IMF, which approved a stand-by credit of SDR91.8 million to support an economic program aimed at boosting GDP growth from zero percent in 1994 to four percent in 1995.

In exchange for the assistance, the IMF asked the government to reduce tariffs and subsidies, to pursue tighter monetary and fiscal policies, and to modernize the economy. As a result of the IMF program, the government dismantled price control, export controls, and regulations governing foreign investment. It also implemented a more liberal tax code, allowing for lower tax rates, faster repatriation of profits, and the sale of public enterprises to the private sector. The agricultural sector employs 50 percent of the population and accounts for one quarter of Moroccan exports, mostly to the EC countries. Sales to foreign markets are tax exempt and do not require an export permit. However, 80 percent of the foreign exchange revenues must be turned to the Treasury within 90 days to be transferred to the central bank, Bank. The exporter has the right to keep the remaining 20 percent to finance the promotion of exports abroad. Imports, under certain circumstances, are subject to stricter regulations. They require a permit that is issued only to persons or institutions registered as importers. To fulfill the requirements for obtaining an import permit, the importer must submit a contract of purchases and make a deposit in a commercial bank equivalent to the value of the transaction. The whole process may take between five and ten days.

The Economies of Morocco and Spain

Population, 1993	Morocco	Spain
Total	28 million	39 million
Population growth	2.16%	0.24%
Labor force	7.4 million	14.6 million
Total area	710,850 square kilometers	504,750 square kilometers
Land area	446,550 square kilometers	499,400 square kilometers

Religion

Muslim	98%	
Christian	1.10%	
Jewish	0.90%	

The Economy, 1994

Gross domestic product	$28.1 billion	$ 514 billion
GDP growth rate	0%	1%
GDP per capita	$1,060	$13,200
Inflation rate	22%	14%
Unemployment rate	17.50%	19%
Exports	$ 4.7 billion	$ 62 billion
Imports	$ 7.6 billion	$ 100 billion
External debt	$ 20 billion	$ 67.5 billion

Most important imports

Capital goods	24%
Semi-processed food	22%
Raw materials	16%
Food and beverages	13%

Currency	Dirhan	Peseta
Exchange rate	Drh/$1	Ps/$1
1988	8.209	116.49
1989	8.488	118.38
1990	8.242	101.93
1991	8.707	103.91
1992	8.538	102.38
1993	9.207	114.59

Source: Central Intelligence Agency, *World Factbook*, September, 1997.

STATISTICAL APPENDIX

Table 14.1
Industrial evolution of the biscuit industry
(Pesetas)

ITEM	1988	1989	1990	1991	1992
Production	188,430	206,769	240,765	230,000	220,000
Exports	2,501	2,969	2,740	4,278	6,878
Imports	8,459	8,869	10,363	16,164	17,229
Consumption	194,388	212,669	248,388	241,886	230,351
(Metric tons)					
Production	622,112	632,534	672,274	645,383	619,567
Exports	4,470	4,792	4,278	6,878	8,926
Imports	8,779	12,120	14,353	16,164	17,229
Consumption	637,401	650,856	696,245	654,669	627,870

Source: Cuetara, Hnos, and *Monografico AlimentaRío*, Alimarket, Madrid, Spain, 1993, p. 119.

Table 14.2
Leading producers in the Spanish biscuit industry

Market Position	Company	Production (Metric tons) 1991	1992
1	Cuetara, S.A.	57,000	57,700
2	Fontaneda	42,000	38,000
3	Royal Brands	30,270	30,000
4	Galletas Gullon	20,000	25,000
5	General Biscuits	13,000	14,000

Source: *Monograma Alimentario*, Alimarket, Madrid, Spain, 1993, p. 117.

Table 14.3
Regional per capita consumption of biscuits in Spain, 1990
(pounds/year)

Region	Consumption	Population
Castilla and León	115.4	More than 500,000
Central – South	113.2	100-500,000
Northwest	105.9	10-100,000
East	99.9	2-10,000
North	97.3	Less than 2,000
Northwest	89.9	
Andalucía	88.1	
Canary Islands	69.3	

Source: DBK from data of MAPA, 1992.

Table 14.4
Cost structure of the alimentary industry in Spain, 1990
(percentage of sales)

Item	Biscuit	Bakery and Pastries
Labor	20	25
Raw materials	60	46
Depreciation	3	3
Distribution	14	21
Gross Profits	3	5

Table 14.5
Cuetara, composition of sales, 1993

Product	Output (metric tons)	Sales (million of pesetas)	Participation (%)
Snacks	19,390	5,950	35
Dry toasted	11,634	3,571	21
Dry plain	9,418	2,890	17
Assorted	6,648	2,040	12
Wafers	3,878	1,190	7
Cookies	2,770	850	5
Sandwich	1,662	510	3
Total	55,400	17,001	

Source: Cuetara Hnos, Madrid, Spain, 1994.

149

Table 14.6
Comparative cost structure, 1994
(pesetas)

Item	Morocco	Spain	Diff
Sugar/kg	37.64	70.4	29.18
Flour/kg	34.82	64	29.18
Milk/liter	23.52	44.8	21.28
Eggs/unit	9.40	10.88	1.48
Wheat	37.5	70.0	32.5
Total	142.88	260.08	113.62

Source: Cuetara, Hnos, Madrid, Spain, 1994.

Table 14.7
Professional salaries in Morocco, 1994
(Dirham/hour)

Degree of Specialization	Salary Range
Unspecialized worker	6.80 - 7.17
Specialized worker	7.59 - 8.36
Semi-qualified worker	8.32 - 8.88
Qualified worker	9.60 - 11.70
Supervisor	15.56 - 20.58

Table 14.8
Urban population in Morocco, 1993

Metropolitan Area	Population (thousand)	Proportion of the Total (%)
Casablanca	2,990	11.9
Rabat-Salé	1,187	4.72
Fez	719	2.9
Oujda	646	2.58
Marrakesh	644	2.5
Mek	484	1.9

Table 14.9
Summary data of the Spanish biscuit industry, 1989 - 1992

	1989	1992
Number of Companies	2,400.0	2,325.0
Number of Employees	34,000.0	33,000.0
Number of Employees/Company	14.0	14.0
Sales (billions of pesetas)	206.0	240.0
Exports (billions of pesetas	2.9	2.7
Imports (billions of pesetas)	8.8	10.3
Market Share of the Top Five	45.0	45.0
Production Growth (%)	1.7	6.3
Market Growth (%)	2.0	7.0

Table 14.10
Key competitors in the Spanish bakery industry, 1991

Company	Sales (tons)	Workers
Donut/Pan Rico, subsidiary of Allied Lyons, U. K.	50,000	2,500
Bimbo, subsidiary of Anheuser Busch	25,083	2,671
La Bella Easo, wholly owned by a Spanish family	4,000	450
Ariete, owned by the Group Fosforera de España	5,308	450
Reposteria Ortiz, owned by United Biscuits, U. K.	4,900	852
Río, Productos Alimenticios, owned by Barilla, Italy	4,000	852
Dulcesa, owned by a Spanish family	3,199	42
Royal Brands, owned by Tabacalera de España	2,550	240

Source: Cuetara, Hnos, Madrid, Spain, 1994.

Notes

1   Tax law n/17-82, published in *Dahir* on January 17, 1983, and modified in 1988.
2   In 1991, the Moroccan population working in EC countries was estimated at two million.
3   *Morocco, EIU, Country Profile, 1991-1994*, The Economist Intelligence Unit Limited, 1994.

15 Exchange rate risk management

Managing exchange rate risk is a hazardous but meaningful task. There are several reasons that justify the importance of this task. First, changes in the exchange rate affect the cost of raw material imports, the price of exports, export revenues, the domestic value of accounts payable and receivable, and the value of inventories having import components. Changes in the exchange rate also affect a firm's income statement and balance sheet, at times with a great deal of severity.

Purpose

The aim of this technical note is to provide the basic concepts required to manage exchange rate risk exposure.

Currency risk and exchange rate risk exposure

Before the exchange rate's affect on the financial performance of a multinational corporation is explained, it is necessary to discuss the difference between foreign exchange risk and foreign exchange rate risk exposure.

Currency risk exists only when the movements of a currency in the foreign exchange market deviate from expectations. Similarly, risk does not exist simply because an anticipated foreign currency cash inflow is expected to be negatively affected by the depreciation of a currency. In short, *currency risk* exists only when the actual appreciation or depreciation of a currency is unknown or when changes in the exchange rate deviate from market expectations.

Exchange rate exposure exists only when the value of a company's assets and liabilities are exposed to unexpected changes in currency values. The degree of exchange rate risk exposure will depend, in turn, on how much of the assets and liabilities are exposed. A US investor holding only assets and liabilities in dollars is not exposed to exchange rate risk. A US Corporation holding a bank deposit worth 10 million German marks has a 10 million German mark exposure. If the marks are converted into dollars, the currency exposure is eliminated.

Exchange rate variability and risk

Exchange rate risk effects on corporate performance are usually classified under the terms of *transaction, economic,* and *translation exposure. Transaction exposure* refers to the effect of exchange rate variations on the value of accounts payable and/or receivable. To explain transaction exposure, two contrasting situations are considered: a US firm holding a yen payable and a German company having a dollar receivable. Under the proposed scenario, the two firms are exposed to unexpected variations of the dollar in the foreign exchange market. A dollar depreciation worsens the financial situation of the US firm by raising the dollar cost of its payable in proportion to the devaluation. The German firm is also affected since the devaluation lowers the mark value of its receivable.

To estimate the market value of the subsidiary of a multinational corporation, the financial managers pay special attention to the present value of the cash flows and the exchange rate forecast. Very often, however, exchange-rate expectations are not fulfilled. As a result, the actual cash flows and market value of the firm are different from the ones originally anticipated. The sensitivity of a firm's cash flows and market value to variations in the exchange rate is known as *economic exposure.*

Translation exposure refers to changes in the value of the income statement and balance sheet items when they are re-expressed at consolidation from local currency terms to the parent company currency terms. Since translation exposure is a measure of the effect of exchange rate variations on a company's financial statements, it is often referred to as *accounting exposure.* Accounting or translation exposure depends on the conditions and composition of the financial statements. To measure the extent of a firm's exposure to exchange rate risk, the financial statement items can be classified either as exposed or non-exposed. To judge the degree of translation exposure is not an easy task, since it depends on the nature of the items and the method used to measure the exposure. The most commonly used methods to measure translation exposure are the *current,* the *current/non-current,* and the *monetary/non-monetary* methods.

Under the *current method,* all assets and liabilities are considered to be exposed at all times. Therefore, they are translated at the current exchange rate when this method is used. Under the current method, if a firm's foreign currency-denominated assets exceed its foreign-currency-denominated liabilities, a devaluation of the home currency results in a local currency gain, while a revaluation or appreciation results in a loss. For instance, if an Italian corporation has 100 million dollar denominated assets and 50 million dollar denominated liabilities, then a depreciation of the lira against the dollar will improve the net worth of the Italian company in terms of lira.

Under the *current/non-current method,* assets and liabilities with maturity exceeding one year are translated at the exchange rate at which they originally entered the records of the subsidiary, that is, at the *historical rate.* Items with shorter maturity are restated in terms of the currency of the parent company at the current rate. A similar procedure is employed to restate the items belonging to the income statement. However, since most of the income statement items originate in periods lasting one year or less, they are usually entered at the current rate. An exception is depreciation, which is translated at the historical rate —the exchange rate in effect at the time the asset was acquired or when the liability was incurred.

Under the *monetary/non-monetary method,* the assets are first classified according to their degree of liquidity. Monetary or liquid assets include cash, accounts receivable, and marketable securities. Monetary liabilities include accounts payable and long-term debt items. In contrast, non-monetary assets include "physical items" such as inventory and fixed assets. Once the items are classified, they are restated according to whether they are monetary or non-monetary. Monetary assets are then translated and consolidated into the financial statement of the parent company in terms of the average rate over the period under consideration.

Income statement items are translated following a logic similar to the one applied to their balance sheet counterpart. Sales revenue, a monetary asset, is translated using the average current rate whereas depreciation and the cost of goods sold are translated at their historical rate.

To estimate the market value of a subsidiary, international managers and investors usually factor into their calculations anticipated changes in the exchange rate because the value of the relevant financial statement items required to calculate the value of the subsidiary vary in accordance with the path of the exchange rate. Naturally, unexpected variations in the exchange rate are not included in the manager's calculations. In consequence, exchange rate divergence from the expected path may lead to a result different from the expected. This variation in the value of a firm resulting from changes in the exchange rate is defined as *economic risk.*

Economic risk may be assessed in the short term, medium term, and long run. *Short-term economic exposure* is the effect of unanticipated exchange rate changes on the one-year cash flows. *Medium-term economic exposure* refers to the consequences of the exchange rate change on the cash flows of the firm during the next two to five years following the unanticipated change. These relative long-term effects are explained by the inability of the firm to adjust its cost and price structure to a new competitive environment. *Long-term economic exposure* pertains to the exchange rate effects on the cash flows of the firm beyond five years.

Managing transaction exposure with hedging techniques

When a firm is in possession of a financial instrument that requires settlement in foreign exchange, it is automatically exposed to transaction risk. To manage this risk, the firm may resort to hedging either in the spot market —also known as the money market— or in the forward market. Other hedging methods are available with futures, options, and swap contracts.

16 Cemex: Debt and exchange rate risk

Introduction

Lorenzo Zambrano, Chief Executive Officer of the Mexican company Cemex, enjoys having breakfast at the local golf club when he is in Monterrey. After a few rounds of golf, he spends time reviewing the latest company reports and economic indicators for the most important countries where the company operates: Mexico, the US and Spain.

The report on Mexico

In the case of Mexico, the economic picture was steadily improving in 1966. Exceeding year-end projections, the country's gross domestic product (GDP) grew 5.1 percent in 1996, spurred by private and public investment and export growth. As a result of Mexico's economic improvements, the demand for cement and ready-mix concrete grew by 3.2 and 8.6 percent respectively.

For 1997, the government planned a 27 percent increase in public spending in the oil, petrochemical, electricity and communication service sectors. These added expenditures, if carried out, should contribute to an upsurge in the demand for cement of about 6 percent.

Other bright aspects of the Mexican operation were exports to Southeast Asia and the Far East, including the Philippines, Indonesia and Malaysia. Exports to this rapidly growing region increased 79 percent, from more than 2.5 million metric tons in 1995 to 4.2 million metric tons of cement and clinker in 1996.[1]

Looking ahead at Mexico's prospects for 1997, Zambrano anticipated a stable cement price, low capital expenditures, increased capacity utilization, and a 31 percent operating margin as the Mexican economy continued its recovery.

The state of the US cement market

The core of Cemex's activity in the United States was concentrated in Texas, California, and Arizona. This latter state was the most dynamic in 1996, achieving a record level of 2.5 million metric tons of sales due to solid, across-the-board construction activity. The demand in California and Texas was less dynamic, though they recorded demand growths of 6.9 and 4.8 percent. For 1997, California's cement consumption is expected to grow 3 percent; Texas' demand is expected to remain flat; Arizona's consumption to decline to 5 percent, due to contraction of the residential and commercial sectors.

Cemex Spain

In 1992 Cemex purchased Compañía Valenciana de Cementos Portland and its associate company, Construcción Sanson. This acquisition provided Cemex with the capacity to serve Spain, the Canary Islands, and the Spanish territories of Ceuta and Melilla. With these purchases, Cemex gained a 28 percent share of the cement market, a leadership position, and additional capacity to produce 12 million metric tons of cement. Unlike in Mexico, 65 percent of the sales were to institutional buyers, and the remaining 35 percent sold directly to individuals and households engaged in small renovation or expansion projects. Since 1993, the Spanish market remained flat, but Zambrano believed that it had great long-term potential, given that the infrastructure in Spain was behind the standards of the majority of the member countries in the EC.

History of the company

The company was founded in 1906 in the village of Hidalgo (in the state of Nuevo León) as Cementos Monterrey. It was a small plant by modern standards, with a capacity to produce 20,000 metric tons of cement. More than a decade later in 1920, it joined forces with Cementos Hidalgo to create what is known today as Cemex.

For a period of 50 years, Cemex remained a family owned company purely focused on serving the domestic market. It was not until 1973 that Cemex became a public company with an export focus. In that year, Cemex issued common stock to finance the purchase of Cementos Guadalajara and began to export from this plant to California.

The business strategy

The oil discoveries of the 1970s compelled Cemex to increase capacity to meet the fast-growing demand for cement in Mexico. However, the oil crisis of 1982 dealt the company a severe financial blow, forcing Cemex to reshape its corporate strategy from a diversified Mexican conglomerate to a North American company focused only on the production, distribution, and marketing of cement, clinker, and ready mix-concrete.[2]

To implement the new strategy, the firm sold hotels, petrochemical plants, and other industrial projects in order to focus on its core business. With the resources generated by the sale of complementary businesses, Cemex bought two domestic competitors, Anahuac and Tolmex, to increase its market share position in Mexico. To expand across borders, it acquired cement producers in Arizona, Texas, and California. At a later stage, in the 1990s, Cemex moved forcefully to become a global company.

The road to globalization

Between 1992 and 1996, Cemex paid $3.36 billion to acquire cement plants in Spain, Venezuela, and Colombia, and invested $1.66 billion to modernize operations. As a result of this expansion, the group's combined production capacity grew to 50 million metric tons from only 10 million in 1986. The expansion efforts also allowed Cemex to have subsidiaries in 22 countries, and establish exports to more than 60 nations. By September 1997, Cemex was considered the third largest producer of cement in the world, the largest in the Americas, and the industry leader in Mexico, Spain, Venezuela, Panama, and the Dominican Republic. In addition, it became the largest producer of white cement in the world, the largest exporter of clinker, and important market player in the Caribbean, the US Southwest, and Colombia.

Financing international expansion

The buying spree was mostly financed with debt. This led many analysts to believe that Cemex had taken on too much debt. The purchase of Valenciana and Sanson in Spain for almost $2 billion was especially controversial. The overall market perception at the time of the purchase was that Cemex had overpaid as a result of an untimely purchase at the peak of a business cycle, and that it would not be able to extract the required cost savings necessary to meet the debt liabilities. Another worrying aspect of Cemex finances was that during the ten-year expansion, cycle, debt increased 300 percent to a total of $5.2 billion, which was equivalent to 49 percent of the company's total capitalization in September 1997.

The criticism against the financing strategy of the firm forced the normally circumspect Lorenzo Zambrano to make a public statement about the company's policy. In his view, Cemex's use of debt had been prudent and cost efficient. "With every acquisition, we moved rapidly to improve efficiency and lower costs." He added that in Spain, Cemex had eliminated 35 percent of the workforce, had switched to cheaper fuels, and had refinanced its debt. These improvements in manufacturing helped the Spanish operation to double its operating margins to 22 percent.

To emphasize the effective debt strategy of Cemex, Zambrano also pointed out the case of Venezuela and Colombia. In 1994, Cemex bought 60 percent of Vencemos, a Venezuelan cement company, for $364 million. As soon as this acquisition was formalized, Cemex moved quickly to slash 60 percent of the workforce, which led to a 50 percent increase in earnings. In 1996, it acquired Diamante and Cementos Samper in Colombia, which were the country's second and third largest cement producers. These two plants were subject to the same treatment as the Venezuelan firm, and the results were equally encouraging.

In addition to seeking improvements in the manufacture of cement, Zambrano added, the company also engaged in an active world search for cheaper means to finance the company's debt. This parallel effort, Mr. Zambrano pointed out, had helped the firm to lower its long-term cost of borrowing from 10.8 to 8.2 percent. This was achieved mainly by transferring expensive, short-term Mexican debt to cheaper Spanish peseta debt taken on by the Valenciana. This move, Zambrano explained, had saved the company $102 million a year in interest expenses.

Mr. Zambrano saw two potential pitfalls for a company going global: 1) doing so in a disorderly fashion and 2) not having the managerial capability of optimizing purchases. On both accounts, he said, Cemex had excelled because it had been both organized and careful in its purchases. To confirm this assertion, he pointed to the company's successful record of turning around under-performing companies.

The role of Mexico

In spite of all the changes introduced to Cemex over the last decade, the most important jewel of Cemex's crown was the Mexican operation. This country provides the firm with a wide manufacturing infrastructure that allowed it to export to Asia and North America at very competitive prices, as well as meet the rapidly growing local demand for cement. In addition to the market opportunities it offered, headquarters in Mexico also constituted the most important source of managerial, technical, and commercial talent. This country was a living laboratory for Cemex. It was the place where the executives learn to live with exchange rate instability, to cope with strong and powerful international competition, and to efficiently serve a market dominated by retail sales. Mexico was also the nerve center where the engineers and technicians of the company were under continuous pressure to find low cost alternatives for manufacturing cement in order to meet the price requirements of a relatively poor, but fast growing market.

But Mexico was also the continuous source of financial instability for the company. During the financial crisis of 1995, the devaluation of the peso and the recession that followed slashed cash flow from Cemex's Mexican operation by more than 50 percent, in dollar terms, to $394 million. Fortunately for the company, the group's foreign subsidiaries in Spain, the US, Venezuela, Panama, and the Caribbean, all acquired after 1992, saved the day for the company. They brought in $440 million and allowed Cemex to keep afloat while others Mexican companies were sinking.

To Lorenzo Zambrano, the resilience of the company during the peso crisis also had helped to vindicate the debt strategy. To him, geographical diversity had stabilized the multinational's cash flows, and had provided an insurance policy against foreign predators. "Had we remained a purely Mexican company, the local stock market would have penalized our company and we might become vulnerable to a takeover," Mr. Zambrano said.

The Asian venture

To further show that concerns about the company's debt were misplaced, Mr. Zambrano went ahead and authorized the company's first acquisition in Asia. It was the purchase of a cement plant in the Philippines, and it was looking for other deals. However, to avoid a further accumulation of debt, Mr. Zambrano tried to put together a $300 million venture capital fund with other financial investors in order to acquire more cement plants in Southeast Asia. According to this plan, Cemex could contribute $100 million and have control over the operation. Venture capital investors, in turn, would be asked to contribute the additional $200 million. With 40 percent leverage, Mr. Zambrano further explained, the fund could have $500 million to fund the Asian expansion. Assuming that the fund could take simple majority stakes, Cemex could effectively control $1 billion of cement assets with a $100 million investment.

"This is most definitely the right time to buy in Asia," the Cemex chairman enthused. In his view, Cemex had the managerial skills and the technology "to squeeze profitability" from new investment assets in Asia, even if the region headed into a Mexican-style recession. At their peak, Asian cement companies were valued at $500 per ton of capacity, he said. But, after the Hong Kong crisis in November 1997, they came down to $100 per ton.

Some analysts, while acknowledging the benefits of globalization for Cemex, disagree with Mr. Zambrano's interpretation of the financial results inspired by the Mexican crisis. In their view, this event provided the company with an example of what might follow if it did not take care of its debt size and its exposure to exchange rate instabilities both in Mexico and the world economy.

Debt highlights

- In December 1996, the subsidiary of Cemex in Spain signed a syndicated credit for Ps108,375 million (approximately $830 million) at a rate of 7.875 percent. The loan is to due to mature in the year 2003. The settlement of this debt is in the form of equal semi-annual installment payments beginning in January 1997.

The assets held by the Spanish subsidiary were used as collateral to guarantee this loan.[3]

- In November 1996, the Venezuelan subsidiary issued bonds totaling $200 million. Half of the issue was due in 1998 and the remainder in the year 2000. The coupon rates were 8.625 and 9.5 percent respectively.

- In August 1996, the Colombian and US ancillaries obtained syndicated credits for $259 and $125 million due in the year 2000.

- In July 1996, headquarters issued bonds for $600 million in two series. The first at 10.75 percent, due in the year 2000; the second series is at 12.75 percent due in the year 2006.

Table 16.1
Distribution of assets and sales, December 1996

Country	Distribution of Assets %	Distribution of assets $ million	Distribution net sales %	Distribution net sales MxP million
Spain	27	2,814	24	808
Venezuela	10	1,042	11	370
Colombia	12	1,251	5	168
USA	5	521	13	437
Caribbean	3	313	3	101
Mexico	43	4,481	44	1,481
Total	100	10,422	100	3,365

Table 16.2
Mexico, inflation, exchange rates and interest rates

Year	Consumer price Index	Inflation %	Exchange rate Mxp/$	Interest rate %
1997	358.4	18.79	7.8656	20.08
1996	301.7	34.39	7.5994	31.39
1995	224.5	35	6.4194	48.44
1994	166.3	6.95	3.3751	14.1

Table 16.3
Spain, inflation, exchange rates and interest rates

Year	Consumer price Index	Inflation %	Exchange rate Mxp/$	Interest rate %
1997	135.4	1.68	145.79	5.14
1996	133.2	3.58	126.66	7.23
1995	128.6	4.64	124.69	9.79
1994	122.9	4.77	133.96	8.11

Table 16.4
The US, inflation and interest rates

Year	Consumer price Index	Inflation %	Interest rate %
1997	122.6	2.17	5.06
1996	120	2.92	5.04
1995	116.6	2.82	5.51
1994	113.4	2.53	4.27

Table 16.5
Short-term loans, and other short-term liabilities
(thousand, Mexican pesos)

Currency	1996	1995
US Dollar	5,415,665	723,414
Peseta	323,857	970,087
Bolivar	127,988	259,614
Mexican Peso	39,398	138,345
Colombian Peso	473,111	0
Dominican Peso	43,106	0
Total	6,425,121	2,091,460

Table 16.6
Debt structure, 1966
(thousand of Mexican pesos)

Structure of Debt	Mexican peso	Interest rate	Foreign currency	Interest rate	Total
Collateralized					
1997-2003	12,634	28.80%	9,689,801	6.90%	9,702,435
Non-collateralized					
1997-2001			228	8.00%	228
Bank loans					
1997-2001			4,441,359	8.20%	4,441,359
Payables					
1997-2006	60,473	31.50%	21,725,138	8.70%	21,785,611
Total	73,107		35,856,526		35,929,633

Table 16.7
Maturity of long-term debt, 1996
(thousand of Mexican pesos)

Year	Mexican peso	Foreign currency	Total
1998	2,103	9,043,738	9,045,841
1999	12,686	4,654,303	4,666,989
2000		5,791,735	5,791,735
2001		5,651,339	5,651,339
Beyond 2001	0	5,981,422	5,981,422
Total	14,789	31,122,537	31,137,326

Table 16.8
Long-term liability by type of currency
(thousand of Mexican pesos)

Currency	1995	1996
Dollars	28,527,869	24,460,782
Pesetas	2,261,146	3,767,274
Bolivares	199,902	600,170
Mexican Pesos	33,709	1,117,711
Colombian Pesos	133,620	0
Total	31,158,242	29,947,932

Table 16.9
Foreign exchange rate position, 1996
(thousand of Mexican pesos)

Item	Mexico	Abroad	Total
Current assets	177,218	913,483	1,090,701
Fixed assets	812,739	4,848,045	5,660,784
Total assets	989,957	5,761,528	6,751,485
Current liabilities	587,723	666,161	1,253,884
Long-term liabilities	2,440,909	1,594,486	4,035,395
Total liabilities	3,028,632	2,260,647	5,289,279
Net	-2,038,675	3,500,881	1,462,206

164

Table 16.10
Key financial figures

Accounting Period Figures in	12-month Ended Dec 94 $ million	12-month Ended Dec 95 $ thousand	12-month Ended Dec 96 $ thousand
Profit Before Interest & Tax	797	1,231,574	914,667
Ordinary Dividends	77	104,681	73,789
Total Assets	8,120,801	8,814,767	7,524,516
Net Current Assets	384	418,849	

Table 16.11
Performance ratios

Accounting Period	12-month Ended Dec 94	12-month Ended Dec 95	12-month Ended Dec 96
Profit Margin (%)	36.853	38.67	41.313
Debt/Equity (%)	190.441	165.411	167.082
P/E Ratio	13.785	17.438	
Current Ratio	1.354	1.359	
Interest Cover	2.154	2.286	
Dividend Cover	5.364	5.452	

Source: *Financial Times*, October 1997.

Table 16.12
Net sales, net income, and total assets
(thousand Mexican pesos)

Country	Net sales 1996	1995	Net income 1996	1995	Total assets 1996	1995
Mexico	11,761	9,798	3,638	3,018	37,864	37,611
Spain	6,097	7,474	1,442	1,841	20,773	29,063
Venezuela	3,163	3,592	1,109	1,165	7,957	9,695
US	3,427	3,725	266	321	4,854	4,901
Colombia	1,321		290		9,643	
Other	4,494	3,291	-427	-303	11,732	14,918
Total	30,263	27,880	6,318	6,042	92,823	96,188
Adjustment	-3,746	-2,569			-14,474	-13,567
Total	26,517	25,311	6,318	6,042	78,349	82,621

Source: Cemex, S.A. de C.V. *Annual Report*, 1996.

Table 16.13
Consolidated income statement, December 1995 and 1996
(million, constant pesos)

	1996	1995
Net sales	26,517	25,311
Cost of sales	16,079	15,437
Gross profit	10,438	9,874
Operating expenses		
Administrative	2,787	2,538
Selling	1,330	1,293
Total operating expenses	4,117	3,831
Operating profits	6,321	6,043
Finance income/expense		
Interest income	646	716
Interest expense	5,260	6,435
Foreign exchange losses	794	3,605
Effect of monetary position	9,577	14,918
Total Finance position	4,169	5,594
Other expenses net	1,344	1,597
Income before taxes	9,146	10,040
Provision for taxes	738	1,628
Profit sharing with workers	44	18
Net profit for year	8,364	8,394
Participation from associates	271	174
Consolidated net profits	8,635	8,568
Distribution to common stock	7,699	7,494

Source: Cemex, S.A. de C.V. *Annual Report*, 1996.

Table 16.14
Consolidated balance sheet, December 31, 1995 and 1996
(million, constant pesos)

Assets	1996	1995	Liabilities	1996	1995
Current assets			Bank loans	901	1,026
Cash	3,220	3,500	Accounts payable	749	4,515
Marketable securities			Notes payable*	4,773	3,051
Accounts receivable	4,649	5,300	Suppliers	1,669	1,536
Inventories	3,289	3,338	Other	2,703	2,667
Other current assets	829	1,082	Total current liabilities	10,795	12,795
Total current assets	11,987	13,220			
			Long term liabilities		
Investment and other			Bank loans	14,144	9,225
Investment in subsidiaries	3,187	2,042	Liabilities to pay		62
Other investments	297	339	Documents to pay	21,785	23,708
Other accounts receivable	131	1,510	Maturity of long-term debt	4,773	3,050
Total of Investment	3,615	3,891	Total of long-term liabilities	31,156	29,945
Fixed assets			Other liabilities		
Land and buildings	19,999	20,834	Pensions	639	674
Machinery and equipment	64,216	70,255	Deferred taxes	1,074	1,372
Investment in process	1,804	1,029	Other liabilities	502	486
Total plant and equipment	86,019	92,118	Total of other liabilities	2,215	2,697
Less depreciation	40,768	43,369			
Net fixed assets	45,251	48,749	Total liabilities	44,166	45,437
Deferred liabilities	17,488	16,763	Stockholder's equity		
			Common stock	1,806	1,803
Total assets	78,341	82,623	Capital surplus	9,965	8,141
			Excess (insufficiency in the Updating of common stock)	-20,540	-9,905
			Accumulated retained earnings	27,362	20,878
			Earnings for the year	7,699	7,495
			Total Stockholder's equity	26,292	28,412
			Preferred stock	7,883	8,774
			Total equity	34,175	37,186
			Total liabilities and Stockholder's equity	78,341	82,623

Source: Cemex, S.A. de C.V. *Annual Report*, 1996.

Notes

1   Exports to Asia in 1996 represented more than a fourfold increase over sales in 1994.
2   Clinker is a chemical component required for the manufacture of cement. Ready-mix concrete is a mixture of cement, sand and water.
3   All the financial information included in this section was taken from Cemex, *Annual Report*, December 1996.

17 Managing transaction exposure with spot and forward contracts

Introduction

Due to the nature of their business activity, multinational corporations are always exposed to exchange rate risk. This risk may affect the value of payables and receivables stated in terms of a foreign currency. This is known as transaction exposure.

Purpose

The aim of this technical note is to explore ways in which the financial officer of a multinational corporation can manage transaction risk. Specifically, this note explains how the executive of an international entity can use spot and forward contracts to eliminate or reduce transaction exposure.[1]

Transaction exposure

To provide a flavor for transaction risk, consider the case of MCI, a US telecommunications company which is known to hold accounts payable and receivable stated in terms of French francs, Mexican pesos, British pounds and many other currencies. In the event of a dollar depreciation across currencies against the franc, the peso, and the pound, the dollar value of the payables held by MCI increase in proportion to the dollar devaluation. In the case of the receivables, the opposite occurs. Their dollar value increases with the dollar depreciation. The net financial result of a dollar devaluation on the assets and liabilities held by MCI will depend on the balance between payables and receivables, the currency in which these items are stated, and the degree of the devaluation. To minimize the transaction risk associated with variations in the exchange rate, the multinationals may hedge their payables or receivables.

Hedging a receivable with a spot contract (money market hedge)

To describe how a firm can hedge a receivable using spot contracts, consider the case of a US exporter who is scheduled to receive a 10 million French franc (Ff10,000,000) payment for exports to France in 90 days. If the exporter fears a French franc devaluation against the dollar, this person can hedge the risk of the French franc devaluation by implementing a spot hedge, also known as a *money market hedge*. The first step in implementing this hedge is either to borrow (in French francs) the equivalent of the present value of the receivable or to submit the French franc receivable for discount. The second step is to trade the French francs in the spot. At this point, regardless of what happens to the dollar, the trader has secured dollar revenue for the 90-day French franc export. The hedging procedure is described in detail below, using the foreign exchange and money market information provided in Table 17.1. It is also described in page 173.

Table 17.1
Foreign exchange and interest rate quotes

Country	$ equivalence		French franc equivalence	
	Wed	Tues	Wed	Tues
France (Franc)	0.17234	0.17460	5.8025	5.7274
90-day Forward	0.17122	0.17321	5.8405	5.7734

	US	France
90-day interest rate	5.97%	10.25%

Steps required to perform a spot hedge

1. Borrow French francs. The maximum amount of French francs that the firm can borrow, when using the French franc receivable as collateral, is the present value of the receivable discounted at the French franc interest rate provided in Table 17.1.

   The present value of the French franc receivable is
   PV(Ff) = Ff10,000,000/(1.025625) = Ff9,750,152.3

2. Once the loan has been realized, the US exporter can convert the French francs just borrowed into dollars by trading the francs in the spot market.

169

The present value of the French franc loan expressed in dollar terms is PV($) = Ff9,750,152.3*($1/Ff5.8025) = $1,680,336.5

3.   At maturity, use the French francs to settle the French franc loan.

Hedging a receivable with forward contracts

To perform a forward hedge on the 10 million French franc receivable, the exporter needs to find the best forward rate, and a bank willing to pre-purchase the francs at that rate. To compare the forward option with a money market hedge, the hedger has to bring the forward values to present value. If the present value of the forward hedge provides a higher dollar income than the spot hedge, then the US trader can enter into a forward contract. At the maturity of the receivable, the US firm should collect the French francs and deliver them to the bank to honor the forward contract.

In a step-by-step fashion, the illustration below describes how to implement a forward hedge on the 10 million French franc payable.   This process is also described in page 174.

Hedging with forward contracts

1.   Sell the French francs to be received at the best forward rate available. If the francs can be sold at the best forward rate, the dollar value of the forward transaction is $1,712,182.2.

The dollar value of the forward contract
= Ff10,000,000*($1/Ff5.8405) = $1,712,182.2

2.   To compare the forward with the spot hedge, the trader has to bring the dollar value of the forward transaction to present value. This happens to be $1,687,003.7.

PV($) = $1,712,182/(1+(0.0597/4)) = $1,687,003.7

3.   Since the present value of the forward transaction is higher than the value of the spot hedge, the US exporter should enter into the forward transaction.

4.   At the maturity of the receivable, the US exporter can collect the French francs and deliver them to the holder of the forward contract to honor his/her commitment.

Hedging imports

To illustrate how to hedge a payable, consider the case of a US importer who has agreed to import Swiss watches for distribution and sale in the United States. The value of the transaction is 6.5 million Swiss francs per year over a two-year period. The delivery of the product is quarterly, and the payment on the cargo is at delivery of the goods. The Swiss franc value of each quarterly delivery is SwF1.625 million. Given the size of the commitment and the fact that the US importer is expecting a Swiss franc appreciation against the dollar, the trader decides to hedge the Swiss franc payable.

Hedging imports with a spot contract (money market hedge)

To implement a spot hedge, the trader has to first estimate the present value of the Swiss franc payable by discounting the eight quarterly payments using a Swiss franc interest rate. Once the Swiss franc present value of each payable is known, the US importer has to find out the dollar value of each one using the spot rate. The dollar value of each payable is the amount of dollars that the importer needs to cover his Swiss franc payables. The US importer has to trade the dollars in the spot market and open eight time deposits with eight different dates to maturity. At maturity, each one of the Swiss franc deposits will be of sufficient value to meet the importer's liabilities regardless of what happens to the dollar/Swiss franc parity. A detailed, step by step analysis of how to implement a money market hedge is presented in Table 17.2.

Hedging a payable with a forward hedge

To cover the payable with a forward hedge, the US importer has to find forward quotations meeting the maturity of each one of the eight payments. Once these rates are known, he can estimate the present value of the forward hedge to compare it with the cost involved with a money market hedge. If the forward hedge is cheaper, the US importer should purchase eight forward contracts to secure the cost of each one of the payables. A detailed analysis of how to hedge the Swiss payable is presented in Table 17.2, which shows that forward contracts on Swiss francs are only available to cover the first payment. The remaining Swiss franc liabilities can be covered in the same fashion.

171

Table 17.2
Hedging imports with spot contracts

Information	US	Switzerland
Spot rate	$0.8222/SwF1	
90-day forward rate	$0.8295/SwF1	
Interest rate in the US	8.50%	
Interest rate in Switzerland		3.88%

Transaction

Imports	SwF 6.5 million/year	
Period	2 years	
Equal quarterly payments		

Spot Hedge

Period	Swiss Franc Payment	Discount Factor at 3.88%	Discount Factor	Present Value in SwF
1	1.625	1/(1+(0.0388/4))^1	0.99	1.61
2	1.625	1/(1+(0.0388/4))^2	0.98	1.59
3	1.625	1/(1+(0.0388/4))^3	0.97	1.58
4	1.625	1/(1+(0.0388/4))^4	0.96	1.56
5	1.625	1/(1+(0.0388/4))^5	0.95	1.55
6	1.625	1/(1+(0.0388/4))^6	0.94	1.53
7	1.625	1/(1+(0.0388/4))^7	0.93	1.52
8	1.625	1/(1+(0.0388/4))^8	0.93	1.5
		PV (SwF)		12.45
		Spot rate		$0.82
		PV ($)		10.24

Money market hedge of first payment

	Present value ($)	1.61*0.8222	1.32

90-day forward hedge of first payment

Principal * forward rate	Future value in $	1.625*0.8295	1.35
	Present Value ($)	1.35/(1+(0.085/4))	1.319

A comparison of the costs involved in both the spot and the forward hedge to cover the first of the eight payments suggests that the US importer is indifferent between one or the other since the costs are practically the same. Not surprisingly, this result reflects interest rate parity. Normally, due to arbitrage, interest rate parity holds pretty well in the international financial markets. As a consequence, both the money market and the forward hedge options should yield similar results most of the time. If this is true, interest rate parity renders the practice of comparing spot and forward hedges somewhat meaningless. There are, however, some compelling reasons to recommend an understanding of how to hedge in either one of these two markets.

The first reason is the existence of market imperfections that may lead to short-term discrepancies between spot and forward hedges. Another reason is the fact that even if forward contracts exist, they are not always offered with the maturity required to meet the needs of the traders. In this last instance, the executive may be forced to engage in a combined hedge —that is, to cover some portion of the transaction with a forward hedge, and the remaining with a spot hedge. To determine the most convenient mix of hedging, the trader has to compare both money market and forward hedge results.

MONEY MARKET HEDGE

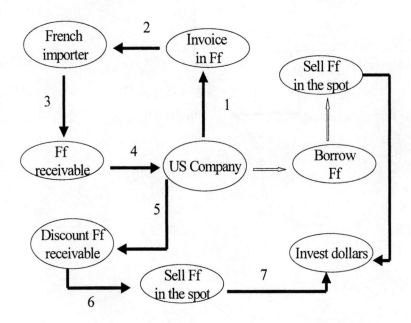

FORWARD HEDGE

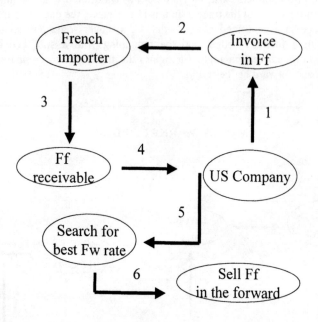

Problems

1. A US firm has a Ff200,000 payable due in six months. Assume that the 180-day French interest (annualized) and the spot rates are 7 percent and $.1/Ff1 respectively. Indicate the cost of the payable if the company implements a money market hedge.

2. A French firm has contracted to buy parts from Japan worth ¥15 million payable in three months. The firm has receivables for goods sold to a Japanese firm valued at ¥5 million, also due in three months. It is the policy of the firm to hedge all residual currency positions.

Information	France	Japan
Spot rate	Ff1/¥27.00	
90-day forward rate	Ff1/¥26.65	
Interest rate	13.2%	8 percent

   a. What is the amount of the payable in French francs if the French company hedges in the money market?
   b. What is the amount of the payable in French francs if the French company hedges in the forward market?
   c. Which option is the best alternative?

3. International Instruments, Inc. has just imported a shipment from a German firm valued at DM5,000,000 payable in 180 days.

Information	United States	Germany
Spot	DM2.66/$1	
180-day forward rate	DM2.5802/$1	
Interest rate	13%	8%

   a. What is the dollar cost of the imports if the company hedges in the money market?
   b. What is the dollar cost of the imports if the company hedges in the forward market?
   c. Which is the best alternative?

4. Assume the following information:

Rate	Germany	United States
Spot	$0.39/DM1	
One-year forward	$0.40/DM1	
Bid interest rate	8%	11%
Offer interest rate	10%	12%

Additionally, assume that a US exporter denominates its German exports in marks and expects to receive DM600,000 in one year. What will be the appropriate value of these exports in dollars if the firm executes a money market hedge?

5. Pitou, a Swiss based multinational corporation, has a $1,000,000 90-day payable. The company wants to eliminate the exchange risk using the lowest cost alternative.

Rate	United States	Switzerland
Spot	$0.6/SwF1	
90-day forward rate	$0.6075/SwF1	
Interest	10% (annual)	7% (annual)

a. What is the Swiss franc value of the money market hedge?
b. What is the Swiss franc value of the forward hedge?
c. Which hedge is the best alternative?

6. The US subsidiary of the Mexican corporation Vitro, S.A. is filling an order from a Taiwanese industrial company for machinery worth Tai$4,800,000. The export sale is due in 90 days and is denominated in Taiwanese dollars. The opportunity cost of funding for Vitro in the United States is 8 percent. The interest rate on 90-day securities in Taiwan is ten percent. The spot rate is Taiw$20/$1, and the 90-day forward rate is selling at a 20 percent discount per year. The finance staff of Vitro forecasts that the Taiwanese dollar will depreciate ten percent at a steady rate over the next year. Vitro faces the following choices: hedge in the spot or forward market. Which is the best option for hedging?

Note

1 Transaction exposure can be hedged with futures and option contracts. However, an explanation of how to use these contracts has been postponed to another technical note.

18 Managing transaction exposure with futures and options

Introduction

The futures and options markets offer highly standardized foreign exchange contracts written against the futures clearing house for a fixed number of currency units to be delivered on a specific date. Futures and options contracts provide firms and individuals with the opportunity to limit their exchange rate exposure by taking futures and/or options positions.

Purpose

The purpose of this technical note is to describe, in a step-by-step approach, the nature of futures and options markets and how individuals and corporations can use futures and options contracts either to hedge exchange rate risk or speculate.

Hedging with futures

To describe how futures contracts can be used to hedge, assume the case of an investor who is planning to invest in Mexican Treasury bills, better known as CETES (Certificado de Tesorería, CETES). Historically, these instruments have offered much higher yields than comparable US Treasury bill rates. These high yields have made CETES an attractive investment possibility. However, the foreign exchange risk associated with holding a peso-denominated investment has deterred more than one investor from taking advantage of the high yields offered by CETES. The fear attached to investing in the peso is more than justified. However, the availability of future contracts on pesos in the Chicago exchanges has opened up the opportunity to eliminate the exchange rate risk associated with peso denominated CETES, and for that matter on other foreign assets.

To describe the process of hedging a peso investment, assume the case of a US investor who decides to purchase a one million peso, 91-day CETES. The investor buys the CETES at a 50.01 percent discount on June 7 and receives MxP1,000,000 at the end of the 91-day period (the third Wednesday of September). The risk involved in this transaction is that the Mexican peso may depreciate against the dollar within that time span. If this happens, the investor will end up receiving fewer dollars at the maturity of CETES. If the peso falls far enough, the investment in CETES may even result in a dollar loss. To minimize the exchange rate risk of this transaction, the US investor may hedge his/her peso position by entering into a Mexican peso futures contract.[1]

The peso futures contract

A futures contract is a standardized fixed-date obligation to make or receive delivery of the underlying commodity at the defined delivery date. A Mexican futures contract reflects the dollar value of the Mexican peso at some time in the future. This future value is determined by four variables: 1) the current spot rate between the peso and the dollar, 2) the time to maturity, and the interest rates both in 3) Mexico and 4) the US. The maturity date to make or receive delivery of pesos is the third Wednesday of the month of maturity. These are March, June, September, and December. The size of peso contracts is MxP500,000.[2]

The hedging process

On June 7, a US investor purchases, at a 50.01 percent discount, a 91-day Mexican Treasury Bill with a face value of MxP1,000,000, for a price of MxP873,585.83. The market price of the CETES is equivalent to its present value. This is equal to the face value (MexP$ 1,000,000) discounted at the yearly rate of 50.1 percent, and adjusted by the maturity period (91 days). That is:

Price = MxP1,000,000/[1 + (0.501*91)/360] = MxP1,000,000/1.1266) = MxP887,593.6

If the spot rate is MxP6.14/$1 on June 7, it will take $144,513.2 to purchase MxP887,311.4. To cover the peso exposure with a peso futures contract, the investor must take into consideration three aspects: 1) whether to purchase or sell future contracts, 2) for what expiration date, and 3) how many contracts are required to cover the peso risk. To solve the first problem, the investor must remember that he/she will receive pesos in the future. Then, as a rule of thumb, the investor should take the same action in the futures market that he will take at a later date in the cash market. In this case, the investor will want to pre-sell pesos with futures contracts, since he/she expects to receive pesos at the maturity of the Mexican investment. Regarding maturity, the investor will want to sell the futures contract that matures at or near the time that the CETES investment does. In this

178

case, the investor will want to pre-sell pesos with future contracts expiring in September. To find out how many futures contracts are needed to cover the exposure, the investor has to divide the number of pesos to be received in the future by the contract size in pesos. Since the investor expects to receive MxP1,000,000, and the futures contract size in pesos is 500,000, the investor should enter into two futures contracts at $.144825 per peso, which is the futures quotation available on pesos at that point in time. On September 7, at the maturity of the CETES, the US investor receives MxP1,000,000. He trades in the spot, since September contracts are not due yet. To close his futures position, the investor should buy back the two September contracts that he had sold previously on June 7. In practice, it is impossible to know in advance the level of the spot and futures. Therefore, to consider the profitability involved in the peso investment, it is convenient to consider some possible scenarios to determine the range of the dollar proceeds from this investment.

Scenario A

- Column one shows the initial date of the investment and the date of settlement (September 7).

- Column two shows the face value of the investment (one million pesos).

- Column three shows the peso market price of the one CETES, which sells at a discount of 50.1 percent per year or 12.6 percent per quarter [0.501*91)/360].

- Column four exhibits the initial and settlement spot rates. This information suggests that the initial dollar investment was sold at a price of MxP6.14 per dollar in the spot, and that at the maturity of the CETES investment, the dollars were purchased back at only MxP5. These two transactions result in a gain in the spot market of 1.14 pesos per dollar traded.

- Column five indicates that the total spot gains measured in terms of dollars amounted to $55,441.

- Column six shows two futures rates -- one on June 7 used to pre-sell the pesos, and the September 7 rate applied to repurchase pesos. Since the dollar repurchase price is higher than the dollar pre-selling price, then the transaction nets a loss of $0.053250 per peso traded.

- Column seven exhibits the futures position. Initially, the investor is holding two futures contracts where heshe is pre-selling pesos. To close the position, the investor enters into two contracts to pre-purchase pesos.

- Column eight shows the total loss incurred in the futures market, which is equivalent to $53,250.

- Column nine shows the net dollar value of the transaction, which is $146,750. This was obtained by subtracting the dollar loss in the futures ($53,250 located in column 8) from the sale of pesos in the spot market ($200,000, located in column 5).

Scenario A

1	2	3	4	5	6	7	8	9	10
		Market	Spot	Value of	Futures		Value of		
	Face value	price	rate	CETES	rate	Futures	futures	Net dollar	Rate of
Date	(pesos)	pesos	MxP/$	($)	$/MxP	Position	($)	proceeds	return
7-Jun	1,000,000	887,595	6.14	144,559	0.144825	2 pre-sell	144,825		
7-Sep	1,000,000		5.00	200,000	0.198075	2 pre-purchase	198,075		
Result			-1.14	55,441	0.053250	0	-53,250	146,750	5.99
	Unchanged		gain	gain	loss		loss		

Given the terminal cash flows, it is possible to determine the annualized rate of return on the Mexican investment. This is estimated by dividing the dollar gain in the investment by the original dollar investment. The 91-day return is annualized by multiplying it by the factor that results from dividing 360 days by the investment period (360/91 days).

Dollar rate of return = [(dollar proceed - the initial investment)/(initial investment)]*(360/n)*100 = [(146,750 - 144,559)/144,559]*(360/91)*100 = 5.9%.

Another possible scenario (B) for the same type of investment could be outlined as follows:

Scenario B

1	2	3	4	5	6	7	8	9	10
		Market	Spot	Value of	Futures		Value of		
	Face value	price	rate	CETES	rate	Futures	futures	Net dollar	Rate of
Date	(pesos)	pesos	MxP/$	($)	$/MxP	Position	($)	proceeds	return
7-Jun	1,000,000	887,595	6.14	144,559	0.144825	2 pre-sell	144,825		
7-Sep	1,000,000		10.00	100,000	0.098075	2 pre-purchase	98,075		
Result			3.86	-44,559	-0.046750	0	46,750	146,750	5.99
	unchanged		loss	loss	gain		gain		

Hedging with options

Another hedging strategy available to firms wanting to manage their exchange rate exposure is to enter into the options market. Options provide contract holders with the right to buy or sell foreign exchange at a pre-agreed price prior to or at the expiration of the contract.

Types of contracts

There are two types of options contracts: put and call. **A put option contract** confers its holder the right to sell foreign exchange at the *strike price*. The writer -- or seller -- of the contract is obligated to buy the foreign exchange at the request of the holder if the holder wants to exercise the option. **A call option contract** grants its holder the right to purchase foreign exchange from the writer at the strike price. In this case, the writer has to furnish the foreign exchange if the holder wants to exercise the option.

The *exercise* or *strike price* is the price at which the option buyer (holder) has the right to purchase or sell the underlying currency. Except for the Japanese yen and the French franc, exercise prices are stated in cents of US dollars. For instance, a DM 36 call is an option to buy German marks at $.36 per mark. Exercise prices for options on the French franc are stated in tenths of a cent of a US dollar. For example, the holder of a Ff 115 option has the right to purchase the underlying francs at $.115 per franc. The Japanese yen option exercise prices are stated in hundredths of a cent, such that a □43 price entitles the holder to purchase the underlying yen at $.0043 per yen.[3]

The expiration dates for options on foreign currencies are March, June, September and December. The last day on which an option can be exercised is the Saturday before the third Wednesday of the expiration month. The option premium is the sum of money that the buyer of an option pays when an option is purchased and is, in effect, the price of an option.

An option has an intrinsic value if it is profitable to exercise. In the case of a call, the option has an intrinsic value if the spot price of the underlying currency is above the exercise price. In the case of a put, the intrinsic value exists if the spot price is below the strike price. In both cases, the options are said to be **"in the money."** For example, if the spot D-mark price is $.45, a DM 40 call will have an intrinsic value of $.05 per mark, and a DM 40 put will have no intrinsic value.

Normally, an option whose exercise price is the same or very nearly the same as the spot price is said to be **"at the money."** A call whose exercise price is above the current spot price of the underlying currency, or a put whose exercise price is below the current spot price of the underlying currency are both classified as **"out of the money."** In these two instances, neither of the two alternatives has an intrinsic value.

Hedging a payable in the options market

To explain by example the use of options to hedge, it is assumed that on March 28, 1993, a US importer agrees to purchase a shipment of Swiss cheese for delivery on April 15, 1993, at a cost of SwF375,000. The importer has the choice of paying the import bill at any time between March 28 and April 15. However, the American firm is concerned about a Swiss franc appreciation; therefore, it decides to hedge the Swiss franc account with call option contracts.

181

Chart 1
Option quotes

Swiss Franc (IMM) 125,000 francs, cents per franc

Strike	Calls - Settle		Puts- Settle	
Price	Apr-c	May-c	Apr-p	May-p
6800	.85	....	.67	1.21

Note: Taken from *The Wall Street Journal.*

Given the value of the import bill and the contract size for Swiss francs, the firm can purchase three April option contracts at the strike price of $.68 per Swiss franc. To have these option contracts, the US firm has to pay a call-premium equivalent to $.0085 per unit of foreign currency. If the three contracts are exercised, the total cost of the payable is $258,187.5. The calculations are presented in detail in Chart 2.

Chart 2
Total cost of the call option hedge

Number of options contracts purchased:		3
Type of contracts purchased:		call contracts
Strike price per franc:		$.6800 per franc
Plus call price per franc:		$.0085 per franc
Total cost per franc:		$.6885 per franc
Total cost per contract:	.6885*125,000	$86,062.5
Total cost of payable	.6885*125,000*3	$258,187.5

This contractual arrangement guarantees the owner of the contract a "ceiling cost," since the total cost of the payable cannot exceed $258,187.5. However, if the dollar spot price of the Swiss franc is less than $.6800 per franc at any time within the life-span of the contract, the US importer may end up paying less for the imports of Swiss cheese if he decides to buy "cheap" francs in the spot market. Therefore, any time that the spot rate is less than the strike price, call option contracts are not exercised. The holders of a Swiss franc call contract benefit from a depreciation of the Swiss franc because the depreciation lowers the cost of the Swiss franc account payable. In contrast, a Swiss franc appreciation has no effect on the dollar value of the transaction because the holder of the contract has already secured, with the option contracts, a dollar price for the Swiss francs.

Hedging a receivable

On March 28, 1998, a US exporter agrees to sell a shipment of tennis shoes for delivery on May 15. The invoice is for SwF375,000. The exporter agrees to be paid in Swiss francs. However, the US firm is concerned about a Swiss franc depreciation; therefore, it decides to hedge the Swiss franc receivable by purchasing put option contracts. Given the value of the invoice and the contract size on Swiss francs, the firm can purchase three May-option contracts at the strike price of $.68 per Swiss franc. To have these contracts, the US firm pays a put-premium equivalent to $.0121 per unit of foreign currency. If the three contracts are exercised, the total cost of the option is $250,462.5. The calculations to arrive at the final cost of the option are presented in detail in Chart 3.

Chart 3
Total revenue of the put option hedge

Number of options contracts purchased:		3
Type of contracts purchased:		Put contracts
Strike price per franc:		$.6800 per franc
Minus put price per franc:		$.0121 per franc
Net revenue per franc:		$.6679 per franc
Total net revenue per contract:	.6679*125,000	$83,487.5
Total net revenue of the receivable	.6679*125,000*3	$250,462.5

Hedging with options guarantees the holder a "floor revenue" because the total values of the Swiss franc account cannot fall below $250,462.5. However, if within the life-span of the contract the dollar spot price of the Swiss franc is higher than $.68 per franc, the US exporter may end up having a higher dollar revenue by selling his Swiss francs in the spot market. Consequently, any time that the spot price is higher than the strike price, put options contracts are not exercised. The holders of Swiss franc put contracts benefit from an appreciation of the Swiss franc because the appreciation raises the dollar value of the Swiss francs. In contrast, a Swiss franc depreciation has no effect on the dollar value of the transaction because the holder has already secured, with the option contracts, a dollar price for the Swiss francs.

Problems

1. You purchased a call option contract on Swiss francs. The price of the call was $0.02 per unit. At the settlement of the option, the spot rate was $0.46/SwF1. Should the option contract be exercised if the strike price was $0.45/SwF1 and the quantity traded was 62,500 Swiss francs?

2. You sold a put option on Canadian dollars. The price of the put was $0.03 per unit, the strike price was $0.75/Can$1, and the quantity traded was 50,000 units (Canadian dollars). At the time the option was exercised, the spot rate was $.72/Can$1. What is the amount of profit/loss from this transaction?

3. Assume that a person purchases a put option contract on British pounds. The price of the put is $0.05 per unit, the strike price is $1.50/£1, and the quantity to be traded is 12,500 British pounds. At the time of the purchase of the put contract, the spot rate was $1.51/£1 and continually rose to $1.62/£1 by the settlement date. What is the profit on this transaction?

4. Assume that a speculator purchases a call option contract on British pounds. The price of the call is $.12 per unit, the strike price is $1.50/£1, and the quantity to be traded is 12,500 British pounds. At the time of the purchase of the call contract, the spot rate was $1.51/£1 and continually rose to $1.62/£1 by the settlement date. What is the profit/loss from this transaction?

5. A speculator purchases two European put option contracts on Canadian dollars for $0.025 per unit at the strike price of $0.8823. At maturity, three months later, the spot rate is $0.8771. The size of the option contract on Canadian dollars is 50,000 units. What is the profit/loss from this transaction?

6. A speculator purchases two European call option contracts on Canadian Dollars for $0.013 per unit at the strike price of $0.8823. At maturity, three months later, the spot rate is $0.8771. The size of the option contract on Canadian dollars is 50,000 units. Did the speculator have a dollar profit or loss on this transaction?

7. A writer sells five put option contracts on British pounds at a $0.0105 premium per unit. The strike price is $1.7750. At maturity, three months later, the spot rate is $1.7560. The size of the option contract on pounds is 31,250 units. Did the writer have a dollar profit or loss on this transaction?

8. A writer sells ten call option contracts on British pounds at a $0.017 premium per unit. The strike price is $1.7750. At maturity, three months later when the contract is exercised, the spot rate is $1.7896. The size of the option contract on pounds is 31,250 units. Did the writer have a dollar profit or loss in this transaction?

184

9. A Japanese speculator (the writer) sells a put option on Canadian dollars at Can$0.03 (price of the put option). The strike price in the contract is Can$0.75. The spot at the time of maturity of the contract is Can$0.72. If the speculator (the writer) sells off the Canadian dollars immediately after receiving them, what is the net profit to the writer of the put option if the contract size is 50,000?

10. RALEC is a US company that imports British goods. On November 13, 1997, the company plans to use options to hedge a payable of £287,000 due in 30 days. The following quotations are available on the Philadelphia exchange:

31,250, British Pounds - cents per unit

BP	Strike Price	Nov Calls - last	Dec	Mar	Nov Puts - last	Dec	Mar
	16705	10.00				0.18	
	17205	4.90				0.92	
	17500	2.20	2.95		0.27	1.70	
	17705	0.63	2.10		1.05		
	18000	0.07					
	18205		0.52				
	19000					13.77	

The company wishes to hedge the payable on the imports using the lowest cost alternative. Remember that the cost is determined by the strike price plus the premium. Indicate the dollar savings, considering the following scenarios for the spot rate in December: 1) $1.7640/£1, 2) $1.7430/£1, 3) 17900/£1, and 4) $1.5670/£1. The probabilities are 50, 15, 20, and 15% respectively.

11. On November 13, 1998, Herman and Hakim, a US company, exports equipment to Britain worth £487,000. The company wants to hedge the pound receivable, which is due in 30 days. The company wants to hedge with the highest revenue alternative. Suggest the strike price alternative (it is the difference between the strike price and the premium) which provides the highest revenue, assuming the following scenarios for the spot rate in December: 1) $1.7640/£1, 2) $1.7430/£1, 3) $17900/£1, and 4) $1.5670/£1. The probabilities for each one of the spot quotations are 50, 15, 20, and 15% respectively.

185

Options quotations

31,250, British Pounds - cents per unit

BP	Strike Price	Calls - last Nov	Dec	Mar	Puts - last Nov	Dec	Mar
	16705	10.00				0.18	
	17205	4.90				0.92	
	17500	2.20	2.95		0.27	1.70	
	17705	0.63	2.10		1.05	13.77	
	18000	0.07					
	18205		0.52				

12. To promote its British exports, Dai-Kal has created an inventory of finished goods in London. The value of the British inventory on July 1, 1998 is £500,000, and the spot and December futures rates for the same date are $1.64/£1 and $1.60/£1 respectively. The futures contract size in British pounds is 62,500. The company wants to hedge the foreign exchange rate risk on the 1,000 units of finished goods inventory held when 50% of the exchange rate change can be offset by raising the pound sale price. How could Dai-Kal hedge with futures contracts? On December 1, Dai-Kal sells all its British inventories at a price of £500. At that date, the spot and futures rates are the same at $1.50/£1. What should Dai-Kal do to close its position? After the futures position is closed, did the company have a capital gain or loss in this futures transaction? The table below is provided to facilitate your calculations.

Date	Value (pounds)	Exchange Rate	Value (dollars)	Futures Position	Futures Price	Value (dollars)
July	___	___	___	___	___	___
Dec	___	___	___	___	___	___
Gain	___	___	___	___	___	___

186

Notes

1 The Chicago Mercantile Exchange offers peso futures contracts.
2 For further details, see "Hedging Mexican Money Market Instruments with CME Mexican Peso Futures Contracts," http//www.cme.com/market/insti...I/ strategy papers/mexhedgi.html.
3 For further details on options pricing, see *Understanding Foreign Currency Options, The Third Dimension of Foreign Exchange,* The Philadelphia Stock Exchange, Philadelphia, PA, p. 8.

19 Controlling economic risk

Introduction

After the approval of the North American Free Trade Agreement, Bashas, a retailing company based in Phoenix, Arizona, was assessing whether to expand into Northern Mexico. The initial version of the expansion project considered opening stores in major urban centers located within 500 miles of the Arizona-Mexico border. To assess a preliminary version of the business plan, the financial executives of this company were faced with a major roadblock: how to deal with exchange rate exposure.

By 1993, the Mexican peso had gained stability and inflation was under control. However, at the beginning of 1994, there were some concerns regarding a possible overvaluation of the Mexican currency. To correct the perceived exchange rate imbalance, some experts had been suggesting that a 10-20 percent adjustment was necessary to return the Mexican currency to purchasing power parity equilibrium. As it is known now, the peso depreciation took place in December of 1994, but it was well beyond the proposed 10-20 percent range.

The event previously described suggests that multinational corporations often act upon a project considering some expectations regarding exchange rate risk. Since the fulfillment of these expectations is not certain, companies are always exposed to a risk known as *economic exposure*.

Purpose

The aim of this technical note is to provide an explanation of what constitutes an economic risk, and to furnish the student using this note, with the finance tools required to manage this risk.

Managing economic exposure

Economic exposure to exchange rate risk refers to the impact of unexpected foreign exchange rate fluctuations on the dollar value of cash flows generated by an overseas business venture. Consider, for instance, the case of Bashas. If the company had decided to expand its retail operations in 1993 based on a 10-20 percent peso devaluation, the actual cash flows of the Mexican retailing operations measured in dollars would have been quite different from expected. Unexpected variations in the exchange rate alter either the actual dollar value of the subsidiary's cash flows or the market value of its equity. In the first case, economic exposure is labeled *operating cash flow exposure*. In the second instance, it is referred to as *equity exposure*.

An example of operating cash flow exposure is provided by the increase in the dollar cash flows reported by the Mexican subsidiaries of GM, Ford, and Chrysler after the peso devaluation in December of 1994. The reasons for the cash flow gains were traced to the fact that the operating costs of these plants, which were in pesos, declined in dollar terms. At the same time, the dollar value of the car and truck exports of these subsidiaries to the United States remained steady.

Another example of operating cash flow exposure is provided by the effect of the continuous appreciation of the Japanese yen against the dollar — observed during the period of the 1980s and 1990s — on the cost and revenues of manufacturing plants located within Japan. Operating costs, while steady in Japanese yen terms, have risen in dollar terms. Operating revenues, in turn, have fallen as a result of the higher price fetched by Japanese products in world markets due to the yen appreciation.

An instance of exchange rate equity exposure is illustrated by the experience of the Canadian company, Labat. In December of 1994, Labat purchased $300 million worth of stock in the Latin American corporation FEMSA, which has operations in Mexico, Argentina, Brazil, and other South American countries. Shortly after Labat's purchase of FEMSA stock, the peso collapsed. The effects of this change in the exchange rate quickly extended to the rest of the emerging markets. This phenomenon was later labeled the "Tequila Hangover." The increased riskiness of FEMSA's operations throughout Latin America because of the Tequila Hangover was not ignored by stock markets. In a matter of hours, the dollar market value of FEMSA's stock held by Labat declined by more than 50 percent in Mexico's stock market. The stock price of Labat's parent company also dropped in Toronto and New York.

Managing operating cash flow exposure

To provide an intuitive explanation of operating exposure and how to measure it, consider the case of a US multinational corporation having a Swiss subsidiary. The subsidiary produces and markets its output in Swiss francs and consequently generates cash flows in Swiss francs. The US owners of the Swiss subsidiary, however, do not care for Swiss francs, and prefer to focus on dollar cash flow returns. For instance, if the Swiss franc cash flows are Swf2,000,000 per year and the expected exchange rate is $0.4/Swf1, the expected dollar cash flows of the Swiss subsidiary are $800,000. However, if the exchange rate happens to be $0.35/Swf, the dollar value of the Swiss franc cash flows will deviate from its

189

expected value in proportion to the deviation of the exchange rate from its expected value. That is, the cash flows will turn out to be only $700,000.

After the new exchange rate is observed, investors typically revise their expectations. If they consider the change in the exchange rate as permanent, they will permanently change their expectations about the dollar value of the Swiss franc cash flows. If the variation in the exchange rate is deemed to be temporary, then dollar cash flow expectations will not change.

Measuring cash flow exposure

Operating cash flows consist of operating revenues minus operating costs. Financial costs, such as interest on debt, play no role in determining operating cash flows. Therefore, the operating cash flow exposure of a US subsidiary to currency fluctuations can be defined as the percentage response of dollar cash flows to a one percent change in the dollar value of a foreign currency. This relationship can be expressed as follows:

1) $\varepsilon = [\phi(1) - \phi(0)/ \phi(0)]/[\chi(1) - \chi(0)/\chi(0)]$

where ε is the elasticity response of dollar cash flows to a one percent change in the exchange rate, ϕ is the expected dollar value of the subsidiary's cash flows in periods 0 and 1, and χ is the expected dollar value of one unit of foreign exchange.

Equation 1 can be re-arranged as follows,

2) $\varepsilon = [\phi(1) /\phi(0)] - 1/[\chi(1)/\chi(0)] - 1]$

Solving equation 2 for the dollar value of the cash flow in period one [$\phi(1)$], the following expression is obtained:

3) $\phi(1) = [\phi(0) [1 + \varepsilon \{[\chi(1)/(\chi(0)] - 1]\}$

Equation 3 expresses the new expected dollar value of operating cash flow [$\phi(1)$] as equal to the original dollar cash flow [$\phi(o)$] multiplied by one plus the elasticity response of the dollar value of the cash flows to a one percent change in the dollar value of foreign exchange (ε) times the percentage change (in a decimal format) in the dollar value of one unit of foreign exchange $\{[\chi(1)/(\chi(0)] - 1]\}$.

The elasticity of response of the dollar value of the subsidiary's cash flows, (ε) may be positive or negative, and it may be very high or very low. If the value of (ε) is positive and greater than one, let us say 2.4, then it may be interpreted to mean that a one percent depreciation in the dollar value of the subsidiary's home currency (let us say the British pound) will lower the dollar value of the subsidiary's cash flows by 2.4 percent. Similarly, a one percent appreciation of the subsidiary's home currency will increase the dollar value of the cash flow by 2.4

190

percent. If the value of (ε) is negative, let us say –3, then a one percent depreciation of the subsidiary's home currency will increase the dollar value of the cash flows by three percent.

Example

To apply the concept previously described, consider the case of the US multinational corporation MCI operating in Britain. The spot rate is \$1.6/£1, and the dollar cash flows generated by the British subsidiary are \$60 million per year. If MCI's British subsidiary has an operating cash flow exposure of 2.4 (elastic), and if the dollar appreciates to \$1.5/£1, what is the new level of expected dollar operating cash flows if the change in the exchange rate is deemed to be permanent.

The percentage change in the British pound value against the US dollar is a 6.25 percent depreciation of the British pound. That is $\{[\chi(1)/\chi(0) - 1 = (\$1.5/\$1.6) - 1) = -0.0625 = -6.25$ percent$\}$. Given that the operating cash flow exposure is 2.4, then the operating cash flows should change by -15 percent. That is $[2.4*(-0.0625) = -0.15 = -15$ percent$]$. Since current cash flows are \$60 million, the dollar cash flows should change to \$51 million under the new exchange rate. That is $[\$60*(1-0.15) = \$51]$. Consolidating all the information in expression 3, the same result holds:

$$\phi(1) = [\phi(0) [1 + \varepsilon \{[\chi(1)/(\chi(0)] - 1]\} = [\$60*[2.4*[(1.5/1.6) - 1] = \$51 \text{ million.}$$

Factors determining operating exposure

Customarily, cash flows are defined as operating revenues minus operating costs. Operating revenues can be affected by four kinds of risk: 1) *conversion exposure*: the uncertainty surrounding the dollar equivalence of a given stream of foreign currency cash flows; 2) *price exposure:* the market power of the firm to conveniently adjust prices after an expected change in the exchange rate; 3) *demand exposure:* the response of the quantity of sales to the unexpected variation in the exchange rate and; 4) *competitive exposure*: the change in a firm's competitive position resulting from parity adjustments.

Conversion exposure

Conversion exposure refers to the uncertainty surrounding the dollar value of a foreign currency cash flow at consolidation. Pure conversion exposure is very rare, because it is assumed that the only factor affecting the foreign cash flows is the variation in the exchange rate. This implies that the change in the exchange rate will affect neither the output prices nor the local demand faced by the subsidiary. Experience with exchange rate fluctuations has shown, however, that exchange rate adjustments are usually followed by price and local demand changes.

Price exposure

Price exposure refers to the ability of the subsidiary of a US multinational to adjust its domestic and export prices in response to a dollar appreciation or depreciation. To design an appropriate pricing strategy for exchange rate variations, the management of the subsidiary must have a pretty good understanding of the price elasticity of the firm's products in domestic and foreign markets.

If the price elasticity of the affiliate's output is highly elastic, the best pricing strategy is to maintain the price structure. This approach will lead to higher revenues since the increase in the volume of sales will more than offset the loss in the dollar value of export revenues prompted by the devaluation of the local currency against the US dollar. Lowering prices may also be a sound policy because it may yield even higher revenues than steady pricing. This is not recommended, however, because it invites price retaliation and may result in cutthroat competition. If the subsidiary's products are price inelastic, the best pricing strategy is to raise the price of the company's products by the full percentage of the depreciation. The rationale for this suggestion rests on the fact that the price increase will result in a less than proportional decline in the volume of sales. If this pricing policy is applied, the dollar value of the revenues after the devaluation may remain steady or even increase.

Demand exposure

Sales in an affiliate's domestic market are a function of the number of units sold and the local currency price of output. If the local currency depreciates, the subsidiary's output becomes more competitive in its local market, given that rival imports automatically rise in price with the devaluation.[1] As a result of the change in relative prices, the subsidiary's volume of sales increases. Ultimately, the percentage increase in quantity of domestic sales and exports will depend on the price elasticity of demand of the product, the subsidiary's pricing policy and the effect of the local currency depreciation on real national income.[2]

Competitive exposure

To explain this concept, consider the case of ATT's operations in Singapore. The currency of this country, the Singaporean dollar, has been steadily appreciating against the US dollar. This appreciation has brought substantial gains in the standards of living of Singapore. As a result, sales of the US subsidiary have been steadily increasing in volume. At repatriation, the dollar value of the Singaporean cash flows has increased. Therefore, ATT's operations in Singapore have also enjoyed the benefits of the Singaporean dollar's steadfast appreciation against the US dollar.

As a result of the success enjoyed by ATT's subsidiary in Singapore, however, more companies become inclined to compete for business in Singapore. The additional competition could result in a lower market share for ATT and a lower sales volume in Singapore. Eventually, the increased competition may also lead to price declines, which may further erode the dollar value of ATT's operation in Singapore.

Operating cost exposure

Variations in the exchange rate normally do not affect the price of domestic inputs in the initial stage of the depreciation. Later, if the devaluation has inflationary consequences, input prices may rise. Unlike domestic input, the costs of imported inputs immediately rise with a depreciation of the local currency. A depreciation's effect on the variable costs of a company will depend on the proportion of local and foreign input content and the flexibility of the affiliate to adjust the mix of its inputs as relative costs change. If a company follows a proper pricing policy after a devaluation, it may end up increasing the volume of sales. To meet the excess demand created at home and abroad by the depreciation, the company requires large inventories and an expansion of accounts receivable. To satisfy these requirements, overhead expenses and working capital will have to increase as well.

Controlling operating exposure

If an executive wants to minimize the effects of changes in the exchange rate on the cash flows of his company, he has to keep in mind several factors: 1) the diversity of the firm's markets, 2) the price elasticity of the company's imports and exports, 3) the degree of competition at home and abroad, and 4) the company's cost structure.

Equity exposure

Like operating exposure, the equity risk associated with the subsidiary of a US multinational overseas is measured as the percentage response of the dollar value of a subsidiary's equity stemming from a one percent change in the dollar value of the subsidiary's home currency.

4) $\varepsilon(e) = [\sigma(1)/\sigma(0)] - 1/[\chi(1)/\chi(0)] - 1]$

where $\varepsilon(e)$ is the elasticity response of dollar equity value to a one percentage change in the exchange rate, σ is the expected dollar value of the subsidiary's equity in periods 0 and 1, and χ is the expected dollar value of one unit of foreign exchange.

Solving equation 4 for the dollar value of equity in period one [$\sigma(1)$], the following expression is obtained:

5) $\sigma(1) = [\sigma(0) [1 + \varepsilon(e)\{[\chi(1)/(\chi(0)] - 1]\}$

Equation 5 expresses the new expected dollar value of equity [$\sigma(1)$] as a function of the original dollar cash flow of the subsidiary's equity, multiplied by "1" plus the percentage change (in a decimal format) in the initial dollar value of the subsidiary's equity.

Example

To exercise the concept previously described, consider the case of the multinational corporation Upjohn operating in Germany. The spot rate is $0.64/DM1 and the dollar value of the subsidiary's equity is equivalent to $85 million. If Upjohn's German subsidiary has an equity exposure of two (elastic), and if the dollar appreciates to $0.58/DM1, what is the new level of the expected dollar equity value, if the change in the exchange rate is deemed to be permanent?

The percentage change in the dollar value of the German mark against the US dollar is a 9.375 percent depreciation of the German mark: {$[\chi(1)/\chi(0) - 1]$ = (0.58/0.64) - 1) = -0.09375 = -9.375 percent}. Given that equity exposure [$\varepsilon(e)$] is two, the equity value of the German subsidiary should decline by 18.75 percent. That is [2*(-0.09375) = - 0.1875 = -18.75 percent]. Since the current value of equity is $85 million, the dollar value of equity changes to $69.06 million under the new exchange rate. That is [$85*(1-0.1875) = $69.06]. Consolidating all the information in expression 5, the same result holds:

$$\sigma(1) = [\sigma(0) [1 + \varepsilon(e) \{[\chi(1)/(\chi(0)] - 1]\} =$$
$$[\$85*[2*[(0.58/0.64) - 1] = \$69.06 \text{ million.}$$

To provide a step by step description of the effects of an expected change in the exchange rate on operating income, operating cost, cash flows, and equity, this note next presents the hypothetical operation of a US subsidiary in France.

Economic exposure: The case of Meyer Tools Inc.

Meyer Tools, Inc., a US based multinational corporation, in an effort to diversify its portfolio, decides to acquire the French firm "Instruments L'Express." The operation is fully financed by equity. From the perspective of Meyer Tools, the French subsidiary is expected to provide a 20 percent after-tax return measured in US dollars, and perform as described in Chart 1.

Chart 1
Balance sheet as of December 31, 1997

ASSETS	Ff	LIABILITIES	Ff
Cash	1,600,000	Accounts payable	2,600,000
Accounts receivable	3,200,000	Short-term debt	1,600,000
Inventory	2,400,000	Long-term debt	1,600,000
Net Plant & Common Stock	1,800,000		
Equipment	3,000,000	Retained earnings	6,200,000
	12,000,000		12,000,000

"Instruments L'Express" Expected Income and Cash Flow Statement

Sales (1,000,000 units at Ff12.8/unit)	**12,800,000**
Direct Cost (1,000,000 units at Ff9.6/unit)	(9,600,000)
Cash Operating Expenses (fixed)	(1,200,000)
Depreciation	(240,000)
Gross Income (gross profit or EBT)	1,760,000
Income Tax Expenses	(880,000)
Net Income (net profit or EAT)	880,000
Depreciation (added back to determine cash flow)	240,000
Cash Flow From Operation (Ff)	1,120,000

Existing exchange rate Ff8.00/US$1

Cash flow from operation in US$	140,000

L'Express manufactures in France using French materials and labor. One half of its production is sold within France and the other half is exported to other EC countries. All the sales are invoiced in French francs. A company policy dictated by the Board is to have accounts receivable equal to or less than one-fourth of annual sales. The company is also seeking to implement a just-in-time inventory policy. Until now, however, the management of L'Express in France has considered it a safe and wise policy to have a stock of inventories equivalent to one-fourth of sales. The inventories are carried at direct cost, which is equivalent to 75 percent of the sales price.

L'Express can expand or contract production volumes without any significant change in unit direct costs or in overall general administrative expenses. The depreciation on plant and equipment is Ff240,000 per year; and the corporate income tax in France is 50 percent. *Unexpectedly, on January 1, 1998, the French franc falls 25 percent in value from Ff8.00/US$ to Ff10.00/US$1.*

Measuring the effect of the depreciation of the franc on the firm's cash flows and market value

To evaluate the effects of the French franc depreciation on the cash flows of the firm, several scenarios can be explored. An initial scenario can be created under the assumption that the volume of sales increases without a concurrent increase in local price and costs. Other scenarios can be constructed by changing any one of the previous assumptions regarding sales volume, price, and costs; however, for simplicity, only the first scenario is fully explored.

Volume of sales increases, price and costs remain unchanged

Sales within France double following the devaluation because French-made products are now more price competitive compared to imports. Export volume doubles since French-made instruments are now cheaper in countries whose currencies have appreciated against the franc. The price is kept constant in French franc terms because management of L'Express has not observed any changes in local French operating costs.

Chart 2
Expected income and cash flow statements after the 25 percent devaluation

Sales (2,000,000 units at Ff12.8/unit)	25,600,000
Direct cost (2,000,000 units at Ff9.6/unit)	(19,200,000)
Cash operating expenses (fixed)	(1,200,000)
	(240,000)
Gross income (gross profit or EBT)	4,960,000
Income tax expenses	(2,480,000)
Net Income (net profit or EAT)	2,480,000
Depreciation (added back to determine cash flow)	240,000
Cash flow from operation	2,720,000
Existing exchange rate Ff10.00/US$1	
Cash flow from operations in US$	**272,000**

Analysis of the effects of the depreciation on the cash flows of L'Express

The two-fold increase in sales has increased accounts receivable and inventories. To finance the additional working capital needs, Instruments L'Express decides to use the cash flow from the first year of operation. Accordingly, the cash flow from year one is not available the first year. Other effects of the increase in sales on the income statements are presented in Chart 2.

At the end of the first year, accounts receivable are equal to one-fourth of annual sales, or Ff6,400,000. This amount is twice the value of the receivable of Ff3,200,000 at the end of the prior year. The incremental in the accounts receivable of Ff3,200,000 was financed with cash flows from the first year of operation. At the end of five years, these incremental cash outflows are recaptured, since it is assumed that the investment in current assets rolls over into cash only until the end of the fifth year.

Final evaluation

The devaluation causes a change in the anticipated first year cash flow from US$140,000 (see chart 1) to a negative cash flow of US$288,000.[3] In the remaining years, due to the high price elasticity of the company's products, cash flows are substantially enhanced. A decline of 25 percent in the price of the company's products sold in foreign markets *and* a 25 percent increase in the price of competing imports in the domestic market, both increase the overall sales of L'Express by 100 percent.

A comparative analysis of cash flows and the subsidiary's market value, measured by the present value of the cash flows discounted at 20 percent, is presented in Chart 3 to show the effects of the French franc depreciation.

Chart 3
C a s h   F l o w s

Period	Items	Prior	Present Value	After	Present Value
1	Net Cash Flow*	1,200,000	1,000,000	-2,800,000	-2,400,000
2	Cash Flow from Operation	1,200,000	833,333	2,720,000	1,888,888
3	Cash Flow from Operation	1,200,000	694,444	2,720,000	1,574,074
4	Cash Flow from Operation	1,200,000	578,703	2,720,000	1,311,728
5	Cash Flow from Operation	1,200,000	482,253	2,720,000	1,093,107
5	Working Capital**			5,600,000	2,250,514
	Market Value in Francs		3,588,738		5,718,311
	Market Value in Dollars		448,592		571,831

Note: L'Express' market values were estimated using a 20 percent discount rate on French franc flows.

* Net cash flow is equal to cash flow from operation of Ff2,720,000 less additional investment in working capital equivalent to Ff5,600,000.

** Incremental working capital invested in year one and recaptured in year five at the end of the project.

Notes

1 This statement does not always hold true. During the late 1980s, the yen appreciated vis-à-vis the dollar. To prevent the resulting dollar price increase of the Japanese products in the US market, many Japanese firms lowered the yen price of their exports to the US. This price strategy allowed the Japanese firms to absorb a portion of the effect of the yen appreciation on the price of their products in the US market.

2 A devaluation is often followed by a local recession. In this case, it may be very possible that the decline in income and its subsequent effect on consumption may lead to an overall decline in demand. This decline in demand often overpowers the increased competitiveness of a local product

against imports and yields an overall decline in the dollar value of a subsidiary's cash flow.

3    $288,000 = (Ff2,720,000 − Ff5,600,000) x $1/Ff10.

20 Giant manufacturing and globalization

Taiwan and the bicycle industry

Since 1980, Taiwan has been the largest exporter of bicycles in the world. This island, located between Japan and the Philippines, was established as an independent nation in 1949. The economy of this relatively young nation is deeply rooted in market principles. Nonetheless, the government has played a major role in its development and planning. Old political conflicts between Taiwan and the People's Republic of China kept both nations isolated from each other. However, since the passing of the Cold War leaders, the international relations between the two nations have improved drastically. By 1997, Taiwan was one of the major investors in China.

Given the limited endowment of natural resources existing on the Island, Taiwan had to join the rest of the world to have access to other nations' factors of production. To do so, the government encouraged the creation of one of the most sophisticated communications networks in Asia, second only to Japan. Also, to pay for the imports of raw materials, local industry was forced from the beginning to become export oriented. Subsequent increases in labor costs forced a restructuring of the economy from a labor-intensive manufacturing base to a capital/technological-intensive manufacturing base. This industrial transformation, however, has not changed the exporting spirit of the local industry.

One of the areas where Taiwan has excelled in exports is the bicycle industry. For over sixteen years, beginning in 1980, Taiwan has been by far the largest exporter of bicycles in the world. In 1996, the volume of exports reached 9.7 million bicycles worth $984 million. Most of the Taiwanese bicycles are manufactured in the Taichung region, which is the world leader in the production of bicycles. This region accounts for 90 percent of the national production of bicycles, and 80 percent of the related parts.

199

The Taichung region

Throughout the 1980s, the Taichung region specialized in the production of low quality bicycles, which are exported at very competitive prices ranging from $40 to $50. However, substantial increases in local labor costs forced the region to upgrade its output. In the same decade, the region engaged in the manufacture of higher quality output, such as mountain bicycles, which fetched a higher dollar price in world markets. These items are now produced in the Taichung area using sophisticated materials such as titanium, carbon fiber, chromium, aluminum, steel, and even wood. In the late 1990s, the appreciation of the Taiwanese dollar and increased competition forced a reduction in the dollar price of the Taiwanese bicycle products from an average price of $121 in 1993 to barely $100 in 1997.

The export markets

The most important markets for Taiwanese bicycle exports are the United States (30 percent), Japan (17.5 percent), Britain (6.6 percent), and Germany (5.3 percent). The two leading manufacturers of bicycles in the Taichung province are Giant and Merida. These two companies accounted for more than 25 percent of Taiwanese bicycle exports.

Giant manufacturing

Giant Manufacturing was founded in 1972 in Tachia, 20 kilometers from downtown Taichung, a port city in western Taiwan. This company is both the largest producer and the largest exporter of bicycles in the world. The success enjoyed by Giant Manufacturing appears to be based on two management attributes: imagination to turn a problem into an advantage, and the ability to differentiate between a fad and an enduring shift in consumer demand. Giant was given an opportunity to display both attributes in the 1980s.

Giant's ability to turn a problem into an advantage was first displayed in 1981 when the workers of Schwinn, the largest manufacturer of bicycles in the United States, went on strike at the company's main factory in Chicago. Schwinn's management, unwilling to seek a settlement, closed the plant and sent its engineers and equipment to Giant's factory in Taichung. As part of the new partnership with Giant, Schwinn provided technology, engineering, and volume sales. In return, Giant manufactured and exported bikes to be marketed in the United States under the Schwinn name. By 1984, only three years later, Giant was shipping 700,000 bicycles a year to its partner in the US. During 1985, serious discrepancies arose between US and Taiwanese managers that led to the loss of Giant's biggest customer. Again, however, Giant turned what appeared to be a major problem into another advantage. Forced to replace the lost market, Giant introduced its own brand name in Europe and, by 1987, the US. Giant bought market share in both markets by offering Schwinn's quality bicycles at a 15 percent discount.

In 1976, Giant had 1,089 employees, of which 65 were from the Netherlands operation. In 1996, it produced 2.05 million units, of which 1.5 million were produced in Taiwan, 550,000 in the People's Republic of China, and 300,000 in the Netherlands. The transfer of production facilities from Taiwan to China was prompted by market and cost considerations. According to Antony Lo, Chief Executive Officer of Giant, China will soon be the largest bicycle market in the world. Regarding manufacturing costs, the price of labor and land in China are only about 20 and 13 percent of those paid by the company at home.

In the case of the Netherlands, the main reason for transferring some manufacturing from the Far East to Europe was to speed up innovation, despite the fact that wages in the Netherlands are 70 percent higher than in Taiwan. According to Lo, fashion is changing quickly and market trends must be followed closely. In his opinion, having a production base next to a main market allows the firm to find what the consumers want and to satisfy them faster and better.

Innovation

It is the opinion of Lo that developing new products is as important as manufacturing. "Bicycles are as much a fashion item as a piece of machinery. We sell bikes in several thousand variations. In the early 1990s, we introduced up to three new products every year. Today, however, that figure has grown to between five and ten, reflecting increased demand from customers."[1]

In Lo's opinion, one of the strengths of the company is its ability to introduce regional product lines within the context of an international approach. About three-quarters of the products the company sells abroad are the same, but for the remaining 25 percent, Giant gives the regional managers the freedom to specify products that they think can have a local appeal.[2]

To support design innovation, the firm spends two percent of net sales to back up the work of 65 designers and development engineers. From this total, 45 of the designers are in Taiwan, and the rest are based in China, Japan, the US, and the Netherlands. To take advantage of the pool of available designers, the personnel in China and Japan specialize in commuting bikes. Design in the Netherlands contributes with ideas gathered from the extremely competitive European racing bike tradition. In the US, the engineers from Giant work with variants of mountain bikes. The remaining designers and engineers are located in Taiwan. They incorporate all these ideas into projects aimed at reducing the weight of the frame, such as the use of carbon fiber. To effectively communicate ideas throughout the different research and manufacturing facilities, the company has established English as the official communication language. Also, the company has the policy of getting the entire research team together twice a year in Taiwan.

One of the developments that Giant is very keen on is the project to develop an electric battery-powered bike, which will be available in 1998. The company expects to produce an initial batch of 2,000 units to be sold in Europe and the US. There is an increasing environmental need for such machines to reduce traffic congestion, Lo said. They offer the advantage of easier cycling for a range of about

201

40 kilometers. Once the batteries run out, it is not a huge problem. All the cyclist has to do is pedal home!

Exchange risk management

From its inception, Giant has been global. Therefore, exchange rate exposure has always been a problem. To begin with, most of its sales are to the US market. However, as time has passed, competing in this market has become an increasing problems due to the continuous appreciation of the Taiwanese dollar against the US dollar. Other major problems that have become increasingly difficult to deal with are the volatility of the yen, the increasing uncertainty surrounding the future of EC currencies with monetary developments in Europe, and the unexpected crisis in major Asian economies. To ameliorate these problems, Lo is very convinced that the time has come to re-evaluate the firm's risk management by establishing a healthy hedging policy that can help Giant stabilize revenues in Taiwanese dollars.

So far, the firm has relied on the use of spot and forward contracts to implement its hedging program. The finance staff of the company, however, is aware of many other foreign exchange rate products that they could use to upgrade the hedging program. Among some of the other financial products available in the international financial markets, the company has listed the use of futures, options, swaps, and cross-currency transactions.

The futures contract gives the buyer of the contract the right to purchase or sell a specific amount of a currency for a predetermined price, the futures price, at the expiration date of the contract. The options contract provides its holder the right, but not the obligation, to buy (call contract) or sell (put contract) a specific amount of a currency at a predetermined price, the strike price, on European or American style contracts. The European options contract has the limitation that it can be exercised only at maturity. The American option, in contrast, can be executed at any time within the life-span of the contract. A swap contract gives firms the right to trade a principal, plus interest payments, stated in terms of one currency in exchange for a principal and an associated stream of interest payments in terms of another currency, arranged through a financial intermediary. This contract assumes the proviso that the present value of the two payment streams are of the same value in either one of the currencies. A cross currency alternative allows the direct trade of two currencies without using the US dollar as an intermediary.

Labor Cost

Manufacturing in the bicycle industry is very labor intensive. Therefore, in order to remain competitive, the management of Giant Manufacturing is always attentive to wage rate developments both at home and abroad. In this regard, the Taiwanese operation has often been hurt by the local currency appreciation against the US dollar and other major currencies, as well as salary increases at home due to excess demand for labor in Taiwan.

STATISTICAL APPENDIX

Table 20.1
Major bicycle exporters
(Thousand of units)

Period	Taiwan	Italy	France	Netherlands
1986	10,239.00	1,473	433	247
1987	9,685.00	1,513	492	240
1988	7,151.00	1,500	559	239
1989	5,200.00	1,537	537	344
1990	8,942.00	1,764	583	482
1991	9,831.00	2,196	389	573
1992	8,427.00	2,835	326	669
1993	8,621.00	4,542	361	777
1994	8,751.00	3,777	547	667
1995	9,064.00	3,558	517	411
1996	9,691.64			

Source: Japan Bicycle Promotion Institute, December 1997.

Table 20.2
Taiwan, bicycle exports, 1984-1996

Period	Quantity (units, 000)	Change %	Value ($, 000)	Change %	Average Price ($)	Exchange Rate (Tw$/$1)
1984	6,328		281,596.00		44.5	39.57
1985	7,442	17.6	300,359.12	6.66	40.36	39.76
1986	10,239	37.6	418,058.37	39.19	40.83	39.92
1987	9,685	-5.4	547,008.80	30.85	56.48	32.01
1988	7,151	-26.2	484,980.82	-11.34	67.82	28.07
1989	5,200	-27.3	425,256.00	-12.31	81.78	26.40
1990	8,942	71.9	909,937.92	113.97	101.76	26.80
1991	9,831	9.9	112,761.57	-87.61	11.47	26.80
1992	8,427	-14.3	972,897.15	762.79	115.45	25.13
1993	8,621	2.3	1,044,778.99	7.39	121.19	26.30
1994	8,751	1.5	988,337.94	-5.40	112.94	26.41
1995	9,064	3.5	1,066,379.60	7.90	117.65	26.63
1996	9,692	6.9	984,185.67	-7.71	101.55	26.50

Source: Japan Bicycle Promotion Institute, December 1997.

Table 20.3
Taiwan, bicycle exports, main markets, 1996

	Exports	%
Total	9,692	100.00
USA	2914	30.07
Japan	1696	17.50
Britain	641	6.61
Germany	520.5	5.37
Netherlands	421.4	4.35
Canada	190.3	1.96
Arab Emirates	176.6	1.82
Belgium	170	1.75
Chile	155.8	1.61
Switzerland	136.6	1.41
Sweden	123.4	1.27
Other	2,546	26.27

Source: Japan Bicycle Institute, December 1997.

Table 20.4
Giant manufacturing exports, 1995

Region	Rank	Exports units	%
USA	1	628,126	47.14
EC	2	437,289	32.82
Japan	3	182,054	13.66
Total	1	1,332,418	100.00

Source: Giant Manufacturing, 1996.

Table 20.5
Giant manufacturing exports, 1995-1996

Country	Rank	1995 units	%	1996 Units	%
USA	1	628,126	47.14	671,611	47.14
EC	2	437,289	32.82	467,562	32.82
Japan	3	182,054	13.66	194,658	13.66
Total Giant Exports		1,332,418	14.70	1,424,661	14.70
Total Taiwan Exports		9,064,129	100.00	9,691,636	100.00

Source: Japan Bicycle Promotion Institute, December 1997.

Table 20.6
Financial performance, Giant manufacturing, 1994-1995

Financial Performance	1995 $ million	1994 $ million
Turnover/Gross Revenue	330	331
Profit Before Interest and Taxes	18	24
Interest Payments	9	7
Taxes	1	7
Earnings	8	10
Ordinary Dividends	5	4
Total Assets	278	259
Net Current Assets	91	17
	$	$
Earnings Per Share	0.06	0.10
Dividends Per Share	0.04	0.04
Price Per Share	1.52	2.39
	%	%
Debt/Equity	143.00	144.00
Price Earnings Ratio	25.30	25.20
Current Ratio	1.74	1.10
Interest Cover	2.00	3.42
Dividends Cover	1.56	2.50
Shares outstanding	Million 135.13	million 105.26

Source: Giant Manufacturing.

Table 20.7
Country statistics, Taiwan and main world markets, 1996

Key Statistics (1996)	Taiwan	China	Netherlands	USA	Germany	Japan
Area (sq km)	35,980	9,596,960	37,330	9,372,610	356,910	337,835
Population (million, 1995)	21.30	1,210.00	15.50	266.40	83.50	125.40
Population growth (%)	0.89	0.98	0.56	0.91	0.67	0.21
Life expectancy (years)	76.02	69.60	77.30	75.90	73.90	79.50
Labor force (million)	8.90	583.60	6.40	132.20	36.80	65.80
GDP ($ billion)	291	3,500	301	7,240	1,452	2,675
GDP growth (%)	6.00	10.30	2.50	2.10	1.80	0.30
GDP per capita ($)	13,510	2,900	19,500	27,500	17,900	21,300
Inflation (%)	4.00	10.10	2.30	2.50	2.00	-0.10
Unemployment (%)	1.60	5.20	7.10	5.60	8.70	3.10
Hourly wage rate ($)	5.41	1.16	9.38	13.22	8.61	10.24
Wage rate/Taiwan's wage rate	1.00	0.21	1.73	2.44	1.59	1.89

Source: *CIA World Fact Book*, 1996.

Table 20.8
Exchange rates
(currency/US dollar)

Period	Taiwanese Dollar	Yuan	Guilder	Mark	Yen
91	26.80	5.32	1.87	1.66	134.71
92	25.13	5.51	1.76	1.56	126.65
93	26.30	5.76	1.86	1.65	111.20
94	26.41	5.62	1.82	1.62	102.21
95	26.63	8.35	1.61	1.43	94.06
96	26.50	8.31	1.64	1.46	105.84

Source: *CIA World Fact Book*, 1996.

Table 20.9
Foreign exchange rates trends, December 1997
(Currency/US dollar)

Country	Spot Rate	30-day Rate	90-Day Rate	One-Year Rate
Japan (Yen)	129.48	128.73	127.55	122.37
Germany (Mark)	1.77	1.77	1.76	1.74
Netherlands (Guilder)	2.00	1.99	1.98	1.96
China (Yuan)	8.28			

Source: *The Financial Times*, Dec 5, 1997.

Table 20.10
Eurocurrency rates, December 1997
(percentage)

Euro-Interest Rates	30 Days	90 Days	180 Days	One Year
USA (Dollar)	6.00	5.90	5.90	6.03
Japan (Yen)	0.18	0.15	0.21	0.28
Britain (Pound)	7.62	7.75	7.81	7.90
Germany (Mark)	3.78	3.75	3.87	4.12
Netherlands (Guilder)	3.59	3.81	4.00	4.09
China (Yuan)				
Canada (Dollar)	4.00	4.25	4.34	4.68

Source: *The Financial Times*, Dec 5, 1997.

Notes

1   Lo, Antony Interview, *The Financial Times*, London, October 24, 1997.
2   Ibidem.

21 International arbitrage

Introduction

Arbitrage is a very common transaction in international currency markets. It refers to simultaneously buying currency from a segment of the market where it is cheap, and selling it in another section where it is expensive. The fact that the trader acts simultaneously on both ends of the market with full price information makes this type of trading a risk-free activity.

Traders who specialize in arbitrage (also known as **"arbitrageurs"**) create an excess demand in the section of the market where the quotation for a currency is low and excess supply in the segment where the price for the same currency is high. Executed simultaneously, both actions produce a currency price equalization within and across foreign exchange markets.

Purpose

The aim of this note is to provide the business executive with the financial tools required to identify and manage arbitrage opportunities.

Forms of arbitrage

The practice of arbitrage can take any one of the following forms: locational, triangular, and covered interest.

Locational arbitrage

Locational arbitrage refers to profiting from the variance in spot quotations between two or more locations. To capitalize on the price difference between sites, the offer price (the commercial bank's selling price) in the low price location must be lower than the bid price (the commercial bank's purchasing price) in the high currency-price location. Otherwise, locational arbitrage is not profitable.

Table 21.1
Exchange rate quotations (DM/$)

Bank in Location One		Bank in Location Two	
Prices		Prices	
Bid	Offer	Bid	Offer
DM1.6780/$1	DM1.6938/$1	DM1.7098/$1	DM1.7100/$1

A trader can profit from the exchange rate scenario presented in Table 21.1 by buying dollars with German marks from the bank in location one at the offer price of DM1.6938/$1, and simultaneously selling them to the bank in location two at the bid price of DM1.7098/$1. The profit from this operation is DM.016 per dollar traded.[1]

Triangular arbitrage

Triangular arbitrage refers to the immediate repurchasing of a currency previously sold in a different location. To identify triangular arbitrage opportunities, the traders compute reciprocal rates and cross rates to facilitate the comparison of spot quotations given in different terms at different locations.

Table 21.2
Cross rates and triangular arbitrage

	New York	London
Spot rates	$1.6487/£1	DM2.5806/£1
	$.64/DM1	
Cross rate	(DM1/$.64)*($1.6487/£1) = DM2.5761/£1	

The New York quotations presented in Table 21.2, worked out in terms of marks per pound, allows traders to observe a discrepancy between cross rates in New York and London that may permit triangular arbitrage. To profit from this situation, the arbitrageur can *sell pounds* at DM2.5806 in London, and reverse that transaction in New York by taking two steps: 1) buying dollars with marks and 2) buying back pounds with dollars. The result is a profit of DM.0045 per pound traded (2.5806-2.5706). This transaction is described in Chart 1.

Chart 1

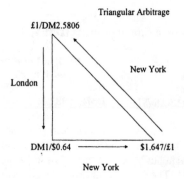

Triangular Arbitrage

£1/DM2.5806

London

New York

DM1/$0.64 ⟶ $1.647/£1

New York

Alternatively, if a trader wants to buy pounds with marks, he will be better off by *buying* dollars with marks in New York, using the marks in New York to purchase pounds, and, finally, using the pounds to buy back marks in London. This transaction will also result in a profit of similar value. In locational and triangular arbitrage operations, there is no risk involved because the traders operate simultaneously on both ends of the market and know the relevant quotations prior to the transaction. Also, both arbitrage transactions are self-financed, since the sale of a currency always finances its purchase.

Covered interest arbitrage

Covered interest arbitrage refers to investing local funds in terms of a foreign currency at higher rates of return and without exchange rate risk. Therefore, covered interest arbitrage is convenient only if the rate of return of the foreign investment, measured in terms of the local currency, is higher than the domestic rate of return. This is a risk-free transaction only when the investor can find a way to lock-in, from the beginning, exchange rate quotations to trade the proceeds of a foreign investment back to the initial currency upon maturity.

To identify covered interest arbitrage opportunities, investors apply the *interest-rate-parity principle*. Under this principle, there are incentives for covered interest arbitrage when the interest rate differential between two currencies differs from the forward premium or discount observed in foreign exchange markets. However, if both are equal, interest parity holds and arbitrage opportunities do not exist.

Table 21.3
Identifying covered interest arbitrage opportunities

Rates	United States	Britain
Spot rate	$1.4000/£1	
90-day forward rate	$1.3860/£1	
90-day interest rate	7%	12%
Transaction size	$2,800,000	£2,000,000

The calculations shown in the box below, which are based on the information provided in Table 21.3, indicate that it is profitable for a US investor to transfer his funds from the United States to Britain. The higher rate of return in the British money market, 12 percent in Britain versus 7 percent in the US, is large enough to offset the four percent loss incurred in the foreign exchange market if the investment takes place. The end result of covered-interest rate arbitrage, based on the information provided in Table 21.3, is a one percent return above the return that the investor could have obtained if he had kept his investment in the US. This one percent return is a secured return, already free of exchange rate risk.

Estimation of the dollar forward premium or discount (annualized)

The forward premium or discount is estimated by using expression 1, which was derived from the interest rate parity principle.

1) [(forward quote - spot quote)/spot quote]*100*(12/n)

Using the information provided in Table 3 on expression 1, the following result is obtained:

P/D = [($1.3860/£1 - $1.4000/£1)/$1.4000/£1]*100*(12/3) =

= [(1.3860 - 1.4000)/1.4000]*100*(12/3) = - 4 percent per annum.

These results indicate that the pound is selling at a 4 percent annualized discount against the dollar.

Interest rate differential

$r_£ - r_s$ = (12 percent - 7 percent) = 5 percent higher return in the British money market.

Inference

The pound is selling only at a 4 percent discount against the British pound when the interest rate differential between the two currencies is 5 percent. This difference provides covered interest arbitrage opportunities by trading dollars in the spot and investing them in Britain, and at the same time securing a contract to bring the pounds back into dollars.

Implementing covered interest arbitrage

To illustrate the covered interest arbitrage technique, it is assumed that a multinational corporation has $2.8 million in cash available to redeem a dollar payable in 90 days. As a result of this discrepancy between cash availability and the maturity of the short-term debt, the corporation has cash available for a short-term investment of 90 days. Further, it is assumed that the firm has only two investment options: invest in the US or in the British money markets.

In principle, the firm prefers to invest in the US because there is no exchange rate risk involved. However the higher British rate of return is an incentive to invest in that market if there is a forward cover to negate the exchange rate risk. To cover the exchange rate risk, the company needs to implement several actions. First, it must buy British pounds in the spot market. Simultaneously, it must invest the pounds for 90 days at 12 percent in the British money market and sell the investment's proceeds in the forward market at the best forward rate. At maturity, it will deliver pounds to fulfill its forward contract commitment and settle the dollar payable. The actions needed to implement covered interest rate arbitrage are described in Chart 2.

Chart 2
Steps Required to Perform a Covered-Interest Arbitrage Transaction

Initial Date

Step 1: Sell the $2,800,000 in the spot market (the corporation obtains £2,000,000).

Step 2: Invest the £2,000,000 for three months in the British money market at 12 percent (annual rate).
Total return after 90 days is £2,060,000 = £2,000,000*[1 + (.12/4)].

Step 3: Sell £2,060,000 forward three months at $1.3860.
The amount to be sold forward includes both the principal (£2,000,000) and the three month's interest generated by the investment in Britain (£60,000).

Three Months Later

Step 4: Fulfill the forward contract by delivering £2,060,000 at $1.3860/£1 in exchange for $2,855,160 to be received this day.

Step 5: Settle the $2,800,000 payable outstanding.

The profits from this covered interest arbitrage operation are estimated as follows:

Proceeds received from forward contracts (step 5) $2,855,160

Less principal   2,800,000

Less opportunity cost of money in the US money
market ($2,800,000)*(.07/4)   49,000

Net profits before taxes   **$ 6,160**

Note: Net profits before taxes are calculated assuming that there are no transaction costs.

Factors to consider in the implementation of covered-interest arbitrage

If the interest rate differential is higher than the forward discount, firms should invest in the currency with the higher rate of return. However, if the forward discount becomes larger than the interest rate differential, it pays to invest in the currency with the lower rate of return in order to take advantage of the excessive forward premium on this currency. Nonetheless, to fully evaluate the advantages of covered arbitrage, the firm has to take into consideration other factors that may limit the benefits of a covered interest transaction, such as spreads between bid and offer exchange rates, transaction costs, taxes, and exchange rate controls. Similar to other arbitrage methods, covered interest arbitrage does not require financing, since the funds needed to implement it can be borrowed. Also, it does not involve any exchange rate risk because the firms know the relevant interest and exchange rates prior to investing.

Note

1   Profit = DM1.7098-DM1.6938 = DM.016 per dollar traded.

Problems

1. Assume the following bid and ask rates of the pound for the two banks,

Institution	Bid	Ask
Citicorp	$1.41/£1	$1.42/£1
Chase	$1.39/£1	$1.4/£1

   a) Is *locational arbitrage* possible?
   b) What are the profits per unit of currency traded?

2. Two banks in Los Angeles provide the following spot quotations for the Swiss franc:

	Bank of America	Wells Fargo
Bid	$.6885/SwF1	$.6899/SwF1
Offer	$.6887/SwF1	$.6911/SwF1

   a) Are there any opportunities for *locational arbitrage*?
   b) If arbitrage is possible, what are the profits per unit of currency traded?

3. Assume the following information:

Institution	Bid Rate	Ask or Offer Rate
Citicorp	$.40/DM1	$.41/DM1
Chase	$.42/DM1	$.425/DM1

   a) Are there locational arbitrage opportunities?
   b) What is the profitability per unit of currency traded associated with the arbitrage transaction?

4. Assume the following information:

Rate	New York	Frankfurt
Spot	$1/DM3	DM1/FF2
	FF5/$1	

   a) Given the previous information, is *triangular arbitrage* possible?
   b) What is the profitability per unit of currency traded from a *triangular arbitrage* transaction?

5. Given the quotations presented in the table below, indicate whether there are opportunities for *triangular arbitrage* and the potential amount of profits per unit.

Rates	Toronto		Frankfurt
Bid	$.8712/Can$1	$.6088/DM1	
Offer	$.8754/Can$1	$.6097/DM1	
Spot			Can$.6900/DM1

6. Mr. Roberto Marino, currency specialist of the Central bank of Mexico, has $10,000,000 of the bank's funds available for investment. He receives the following quotations from Citicorp:

	Spot rates	
	Toronto	Frankfurt
	$.9/Can$1	
	$.3/DM1	DM3.02/Can$1

a) Given these rates, are there *triangular arbitrage* opportunities?
b) Indicate the value of profits per unit of currency trade.

Hint: To solve this question, find out the required cross rates and compare them with the quoted spot rates.

7. You have $1,000,000 to invest and you are given the following information:

Rates	United States	Britain
Interest	9% (annual)	12% (annual)
Spot rate	$1.30/£1	
90-day forward	$1.28/£1	

Would you recommend a 90-day covered-interest arbitrage? Explain.

8. Given the quotations provided in the table below, are there opportunities for *covered-interest arbitrage* for a company having $1,000,000 of idle cash or a line of credit in Swiss francs equivalent to the value of the dollar holdings?

Rates	Switzerland	United States
Spot	$.6085/SwF1	
90-day forward	$.6122/SwF1	
90-day interest	4.3% (annual)	6% (annual)

If arbitrage is possible, what is the profit potential?

9. Assume that Bayer, the German concern, has DM1,000,000 available in cash and the following information:

Rates	Germany	Britain
Spot	$.5896/DM1	$1.823/£1
90-day forward	$.5947/DM	$1.8149/£1
Interest rate	6% (annual)	8.5% (annual)

a) Is *covered interest arbitrage* possible?
b) If *covered arbitrage* is implemented, indicate the net return on this investment.

10. Dai Kal, a US corporation, has a borrowing capacity of $10 million in the United States or the equivalent of that amount in British pounds.

	Lending Interest Rates	
	Bid	**Offer**
US dollar (180-day)	4.0%	4.3%
British pound (180-day)	8.5%	8.7%
Spot rate	$1.64/£1	
180-day forward	$1.595/£1	

Are there *covered interest arbitrage* opportunities?

11 Bankers Trust provides the following quotations:

Quotes	France	United States
Spot	FF1 = $0.14	
90-day forward	FF1 = $0.1386	
Interest rate	10% (annual)	8% (annual)

a) Is there an opportunity for *covered interest arbitrage*?
b) What is the value of profits expressed in percentage terms?

22 Note on international currency swaps

Introduction

In the last decade of the 20th century, the world economy has provided enormous international expansion opportunities even, for those companies that initially planned to stay focused on the domestic market. In the case of the US fast food industry, for instance, sales abroad have grown faster than at home, and profitability has also been more elevated in foreign markets. To finance this kind of expansion, while keeping interest rate and exchange rate risk low, firms have resorted, to a certain extent, to entering into swap contracts.

Currency swaps evolved from the parallel loan concept, which was devised by multinational firms to circumvent cross-border capital controls. To understand how a parallel loan agreement worked, consider the case of Nestlé in China. The subsidiary of the European firm, which has been operating in China for a number of years, has been very profitable. However, the repatriation of profits back to Switzerland, used to meet the liabilities incurred by the Asian subsidiary in global markets, was a continuous source of tension between Nestlé and the Chinese Central Bank. The latter institution often delayed the remittance of profits, without the benefit of an interest payment, for periods lasting a year or longer. The Chinese government's rationale for the delay was grounded in the belief that the control would encourage Nestlé, and other multinationals operating in China, to invest these profits locally to further enhance employment opportunities for the Chinese labor force. In search of ways to avoid the exchange controls, Nestlé found that there was no law preventing multinationals from raising Chinese yuans to lend them to firms interested in investing in China. In return, the parent of the subsidiary receiving the Chinese yuans could raise the equivalent amount abroad and lend it to Nestlé in Switzerland.

Purpose

The aim of this note is to provide an explanation of what constitutes an international currency swap and the tools required to engineer and execute swap contracts.

Definition of a currency swap

The term currency swap is applied to describe a transaction between two borrowers, coordinated by a financial intermediary. Under a swap agreement, one party agrees to make periodic payments in a given currency, for a specific period, to meet a liability incurred by the other party in terms of the said currency. In return, the second party agrees to do the same thing on behalf of the first one, but in a different currency. A currency swap is possible when the parties involved in the transaction have absolute or comparative advantages in borrowing, and when each one of the streams of payments to be swapped has the same present value, regardless of whether the streams are stated on fixed or fluctuating interest rates.

The case of absolute advantages in borrowing

To explain a currency swap engineered on the basis of absolute advantages in borrowing, consider the case of two multinational corporations, one from the United States and the other from Germany. The US Company needs to borrow DM1,600,000 for two years. The German firm, in turn, needs to borrow $1,000,000 for the same period. The existing spot rate is $0.625 per one mark. Each company is highly respected in its home country and can borrow at premium interest rates locally. However, outside of their local financial markets, their borrowing ability is somewhat limited, as shown in Table 22.1.

Table 22.1
Case of absolute advantages

Borrowing Interest Rates

	US Dollar	German mark
US company	6.00%	5.00%
German company	7.50%	3.50%
Absolute Advantage	1.50%	1.50%

The information presented in Table 22.1 indicates that the US Company has an absolute advantage of 1.50 percent in borrowing dollars as compared with its German counterpart. The European firm, in turn, has an absolute advantage of 1.50 percent in borrowing marks. The fact that each company possesses absolute advantages borrowing at home provides grounds for a swap agreement where the financial intermediary earns an interest rate profit, and each participating firm lowers its cost of borrowing in foreign exchange. Total gains of the currency swap equivalent to 3.00 percent can be distributed among the participants in many different ways. Under a scenario where the gains of the currency swap are shared evenly, the US and German companies can simultaneously borrow $1,000,000 and DM1,600,000 at six and 3.5 percent respectively, as described in Chart 1.

Chart 1
Case of absolute advantage

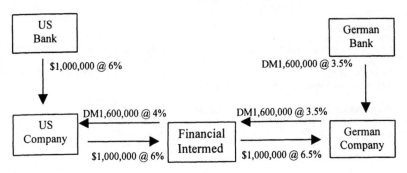

Next, the two firms can deliver the principal of each loan to the financial intermediary, which will make the $1,000,000 available to the German firm at 6.50 percent, and deliver the DM1,600,000 to the US firm at an interest rate of four percent.

Under this agreement, the US firm will be able to borrow German marks at four percent. This will represent a one percent savings in the cost of borrowing marks. Similarly, the German firm can borrow dollars at only 6.5 percent, which is one percent below the cost that this firm can borrow in the US. The benefit to the intermediary is a one percent per year profit. It receives the dollar principal from the US firm at a dollar-bid rate of six percent and transfers it to the German company at a dollar-offer rate of 6.5 percent. This transaction provides a 0.50 percent per year gain. Regarding the German principal, the intermediary receives it at the mark-bid rate of 3.5 percent and transfers it to the US firm at a mark-offer rate of four percent, which also yields a half percent profit.

Upon swapping principals, each firm has benefited from a reduction in the interest cost of borrowing. However, they are still exposed to exchange rate risk. The US company must make four mark-coupon payments and repay the principal in marks at maturity two years after the swap agreement, while the German company has to do the same thing in dollar terms. To eliminate the exchange rate risk involved in the transaction, each firm may further agree to swap the stream of payments. This stream includes four semi-annual interest payments and the repayment of the principal at maturity. That is, if the US firms agrees to take over the dollar coupon payments and the repayment of the dollar principal on behalf of the German firm, it will have to make dollar payments to the bank each six months, as shown in line 3 of Table 22.2 In turn, the German firm must agree to meet interest and principal payments in German marks on behalf of the US firm. This transaction is described in line 8 of Table 22.2 If the currency swap agreement goes this far, both firms benefit from lower interest cost in a foreign currency loan and eliminate the exchange rate risk associated with external borrowing.

Table 22.2
Description of the dollar – German mark swap agreement

Line	ITEM	0	1	2	3	4
1	Exchange rate	$0.625/DM1				
2	Principal swapped ($)	1,000,000				
3	Coupon swapped @ 6.5% ($)		65,000	65,000	65,000	1,065,000
4	Discount Factor @ 6.5%	1.00	0.94	0.88	0.83	0.78
5	Present value ($)		61,033	57,308	53,810	827,849
6	Accumulated present value ($)	1,000,000				
7	Principal swapped (DM)	1,600,000				
8	Coupon swapped @ 4% (DM)		64,000	64,000	64,000	1,664,000
9	Discount Factor @ 4%	1.00	0.96	0.92	0.89	0.85
10	Present value (DM)		61,538	59,172	56,896	1,422,394
11	Accumulated present value (DM)	1,600,000				

A case of comparative advantage in borrowing

In the example previously described, it is easy to justify a swap agreement, since each participant has absolute advantage in borrowing locally. However, there are cases where a company can borrow at lower rates than its counterpart in all markets. Would a currency swap still makes sense under this scenario for the company exhibiting absolute advantages in borrowing in all markets? To provide an answer to this question, consider two companies, one from the United States and the other from France. The US corporation needs to borrow Ff25,000,000 for two years. The French firm needs a $5,000,0000 loan for the same period. The two companies can borrow at fixed two-year interest rates in dollars and francs as shown in table 22.3 At the time that this is happening, the spot rate is Ff5 per dollar.

Table 22.3
Borrowing interest rates

	US Dollar	French Franc
US company	6.00%	10.50%
French company	8.00%	11.00%
Comparative Advantage	2.00%	-0.50%

The information provided in Table 22.3 is very important because it indicates that the interest rates are higher in France than in the United States. It also suggests

220

that the US firm can get lower interest rates in either one of the two currencies. The most relevant aspect of this information, however, is the fact that the difference between the rates offered to the companies is not the same in both markets. For instance, in the dollar market, the US Company has a 2.0 percent competitive edge against the French company. In francs, the French company holds a borrowing disadvantage of only 0.50 percent in the French market. This difference in the interest rates means that the US Corporation has a comparative advantage in borrowing dollars, and that the French corporation has the same advantage in francs.[1] This situation provides the financial intermediary an ideal opportunity for the engineering of a swap because each company can borrow along comparative advantages and profit by swapping the loans. Given the interest differential of 2.0 percent and -0.50 percent respectively, the total gain available to the participants in the swap is 1.50 percent (2.0 percent-0.5 percent).

Chart 2
Case of comparative advantage

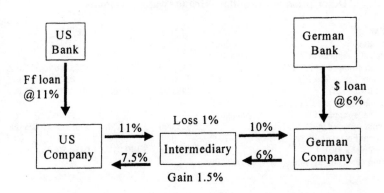

If the gains are distributed evenly among the US firm, the French corporation, and a commercial bank, then the US and French companies need to simultaneously borrow $5,000,000 and Ff25,000,000 at six percent and 11 percent respectively. Then, they can provide the dollar and franc principals to the financial intermediary. The intermediary, in turn, will transfer the dollar principal to the French firm at a rate of 7.5 percent. This will imply an interest savings of 0.5 percent for the European firm. In a similar fashion, the bank will transfer the French franc principal to the US firm at ten percent. At this rate, the US firm saves 0.50 percent on the franc loan.

With respect to the financial intermediary, it receives the dollar principal at a dollar-bid rate of six percent and provides it to the French firm at a dollar-offer rate of 7.5 percent. This transaction nets to the bank a gain of 1.5 percent per year. However, on the French franc principal, it suffers a loss of one percent, since it receives it at a bid rate of 11 percent and loans it out at the offer rate of only ten percent. Therefore, the swap provides the bank is a net gain of 0.5 percent.

Up to this point, the US and French companies have realized interest savings of 0.5 percent each. But they are still exposed to exchange rate risk, since the US firm has the commitment of making four semi-annual franc-coupon payments and the repayment of the principal at maturity to the financial intermediary. To eliminate exchange rate risk, the US firm may further agree to take over the dollar-coupon payments and the repayment of the dollar principal at the maturity of the dollar loan on behalf of the French firm. By the same token, the French firm has to agree to take over the French franc liabilities of the US firm. If the two firms agree to swap the two streams of payments, then they are voiding the exchange rate risk associated with the swap. The switching of principals is shown in lines 2 and 7 of Table 22.4. To cover for exchange rate risk, the US firm agrees to meet the semi-annual coupon payments shown in line 3 of the same table. In the same fashion, the French firm takes over the French franc liabilities of the US firm shown in line 8.

Table 22.4
Description of the dollar – franc swap agreement

Line	ITEM	0	1	2	3	4
1	Exchange rate	Ff5/$1				
2	Principal swapped ($)	5,000,000				
3	Coupon swapped @ 7.5% ($)		375,000	375,000	375,000	5,375,000
4	Discount Factor @ 7.5%	1.00	0.93	0.87	0.80	0.75
5	Present value ($)		348,837	324,500	301,860	4,024,803
6	Accumulated present value ($)	5,000,000				
7	Principal swapped (Ff)	25,000,000				
8	Coupon swapped @ 10.5% (Ff)		2,625,000	2,625,000	2,625,000	27,625,000
9	Discount Factor @ 10.5%	1.00	0.90	0.82	0.74	0.67
10	Present value (Ff)		2,375,566	2,149,833	1,945,550	18,529,051
11	Accumulated present value (Ff)	25,000,000				

Valuation of currency swaps

To evaluate a currency swap, it is first necessary to understand the meaning of the expression "structure of interest rates." This expression refers to the range of yields for securities with varying maturities. It can also be understood as the relationship between the interest rates and time to maturity, or the yield curve for a currency. If the yield to maturity increases as the time to maturity increases, the yield curve is termed to be upward sloping. A downward sloping yield curve shows yields to maturity, which decrease as the time to maturity increases. In contrast, a flat yield curve shows the same yield to maturity for all periods.

In the absence of default risk, a currency swap can be decomposed into a position of two long-term debt instruments — bonds. For instance, in the previous case of the dollar–French franc swap, prior to the swapping of interest payments to cover for exchange rate risk, the position of the US corporation is initially long in a French franc bond that pays a 10.5 percent coupon. It is short in the dollar bond that pays a 7.5 percent annual coupon rate. From this example, it is possible to derive an expression to value a currency swap as follows:

1) $PV(V) = S*PV(B_{FF}) - PV(B_\$)$

PV (V) is the dollar present value of the currency swap. S is the spot rate existing at the time when the swap is negotiated expressed in terms of the number of dollars per unit of foreign exchange. B_{FF} is the present value, in terms of foreign exchange of the non-US bond. And, $B\$$ is the dollar present value of the US bond. Given the definition in (1), the value of a currency swap can be determined from the term structure of the interest rates in the domestic currency (the dollar), the term structure of the interest rate in the external currency (the French franc), and the spot exchange rate.

To provide an example of how to evaluate a currency swap, consider the case of a financial intermediary who has arranged a three-year dollar–yen swap, where the principals swapped are $10 million and ¥1,250 million, and the spot rate is $0.8/¥100. The US and Japanese rates are five and 2.5 percent percent respectively. Given these rates, the bank has engineered a currency swap where it will receive semi-annual yen coupon payments of 1.5 percent (3 percent annual rate) from the US firm. It will pay to the same US firm semi-annual coupon dollar payments at two percent. This implies that the bank is having the benefit of one percent annual savings on the dollar coupon payment and a 0.5 percent annual gain in yen terms. All the relevant information for this transaction is shown in Table 22.5.

Table 22.5
Description of the dollar – yen swap agreement

ITEM	Spot Rate	Principal Swapped	$ Rate	Borrowing $ Rate	¥ Rate	Lending ¥ Rate
US	$0.8/¥100	$10 million	5%			
Financial Intermediary				4%		3%
Japan		¥1,250			2.5%	

Using the information from Table 22.5, the accumulated present dollar value of the dollar transaction ($B_\$$) is $9.72 million, as shown in line 7 of Table 22.6. Similarly, the accumulated present value of the yen transaction underlying the swap ($B_¥$) measured in yen is ¥1,375.69 million, as shown in line 11 of Table 22.6. Finally, the value of the swap is $1.28 million dollars.

Table 22.6
Dollar present value of the 3-year semi-annual coupon payments of a $/¥ swap

Line	Period	0	1	2	3	4	5	6
1	Exchange rate ($/100 yen)	0.8/100						
2	Principal ($ million)	10.00						
3	Principal (yen)	1250.00						
4	Coupon payment @ (4/2)% ($)		0.2	0.2	0.2	0.2	0.2	10.2
5	Discount rate @ (5/2)%		0.98	0.95	0.93	0.91	0.88	0.86
6	Present value ($ million)		0.20	0.19	0.19	0.18	0.18	8.80
7	Accumulated present value ($)	9.72						
8	Coupon receipt @ (3/2)% (yen)		37.5	37.5	37.5	37.5	37.5	1287.5
9	Discount rate @ (2.5/2)%		0.99	0.98	0.96	0.95	0.94	0.93
10	Present value (yen million)		37.04	36.58	36.13	35.68	35.24	1195.03
11	Accumulated present value (yen million)	1375.69						
12	Accumulated present value ($ million)	11.01						
13	Value of the swap ($ million)	1.28						

Swap formats

A currency swap, in its most general form, is a contract that involves the exchange of cash flows according to a formula that will depend on the values taken by the different cash flows. As such, there is no limit to the number of different swaps that can be invented. The variables affecting cash flows are the currencies involved, the spot rate, the principal in both dollar and non-dollar terms, the term to maturity of the swap, the cost of borrowing on the two currencies, and the interest rates underlying the coupon payments.

Currently, the most common form of a swap is the fixed-for-fixed currency swap. This is known as the basic "plain vanilla swap." Under a plain vanilla currency swap, the cash flows of the swap are based upon the future cash flows of two fixed-coupon bonds in two different currencies. This case is used extensively to explain the currency swap concept in this technical note. Another common form of a swap is the fixed-for-floating currency swap. Under this agreement, one of the payment streams is stated on a fixed coupon rate in one currency, while the other payment stream is based on a floating rate note on the second currency. This currency swap is also referred to as a cross-currency swap.

Another interesting example of a currency swap is the so-called off-market swap. In this case, the parties agree to exchange cash flows having different present values, given a certain spot rate. Obviously, the party receiving the cash flow with lower present value is compensated with a balancing payment from the party receiving the higher present value cash flow. This balancing payment can take place at the mutual agreement of the two partners or at any time within the swap's term to maturity.

Essential ingredients to negotiate a swap

Given the relatively long-term commitment involved in a swap, a successful and risk free swap requires a careful check of both the counter party and the swap intermediary. It is especially important to pay attention to the swap intermediary, which acts as the third party guarantor.[2]

Notes

1 The rationale for the US comparative advantages can be explained as follows: this firm can borrow at both dollar and franc interest rates. However, it will be better off if it borrows only dollars because its borrowing advantage will widen against the French firm. By the same token, the French company can borrow both in dollars and in francs. In both, it shows a borrowing disadvantage against the US firm. However, this disadvantage can be narrowed if the firm specializes only in borrowing francs. At the end of the specialization process, each firm will be better off at nobody's expense.

2 Only financial intermediaries with AAA credit ratings can intermediate swaps.

Problems

1. A company in Japan wishes to borrow dollars at a fixed interest rate. A US multinational, in contrast, wishes to borrow Japanese yen at a fixed interest rate. The amounts required by the two companies, given the existing spot rate, are the same in either one of the currencies. These two companies have been quoting the interest rates described in the table below. These interest rates are net of tax rates.

Company	Yen rate	Dollar rate
US	5.0%	9.0%
Japanese	6.5%	10.0%

Design a swap that will net the financial intermediary 20 basis points profits per year. Also, engineer the swap in such a way that it will be equally attractive to the two companies. Finally, ensure that all the exchange risk is transferred away from the companies to the bank.

2. A currency swap has a remaining life of 24 months. It involves exchanging interest at 14 percent on £20 million for interest at 10 percent on $30 million once a year. The term structure of the interest rate in both the United Kingdom and the United States is currently flat. If the swap were negotiated today, the interest exchanged would be 8 percent in dollars and 11 percent in pounds. Currently, the spot rate is $1.65/£1. What is the value of the swap to the party paying the pound coupon rate? What is the value of the swap for the party paying the dollar coupon rate?

3. A German company wishes to borrow dollars at a fixed rate. A US company, in turn, wishes to borrow German marks at a fixed interest rate. They have been quoted the following yearly rates for semi-annual coupon payments.

Company	Mark Rate	Dollar
German	11.0%	7.0%
US	10.6%	6.2%

Design a swap that will net a bank, acting as financial intermediary, 10 basis points per year, for each one of the companies involved.

4. Suppose that the term structure of the interest rate is flat in the United States and Germany. The dollar interest rate is 11 percent per year, while the mark interest rate is 8 percent per annum. The existing spot rate is DM2.1/$1. Under the terms of a swap agreement, the financial intermediary pays 5 percent per year in marks and receives 10 percent in dollars. The principals are $10 million and DM20 million. The stream of payments is traded on semi-annual payments. The term to maturity of this swap is two years. What is the value of the swap to the financial institution?

226

5. A bank has entered into a 4-year currency swap with a US company. Under the terms of the swap, the bank receives interest at 3 percent per year in Swiss francs and pays interest at 8 percent per annum in dollars. Interest payments are exchanged twice a year. The principal amounts traded are $7 million and Swf10 million. The US company defaults at the end of year three when the exchange rate is $0.64/Swf and the interest rates are 3 and 8 percent in Swiss francs and dollars respectively. What is the value of the swap gain or loss?

23 The balance of payments

Structure of the balance of payments

The balance of payments is a statement of a country's international transactions. Anything imported or exported, anything spent by residents travelling abroad, and anything spent by visiting foreigners is accounted for in the balance of payments. To keep track of such a broad spectrum of transactions, the balance of payments is integrated by three major accounts: the current, the capital, and the official settlement accounts. The *current account* (CA) presents the trade in goods and services between one country and the rest of the world. The *capital account* is a statement of all foreign direct and portfolio investments between one country and its foreign counterparts. The *official settlement account* details the transactions undertaken by a country's central banks to settle a balance of payments deficit or surplus. These balance of payments adjustments undertaken by the central bank include deposits to or withdrawals from the central bank reserves of foreign exchange. Each of these three major accounts is, in turn, divided into sections. The current account encompasses the merchandise, the service, and the transfer balances. The capital account includes foreign direct and portfolio investments.

Purpose

The purpose of this technical note is to provide the student with the tools required to analyze the financial and trade relationships of one country with the rest of the world. To comply with this purpose, the sections that follow describe the balance of payments and its components, and how they are applied to estimate the international financial position of a country.

The current account

The merchandise or *trade balance* is a display of all the transfers of goods between domestic and foreign residents. A *resident* is defined as an individual or a business firm engaged in the export or import of "movable" or "visible" goods. *The service* or *"invisible" balance* includes payments made or received on freight, insurance, travel, tourism, professional services, transfer of profits and interest payments.

Upon first exposure to balance of payments accounting, one is inclined to believe that interest payments and receipts are part of the *capital balance*, but they are not. Interest payments are included in the service balance, because they are considered payments for "service" rendered by foreign investors. The repatriation of a subsidiary's profits is also considered as payment for a service rendered by the capital embodied in a subsidiary's factory. *Unilateral transfers* consist of government and private donations sent or received, remittances by migrant workers to their family members back home, interpersonal and institutional gifts, and government grants. Transfers, unlike loans, do not create a liability on the recipient.

The net current account result should be an indication of the international competitiveness of a country. This is made more obvious if the transfer balance results are excluded. The two other major accounts show the extent to which a country is currently earning its consumption of foreign goods and services. A *current account deficit* occurs when the country is not selling enough to pay for its goods and services imports. This deficit can be offset by a capital account surplus or the sale of central bank foreign exchange reserves. The latter is recorded in the settlement balance.

The capital account

An issue related to the long-term capital balance is the determination of what constitutes a foreign direct investment as opposed to a portfolio transaction. In general, an investment is classified as a portfolio investment if it involves the purchase of a security, a bond, or less than ten percent of the total stock of a corporation. Items considered foreign direct investment include the purchase of more than ten percent of the stock of a foreign corporation, or investment directed to a multinational's subsidiary capital formation.

Direct investment is partially made up of the expenditures of a domestic resident on capital formation abroad. Conversely, direct investment can also be expenditures of a foreign resident on domestic capital formation. A resident's purchase of more than ten percent of the stock of a foreign corporation is also considered direct investment, as is a foreigner's purchase of more than ten percent of the stock of a local corporation. Portfolio transactions can be short-term or long-term. The domestic resident's purchase of foreign securities with a term to maturity of less than twelve months is a short-term portfolio investment. Likewise, the foreign resident's purchase of domestic securities with a similar term to maturity are also short-term portfolio investments. The domestic resident's acquisitions of foreign stock, bonds, and long term deposits represent examples of long-term portfolio investments.

The net result in the capital account is often seen as a measure of the ability of a country to attract foreign resources to speed up its domestic capital formation. Unfortunately, this is not always the case. In many circumstances, the capital account surplus of a country is simply the result of massive transfers of "hot money" in search of high yields. "Hot money" simply refers to wire transfers that are deposited in countries for very short periods of time, from several hours to several days.

The globalization of capital markets and developments in telecommunications have facilitated the international transfer of funds. Fast movement of capital coupled with slow collection of financial data on the part of statistical bureaus has led to information gaps that are often reflected in discrepancies between balance of payments debits and credits. To eliminate these discrepancies, the accounting system of the balance of payments has an *errors and omissions account* that permits the settlement of the discrepancies. The errors and omissions account is often merged with the *short-term capital account*, because it is believed that the source of the discrepancies originates in this account. In other instances, errors and omissions are shown separately.

The settlement account

The last account in the balance of payments is the Settlement Account. It includes purchases and sales of central banks, international official reserves, and transfers of drawing rights between countries. Official reserves are holdings of "hard currencies" or highly liquid assets such as gold, securities and foreign currency checking accounts.

The balance of payments' accounting system

Each transaction recorded in the balance of payments gives rise to two entries: a debit and a credit. A debit entry implies a use of foreign exchange, an outflow of funds, an import, or a payment. A credit entry is a source of foreign exchange, an inflow of funds, an export, or a receipt. If the convention of double-entry bookkeeping is followed, total debits will always equal total credits. In this trivial sense, the balance of payments always balances.

To make the accounting of the balance of payments useful for economic and business analysis, debits and credits have to be classified into significant categories. These categories were discussed in previous paragraphs. If they are incorporated into the accounting system, then it is possible to evaluate the result of each one of the three major balance of payment accounts. Chart 1 contains a description of the different current account transactions already incorporated into the current, the capital, or the settlement accounts.

Chart 1
The balance of payments

DEBITS	CREDITS
Use of Foreign Exchange	*Source of Foreign Exchange*
Merchandise imports	Merchandise exports
Transport service payments	Transport service receipts
Insurance payments from abroad	Insurance income from abroad
Travel expense by residents while abroad	Travel expenditures by non- residents when visiting
Interest and dividends paid to foreigners on loans and investments made in the country	Interest and dividends received on foreign loans and investments abroad
Government and private aid to other countries	Government and private aid received from abroad
Direct investment by residents	Foreign direct investment in the home country
Portfolio investment by residents abroad	Foreign portfolio investment in the home country
Increase in domestic banks' loans to non-residents	Foreign banks' increase in loans to residents
Increase in the commercial bank or central bank's holding of foreign exchange	Increase in foreign loans to domestic commercial banks or to the central bank

To familiarize the reader with double-entry bookkeeping and its use in creating a balance-of-payment statement, some international transactions together with their corresponding entries are presented in Chart 2 below. To make this exercise meaningful the transaction and their financing are presented together.

Chart 2
International transactions

1. *A Mexican manufacturer buys computers from an American firm in Phoenix, Arizona for US$10,000,000; payment is made by issuing a check from an account held by the Mexican manufacturer in a New York bank.*

    Debit: US short-term capital account. The US liabilities to foreigners are reduced by the dollar value of the transaction.
    Credit: US merchandise export to Mexico.

2. *An American tourist travels to France and spends US$250,000 on food, lodging and other. The tourist paid these expenses with travelers checks acquired at departure from a New York bank.*

    Debit: Travel expenditures.

231

Credit: US short-term capital account. The US liabilities to private foreigners increase by the dollar value of the transaction.

The use of foreign exchange by American tourists to purchase French services causes the debit entry, which is credited as a US short-term capital account transaction.

3. *An American importer purchases oil from Saudi Arabia for US$7,000,000; the transaction is settled with a check issued by the American importer from an account held in a Swiss bank.*

Debit: Oil Imports.
Credit: US short-term capital account.

The use of foreign exchange to purchase oil causes the debit entry, which is credited as a short-term capital account transaction.

4. *An Italian bank issues a check from an account held in a New York bank to pay interest and dividends of US$2,000,000 to their American customers on their holdings of Italian securities with the Italian bank.*

Debit: US short-term capital account.
Credit: Investment income received.

Income from portfolio investment as a US source of foreign exchange warrants the credit entry, which is debited as a short-term capital account.

5. *Japanese residents purchase US$200,000 of common stock on the New York Stock Exchange. They issue a check from an account held by the Japanese residents in a New York bank.*

Debit: US short-term capital.
Credit: Long-term capital, private (portfolio).

The use of foreign exchange to acquire the stock justifies the credit entry into the long-term capital account, which is debited as US short-term capital account transaction.

6. *Ford Motors ships a drill press worth US$1,000,000 to Mexico for installation in its branch factory in Hermosillo, Mexico.*

Debit: Foreign direct investment.
Credit: US export to Mexico.

Assembling the balance of payments

The next step is to create the balance of payments of the United States with the information furnished by the transactions discussed previously. To perform this task, the debits and credits have to be allocated to the proper accounts.

Chart 3
US balance of payments

	Debits (-)	Credits (+)	Net
Goods and Services			
Merchandise	(3) 7,000,000	(1)+(6) 11,000,000	+4,000,000
Travel	(2) 250,000		-250,000
Investment Income		(4) 2,000,000	+2,000,000
Current Account	**7,250,000**	**13,000,000**	**+5,750,000**
Long-term Capital			
Direct Investment	(6) 1,000,000		-1,000,000
Portfolio		(5) 200,000	+200,000
Basic Balance	**8,250,000**	**13,200,000**	**+4,950,000**
Private short-term	(1) 10,000,000	(2) 250,000	9,750,000
	(4) 2,000,000	(3) 7,000,000	+5,000,000
	(5) 200,000		-200,000
Net	12,200,000	7,250,000	-4,950,000
TOTAL	**20,450,000**	**20,450,000**	**0**

The analysis of the balance of payments

The information provided by the balance of payments has a wide variety of applications. Commercial banks use it to determine the risk involved in foreign lending. Multinational corporations use the information contained in the balance of payment to determine the risk and return associated with foreign direct investment. Government officials and monetary authorities employ it to forecast macroeconomic variables, and to set commercial and exchange rate policies. Multinational financial institutions such as the International Monetary Fund (IMF) and the World Bank often utilize balance of payments information to design adjustment programs for countries suffering from price instability and trade imbalances.

The information presented on countries A and B in Chart 4 will be used to illustrate how the analysis of the balance of payments assists the decision making process of either the corporate executive or the government official managing foreign affairs.

Chart 4
Comparative analysis of the balance of payments

ITEM	COUNTRY A	COUNTRY B
Merchandise Trade	-1,000	+2,000
Services	-500	-1,200
Transfers	+900	-100
Current Account	**-600**	**+700**
Long-term Capital		
Portfolio Investment	+1,500	-200
Direct Investment	-100	+300
Basic Balance	**+800**	**+800**
Short-term capital	-400	-580
Errors and Omissions	-200	-20
Settlement Balance	**+ 200**	**+ 200**
Official Reserve Transactions	-200	-200

Country A's balance of payments shows a large surplus in portfolio investment, which helped to finance both the current account and foreign direct investment deficits. Overall, the basic balance shows a surplus of $800, which is eroded by short-term capital movements plus errors and omissions. After these changes have been considered, the settlement balance presents a $200 surplus, which was used to increase Country A's central bank reserves.

Similar to country A, country B's balance of payments presents a basic balance surplus of $800. However, unlike country A, this surplus was generated by a strong export performance. Adjustments for short-term capital movements and errors and omissions consume a portion of the basic balance surplus and leads to a net balance of payments surplus of $200 which, like country A, ends up as an increase in Country B's central bank reserves.

A financial analyst faced with the responsibility of recommending the site for a new subsidiary will notice that the balance of payments performance of countries A and B, while similar in overall balance performance, has quite different meanings. Country B has earned its balance of payments surplus by exporting and creating a climate favorable to foreign direct investment, while Country A has "borrowed" it. The government official confronted with the responsibility of approving long-term government loans to either country will notice that country A's balance of payment stability and performance is heavily dependent on external debt and the good will of foreign residents, while country B's performance is based on its export strengths.

Both the analyst and the government official will conclude from this analysis that, in spite of their similarity at the bottom line, these nations are experiencing very different circumstances. Country A, contingent upon further information, should be considered a "risk" country, while Country B should be assessed as "high profile."

Variations in the real exchange rate and the balance of payments

There are nominal and real exchange rates. Nominal rates are those quoted each day by banks and other institutions. Real exchange rate is the nominal rate adjusted for relative changes in the domestic and foreign price levels. This relationship can be represented as follows:

$$Et = Eo^*[(1 + id)/(1 + if)]$$

where Et is the spot rate in period t, Eo is the spot in the base or initial period, and id and if are the domestic and foreign rates of inflation.

If the domestic inflation (id) is growing faster than its counterpart in a foreign market (if), the local currency must depreciate by the numerical value of the inflation differential. If inflation differentials are fully reflected in adjustments in the nominal exchange rate, then the real exchange rate remains unchanged. Under this scenario, the adjustment in the nominal exchange rate resulting from inflation differentials between two trading partners, say Japan and the US, will not have a significant impact in the trade relations of the two nations. However, the nominal exchange rate often deviates from purchasing power parity. This deviation from PPP may lead to either a real exchange rate appreciation or depreciation. Either one means both good and bad news for the domestic economy.

The good news of a real depreciation is that, by lowering the price of the domestic goods and services relative to foreign counterparts, it raises the quantity of exports and reduces the volume of imports. These adjustments in the balance of trade of goods and services are known as the **volume effect**. The bad news of a real depreciation is that, after the depreciation, each export unit brings a lesser amount of foreign exchange. A depreciation also forces the consumer to pay a larger quantity of local currency to purchase a foreign good. These two aspects of the depreciation are known as the **value effect**.

If both the volume and value effects are measured in percentage terms, it is possible to relate one to the other for both imports and export transactions in terms of the price elasticity, $\eta = -(\Delta Q/Q)/(\Delta P/P)$. After a real depreciation, if the percentage change in quantity of exports $[-(\Delta Q/Q)]$ is equal to the percentage change in the price of exports $(\Delta P/P)$, then the numerical value of the price elasticity of exports (εx) will be one. This may be interpreted to mean that the real depreciation has not changed the value of exports. If the same result were going to be recorded on the import side, then the real depreciation has no overall effect on the value of the flows of trade. Consequently, the net result in the trade balance will remain unchanged.

The only way a real depreciation can improve the trade balance is if both the elastiticities of exports and imports are greater than one, in absolute terms. That is, if the sum of both elasticities is greater than one, $|\eta x + \eta m| > 1$.[1] To illustrate this

235

point, assume that the spot rate between the yen and the dollar is initially ¥320/$1. At this rate, the US imports 840,000 cars from Japan, which sell in Japan for a price of ¥3,200,000. At the same exchange rate, the US companies are exporting 540,000 machine tools to Japan at a price of $2,000 each. Subsequently, the yen appreciates in real terms to ¥130/$1. This real appreciation of the yen reduces US imports of Japanese cars, still priced at ¥3,200,000, to only 600,000 units. Simultaneously, it raises the exports of US machine tools to 720,000 units. The increase in US exports to Japan is due to the fact that the US machines are still priced at $2,000. Chart 23.5 summarizes the elasticity calculations.

Chart 5
Calculating price elasticities

US Imports
Exchange rate = ($1/¥320)

Q_0 = Quantity of US imports = 840,000
P_0 = Price of US imports =
¥3,200,000*($1/¥320) = $10,000

Exchange Rate = ($1/¥130)
Q_1 = 600,000
P_1 = ¥3,200,000*($1/¥130) = $24,615
ηm = [(600 - 840)/840]/ [(24.615 - 10)/10]
= -.19

US Exports

Q_0 = Quantity of US exports = 540,000
P_0 = Price of US exports =
$2,000*(¥320/$1) = ¥640,000

Q_1 = 720,000
P_1 = $2,000*(¥130/$1) = ¥260,000
ηx = [(720 - 540)/540]/[(260 - 640)/640] =
-0.56

$| \eta m + \eta x = (0.19 + 0.56) = 0.75 | < 1$

Since the numerical value of the elasticities is less than one, in absolute terms, the real depreciation of the dollar does not improve the US trade balance. In this hypothetical case, the US is enduring a **J effect**. This means that the real depreciation of the dollar has led to a deterioration of the US current account balance. This is due to the fact that both US imports and exports of goods and services are shown to be price inelastic.

Problems

1. Organize the following information into a balance of payments table for the United States. Attach the correct sign to each entry and incorporate an errors and omissions entry if the accounts do not balance.

ITEMS	VALUE
Merchandise imports	400
Foreign direct investment by US firms	70
Profit remittances to foreigners	40
Merchandise exports	200
Foreign tourist expenditures in the US	40
Foreign purchase of US corporate securities	150

a. What is the numerical value of the current account, the basic balance, and the official settlement accounts?

CA = $ _____

BB = $ _____

ST = $ _____

b. Use the relevant entries in your balance of payments table and some or all of the numbers below to calculate the level of GNP for the United States.

Consumption	300	Government purchases	1000
Savings	650	Investment	700

GNP = $ _____

Note: To calculate GNP you need the current account result of section "a."

2. With the information provided below, estimate the following:

ITEMS	VALUE
Export of goods	4,000
Imports of goods	5,000
Gifts received from foreigners	1,100
Gifts made to foreigners	100
Direct investment abroad	7,000
Direct investment by foreigners	7,200
Debt interest received from abroad	2,000
Debt interest paid abroad	400
Portfolio investment receipts	4,500
Portfolio investment payments	3,800

237

a.   The current account balance _____
b.   The long-term capital _____
c.   The basic balance _____
d.   The settlement account _____

3. The following are hypothetical measures of the international transactions of a nation over a given year.

ITEMS	VALUE
Merchandise exports	26.7
Merchandise imports	29.7
Income from investment abroad	3.2
Income payments abroad	10.7
Private transfers from abroad	2.2
Transfer to foreign residents	6.5
Direct investment	4.5
Direct investment abroad	2.0
Portfolio investment	10.0
Portfolio investment abroad	15.3
Other long-term capital	
Deposits by foreigners in domestic banks	5.2

What is the numerical value of the current account, the basic balance, and the official settlement accounts?

CA = $ _____
BB = $ _____
ST = $ _____

4. Hypothetical Transactions Between US Residents and Foreign Residents:

1. A firm in the US ships merchandise to an overseas buyer with the understanding that the price of $50 million, including freight, is to be paid within 90 days. Merchandise is transported on a US ship.
2. To make payments in dollars for the merchandise he has received from the US, a foreign customer opens a checking account held by his bank in a US bank. Later he transfers the deposit to the US exporter.
3. A US firm has a long-standing capital investment in a subsidiary abroad. The subsidiary transfers to the US parent $10 million of its earnings in the form of a check drawn on a foreign bank.
4. US residents import merchandise valued at $45 million, making payments by transferring $10 million from balances which they hold in a foreign bank, and $35 million from balances held in US banks.
5. US residents transfer abroad balances of $5 million in US banks to foreigners in exchange for foreign currency, which they spend traveling abroad.

6. Recent US immigrants acquire balances worth $1 million (have opened checking accounts in the United States worth $1 million) which US banks have held in foreign banks, and then send them as gifts to relatives living abroad.

7. US residents buy $60 million on long-term bonds issued by Canadian borrowers. The bonds are denominated in US dollars so that the payment for them is made by transferring US dollar demand deposits (paying for the purchase of bonds with a US bank check issued to a Canadian national).

Note: *Use the form provided in the appendix of this note for the solution to balance of payment problems.*

5. What are the appropriate entries (debit and credit) in the US balance of payments for each of the following transactions:

1. An Argentinean exporter ships $50,000 worth of leather to the United States and receives a payment in the form of a dollar deposit in a Los Angeles, California bank.

2. Chrysler ships auto equipment worth $1,000,000 to Mexico for installation in its branch factory in Saltillo, Mexico.

3. A Japanese citizen purchases $500,000 worth of US government bonds; the US seller receives dollar balances in a Tokyo bank.

4. A US citizen purchases $250,000 worth of German bonds; the German seller receives dollar balances in New York.

6. The Mexican government, in an attempt to improve the country's balance of payments, devalues the Mexican peso (MexP) from MexP2.4/$1 to MexP3/$1. The effect of this government policy is a decrease in the quantity of Mexican imports from the United States from 240 to 220 and an increase in the quantity of Mexican exports to the United States from 130 to 160. The domestic price of Mexican exports is MexP6, and the US price of the Mexican imports is $8.

DEVALUATION EFFECTS

ITEM	Before	After
Exchange rate	MxP2.4	MxP3.0
Mexican imports from the U S	240	220
Price of Mexican imports from the US	$8	$8
Mexican exports to the US	130	160
Price of Mexican exports to the US	MxP6	MxP6

a. What is the price elasticity of demand for imports? η_m = _____

b. What is the price elasticity of demand for exports? η_x = _____

c. Has the devaluation produced a balance of payments "*J effect?*"

239

7   Initially, the spot rate between the German mark and the US dollar is DM3.2/$1. At this rate, the US is importing from Germany 840 units of highly specialized equipment used to test the quality of transparent products at a price of DM3,200. In turn, the US exports to Germany 540 personal computers at a price of $2,000.

Due to the high deficits experienced by the US over the last five quarters, the Group of Seven has agreed to support a drive to lower the price of US dollars in world currency markets. This policy ends up in a real depreciation of the dollar against the mark, which is now trading at only DM1.3/$1. This new rate, as expected, changes the flows of trade. The US is both importing less and exporting more. For instance, at the same mark price of DM3,200, the US imports of measurement equipment have declined to 600, while the exports of US computers, still priced at $2,000 have soared to 720 units. This information is reflected in the two tables provided below.

a.   What is the numerical value of the price elasticity of US imports?
b.   What is the numerical value of the price elasticity of US exports?
c.   Did the depreciation of the US currency lead to a "J effect?"

BALANCE OF PAYMENTS

A.		DEBIT (-)	CREDIT (+)	NET
	Merchandise	_____	_____	_____
	Service			
	Transfer	_____	_____	_____
	Current Account	_____	_____	_____
B.	Long-term Capital			
	Direct investment	_____	_____	_____
	Portfolio capital, private	_____	_____	_____
	Basic Balance	_____	_____	_____
C.	Short-term Capital			
	US short-term assets abroad	_____	_____	_____
	US short-term liabilities to foreigners	_____	_____	_____
	TOTAL	_____	_____	00.00

Note: this form can be used to solve the balance of payments problems.

APPENDIX
THE STRUCTURE OF THE BALANCE OF PAYMENTS

Exports _____
Imports _____

Merchandise Trade Balance (A) _____ _____

Income on Investment Abroad _____
Payments for Foreign Investment in the Country _____
Receipts from Travel and Transportation _____
Payments for Travel and Transportation _____
Other services _____

Balance on Services (B) _____ _____

Goods and Services Balance (A + B = C) _____

Government Transfers _____
Private Transfers _____

Balance of Transfer Payments (D) _____ _____

Current Account Balance (C + D = E) _____

Direct Investment Receipts _____
Direct Investment Payments _____
Portfolio Investment Receipts _____
Portfolio Investment Payments _____
Government Loans _____

Balance of Long-Term Capital (F) _____ _____

Basic Balance (E + F = G) _____

Non-liquid Liabilities _____
Non-liquid Claims _____

Balance of Short-Term Private (H) _____

Errors and Omissions (I) _____

Net Liquidity Balance (J) _____

Liabilities to Foreigners _____
Claims on Foreigners _____

Balance on Liquid Private Capital (K) _____ _____

Official Settlement Balance (H + I + J + K = L) _____

24 National income and the balance of payments

Introduction

A firm's total revenue is the result of domestic sales and exports. Local earnings are a function of the level and growth of real income, whereas foreign proceeds are related to the level and growth of foreign real income and the variations of the local currency's parity in the foreign exchange market.

Purpose

The purpose of this technical note is to provide the reader with the analytical tools required to investigate the relationship between national income and the balance of payments.

The circular flow

Every day countless market transactions occur, even in the most simple economies. Individuals work and consume, firms produce and invest, governments and foreigners purchase goods and services. To track down in detail all of these transactions is an impossible task. It is conceivable, however, to organize, classify, and aggregate all of these transactions.

The expenditures of households on all kinds of goods and services, except housing, is classified as consumption. The acquisition of raw materials, parts, and capital goods by firms is aggregated under investment. The expenses incurred by the government are listed under government expenditures. The purchase of domestic goods by foreigners – exports – adjusted by the acquisition of foreign goods by the domestic residents – imports – is incorporated in the current account. The accumulation of all of these transactions determines the level of national income (Y), which is later modified by taxes. The portion of income left after taxes – known as disposable income (Y_d) – is allocated by the households to either consumption or savings, or both. Savings are placed in financial institutions as demand and time deposits. These financial intermediaries then lend these funds to firms, who ultimately invest them.

CIRCULAR FLOW

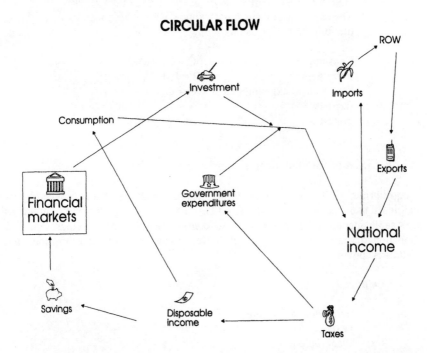

From the description of how the economic system operates, it is possible to identify three critical connections to maintain the stability of the circular flow: the relationships between domestic private savings and investment, imports and exports, and taxes and government expenditures. A surplus in any one of these relationships has to be offset by a deficit of similar magnitude by any one of the other remaining balances.

A statistic frequently used to measure national income is gross national product (GNP), which is the accumulation of consumption (C), investment (I), government expenditures (G), and external sector expenditures (X-M). The creation of GNP is described in Chart 1.

Chart 1

1) $GNP = C + I + G + (X - M)$;
   The expenditures which determine GNP are described by
   the following expressions:

2) Consumption: $\quad\quad\quad\quad\quad\quad$ $C = C_o + cY_d$
3) Investment: $\quad\quad\quad\quad\quad\quad\,$ $I = I_o + iY_d$
4) Government expenditures: $\quad$ $G = G_o$
5) Exports $\quad\quad\quad\quad\quad\quad\quad\,$ $X = X_o$
6) Imports: $\quad\quad\quad\quad\quad\quad\quad$ $M = M_o + mY_d$

The allocation of national income

In equilibrium, GNP is equal to potential income, which is partially reduced by its recipients to meet tax responsibilities (Tx). The remaining, which is known as disposable income (Y_d), is allocated to consumption (C) and savings (S). The allocation of national income in equilibrium between taxes, consumption, and savings is shown in Chart 24.2 .

Chart 2

7) GNP equal to income $\quad\quad$ $GNP = Y$
8) Taxes $\quad\quad\quad\quad\quad\quad\quad\,$ $Tx = tY$
9) Disposable income $\quad\quad\,$ $Yd = Y - Tx$
10) Savings $\quad\quad\quad\quad\quad\quad\,$ $S = Yd - C$

In general, C_o, I_o, G_o, X_o, and M_o are intended to represent autonomous expenditures while c, i, and m express the marginal propensities to consume, invest, and import; t is the marginal rate of taxation.

Transformation of the variables of the model

The expressions for consumption, investment, and imports in equations 2, 3, and 6 are expressed as functions depending on disposable income. However, they can be transformed into variables depending on national income by taking the following steps: First, substituting equation 8 into equation 9 yields a new expression for disposable income as shown in (8'):

(8') Disposable income: $Y_d = Y - tY = (1 - t)Y$.

Replacing the expression $(1 - t)Y$ for disposable income in expressions 2, 3, and 6 turns all of these expressions into variables depending on national income. This transformation permits the standardization of the variables and the determination of a very simple model that can be used to illustrate the creation and determination of Y, Y_d, M, the trade balance (TB), and the other variables pertaining to this model.

National income and the trade balance

Autonomous expenditures are those with disregard for the expected level of national income. An example of these expenditures is the expense made to provide food and shelter for those unable to perform a professional job, such as children and the disabled elderly. Newly made autonomous expenditures have a multiplier effect that produce a change in the level of national income higher than the initial value of the expenditure. This multiplier effect of additional autonomous expenditures is depicted by $[1/(1 - c - I + m)]$, which is the expression to be used to estimate the open economy multiplier.

The open economy multiplier $[1/(1 - c - I + m)]$ is an expression utilized to measure the response of income to changes in autonomous expenditures (A). The numerical value of the multiplier is always greater than one to reflect the fact that the change in income is always greater than the initial value of the autonomous expenditures that generate changes in national income. The degree by which the change in autonomous expenditures will change the level of national income depends on the value of the multiplier. This, in turn, depends on the value of the different marginal propensities. *As a rule of thumb, the larger the marginal propensities to invest and consume, the greater the multiplier effect, and the larger the marginal propensity to import, the smaller the multiplier effect.*

Autonomous expenditures

All the autonomous expenditures, except spending on autonomous imports, are considered an income injection. Accordingly, an increase in C_o, I_o, G_o, and/or X_o disproportionately raises the level of national income in equilibrium in the short run.

Determination of national income in equilibrium

The level of national income is the result of both the autonomous expenditures and their multiplier effect. However, changes in autonomous expenditures – especially government expenditures – can affect the level of income only if the economy is operating at less than potential income. Otherwise, if autonomous expenditures are raised when the economy is operating at its full capability, the addition in autonomous expenditures will raise inflationary expectations rather than output.

Current account balance in equilibrium

Once income and disposable income are estimated, it is possible to use either one of them to calculate the numerical value of the current account. The first step is to substitute the value of disposable income in the import equation. The second step is to subtract imports from exports (**X - M**).

Example

To illustrate how the level of national income affects the balance of payments and the performance of a firm under a fixed exchange rate system, a numerical exercise is presented below in a step-by-step fashion.

Very often in models of the firm, the level of sales (V) are depicted as a function of the level of disposable income (Y_d), that is:

$$V = V_0 + vY_d$$

where V_o are autonomous sales and v is marginal sales. These two parameters, as well as the different marginal propensities required to estimate the open economy multiplier, are often estimated by using regression analysis based on time series or cross sectional data. Assuming that regression analysis has been performed, the estimates will look like the expressions in Chart 3.

Chart 3

V	=	$2 + .01Y_d$
C	=	$20 + .8Y_d$
I	=	$10 + .1Y_d$
G	=	100
X	=	30
M	=	$20 + .05Y_d$
Tx	=	$.2Y$

Step one: estimation of the level of disposable income

$$Yd = Y - Tx = Y - .2Y = .8Y$$

The calculation performed indicates that the government is retaining 20 percent of the income produced, and that the remaining 80 percent is left to the households. The households can allocate their disposable income either to consumption or savings.

246

Step two: re-definition of the variables

Using the estimate of disposable income from step one, it is possible to re-express the variables of the model in terms of total income:

$$
\begin{aligned}
C &= \quad 20 + .8Y_d = \quad 20 + .8(.8)Y = \mathbf{20 + 0.64Y} \\
I &= \quad 10 + .1Y_d = \quad 10 + .1(.8)Y = \mathbf{10 + 0.08Y} \\
M &= \quad 20 + .05Y_d = \quad 20 + .05(.8)Y = \mathbf{20 + 0.04Y}
\end{aligned}
$$

Step three: estimation of the numerical value of the open economy multiplier

The calculations performed in step two provide the values for the marginal propensities, which are required to calculate the open economy multiplier.

$$
\begin{aligned}
\mu &= [1/(1 - c - i + m)] \quad = 1/(1 - .64 - .08 + .04) \\
\mu &= 1/.32 = 3.125
\end{aligned}
$$

Step four: estimation of the level of autonomous expenditures

The numerical value of autonomous expenditures is:

$$
A = (C_o + I_o + G_o + X_o - M_o) = 20 + 10 + 100 + 30 - 20 = 140
$$

Step five: numerical value of income in equilibrium

The numerical value of both the open economy multiplier and the autonomous expenditures calculated in steps three and four furnish the numerical information required to determine the expected level of income in equilibrium. This estimate, in turn, can be utilized to assess the numerical value of the rest of the variables in steps six, seven, and eight.

$$
\begin{aligned}
Y &= (C_o + I_o + G_o + X_o - M_o)*[1/(1 - c - i + m)] \\
Y &= 140 * 3.125 = 437.5
\end{aligned}
$$

Step six: numerical value of the trade balance

$$
CA = (X - M) = [30 - (20 + .04 * 437.5)] = 30 - 20 - 17.5 = -7.5 \text{ (deficit)}
$$

Step seven: level of disposable income

$$
Y_d = .8 * 437.5 = 350
$$

247

Step eight: level of national savings

$$S = Y_d - C = 350 - 300 = 50$$

Step nine: level of sales

$$V = 2 + .01*350 = 5.5$$

Problems

1. Assume the following economy with no government:

$C = 20 + .7Y$ $M = 10 + .12Y$
$I = 12 + .05Y$ $X = 25$

   a) What is the level of income in equilibrium?
   b) What is the current account balance?

2. You are given the following information:

$C = 120 + .7Y_d$ $I = 20 + .2Y_d$
$G = 80$ $X = 125$
$M = 60 + .05Y_d$ $Tx = .1Y$

   a) What is the value of the multiplier?
   b) What is the numerical value of income in equilibrium?
   c) What is the numerical value of disposable income?
   d) What is the numerical value of the trade balance?
   e) What is the numerical value of savings in equilibrium?
   f) What is the numerical value of taxes in equilibrium?

3. In country X, the marginal propensity to consume is .8, the marginal propensities to import and invest are .2 and .15 respectively. If the level of income in equilibrium is 400 million, what is the level of autonomous expenditures?

4. Suppose that the model of the economy is given by:

$Y = C + I + G + CA$ $C = a + bY_d$
$Y_d = (1 - t)Y$ $CA = X - mY_d$

where $I = 650$, $G = 750$, $a = 80$, $b = 0.9$, $t = .3$, $X = 400$, $m = .1$

   a) Determine the value of autonomous expenditures.
   b) Determine the value of the multiplier.
   c) Find the value of national income in equilibrium.
   d) Find the value of consumption in equilibrium.
   e) Find the value of savings in equilibrium.
   f) Find the value of the current account in equilibrium.
   g) Find the level of net private savings (S - I).
   h) Find the level of net government savings (T - G).

249

5. What is the current account balance of a nation with a government deficit of $128 billion, private savings of $806 billion, and domestic capital formation of $777 billion?

6. Devaluation is often used by countries to improve their current account. Explain how a devaluation can affect national savings and domestic investment.

7. Between 1984 and 1985, the money supply in the United States increased to $641.0 billion from $570.3 billion, while that of Brazil increased to $106.1 billion cruzados from 24.4 billion. Over the same period, the US consumer price index rose to 100 from a level of 96.6, while the corresponding index for Brazil rose to 100 from a level of 31.0.

   a) Calculate the 1984-85 rates of money supply growth and inflation for the United States and Brazil.
   b) How would you explain the apparently different response of US prices compared with Brazilian prices?
   c) Assuming that output is $4010 billion in the US and 1418 billion cruzados in Brazil, what is the velocity of money for the two countries?

8. Assume that the following information is provided.

   $C = 400 + .8Y_d$ $T = .1Y$
   $I = 200 + .1Y_d$ $G = 200$
   $M = 100 + .1Y_d$ $X = 300$

   What is the numerical value of the current account?

25 Monetary and fiscal policy, output and exchange rate

Output and the exchange rate — a short-term analysis

In one analysis of the performance of the yen, it was reported that:

> "The Japanese currency (has) been struggling against a background of a faltering economic recovery, falling interest rates, political uncertainty."[1]

Other reports later indicated that:

> "The economic news hit the currency market hard...The yen continued to tumble, undermined by traders disappointed with the pace of the Japanese recovery and the high yields available on investment overseas, particularly the US...There has been a real loss of confidence about whether this (Japan) economic recovery is accelerating."[2]

These two quotations suggest that important business decisions are taken based on expectations regarding the level and direction of output, interest rate differentials between the dollar and other major currencies, and the level and direction of the exchange rates.

Purpose

The purpose of this technical note is to provide a structured and relatively simple economic model to assist the reader in understanding the relationship between output and the exchange rate, and how monetary and fiscal policy affect these two variables.

National income and foreign trade

The gross national product of a nation (GNP) is equivalent to the market value of all *final* goods and services produced by a nation over a period of time, which is usually a year. The *potential* size of gross national product depends on the endowment of national resources and productivity. The *actual size* of GNP is determined by the level of expenditures. When potential and actual GNP are expected to be equal, the national economy is anticipated to operate at full employment equilibrium. Gross national product is estimated by aggregating the expenditures on final goods and services of individuals and families, businesses, governments, and foreigners over the accounting period. Open economy expenditures are usually expressed as:

$$GNP = C + I + G + (X - M)$$

where C represents expenditures by individuals and families for purposes of consumption; I is the expenditures by businesses for gross investment in capital formation and net additions to inventories; G is the expenditures by government for both consumption and investment; X is the expenditures of foreigners on domestic goods (exports); and M is the domestic expenditures on foreign-produced goods (imports).

Allocation of real income

Gross national product measured in terms of domestic output - also known as real GNP - is used by households to pay taxes. What is not spent on taxes is either saved or spent on consumption and imports. Consequently, in this setting, consumption is viewed as depending on disposable income (real income (Y) minus taxes (Tx)):

$$C = C(Y_d)$$

In this specification, a country's desired level of consumption is a function of disposable income (Y_d) where consumption is expected to increase as disposable income increases. Therefore, consumption and disposable income are positively related. To simplify the modeling process, it will be assumed throughout this technical note that government expenditures (G) and investment (I) demand are fixed.

Current account

The current account balance is technically defined as the net result of adding the trade, service and transfer balances. For the purpose of this note it will be defined simply as the demand for a country's exports less the country's own demand for imports. In practice, exports are largely determined by the real exchange rate (E) and foreign real income (Y_f), while imports are ruled by the real exchange rate (E) and real disposable income (Y_d). The current account then can be expressed as:

$$CA = (X - M) \quad = CA(E, Y_d)$$

where: $(X - M)$ = Current account
$\quad$ E $\quad$ = Real exchange rate
$\quad$ Y_d $\quad$ = Disposable income

The relationship between the current account and the real exchange rate is very complex. A change in the exchange rate affects the flow of goods and services in two ways. The first and more obvious is **the value effect**; the second is **the volume effect**.

The value effect of a variation in the exchange rate

After a depreciation, the residents of a nation have to give more domestic goods to buy the same amount of foreign goods. In contrast, foreigners have to give a lesser amount of their goods to purchase the same amount of imports. This change in the trading relationship between residents and foreigners is known as the *value effect*.

The volume effect of a variation in the exchange rate

Domestic consumers usually respond to the price shift on imports by purchasing fewer units of the more expensive foreign goods, while foreigners generally increase their demand for domestic goods. This market response is known as the *volume effect*.

The net effect of the value and the volume effect on both imports and exports, and consequently the current account, is uncertain. It is very difficult to ascertain in advance whether a depreciation of the local currency will improve or worsen the current account. Ultimately, the response of the current account to a depreciation will depend on the relative strength of these two effects. However, when the countries choose a depreciation of their currency, they usually expect the volume effect to outweigh the value effect, so that the depreciation is anticipated to improve the current account. In this technical note, we will have this same anticipation regarding variations in the exchange rate.

Chart 1
Exchange rate, disposable income, and the current account

	Current Account	
Exchange Rate	**Improves**	**Worsens**
Depreciation	X	
Appreciation		X
Disposable Income		
Increase		X
Decrease	X	

Other factors affecting the current account are domestic and foreign disposable income. A rise in local disposable income causes domestic consumers to increase their spending on all goods, including imports. Therefore, an increase in disposable income, assuming foreign income fixed, is expected to worsen the current account. Chart 1, above, summarizes how changes in the exchange rate and disposable income affect the current account.[3]

Aggregate demand

If we combine the four expenditure components, total aggregate demand can be expressed as:

$D = D(E, Y_d)$ where E and Y are the real exchange rate and real output respectively.

Real exchange rate and aggregate demand

Based on the previous description of the effect of changes in the exchange rate on the current account, a depreciation of the real exchange rate should lower the price of domestic output relative to foreign output, and shift domestic and foreign spending from foreign to domestic goods and services. This shift in spending prompted by the depreciation should raise the demand for domestic output, while an appreciation should lower it.

Real income and aggregate demand

An increase in real income, assuming taxes are fixed, persuades domestic consumers to increase their demand for all goods and services. The increase in consumption raises aggregate demand, while the demand for imports lowers it. Since the effect on consumption is far greater than the effect on imports, an increase in real income should raise aggregate demand, while a decline in income should have opposite results.

Determination of output — a short run analysis

The aggregate supply schedule depicted as a 45° line in Figure 25.1 shows the country's real output of goods and services. Its slope, with a numerical value of 1, indicates that gross national product is equal to aggregate expenditures at each point on the schedule. The aggregate demand schedule shows planned expenditures assuming fixed levels of the real exchange rate, taxes, investment, and government spending.

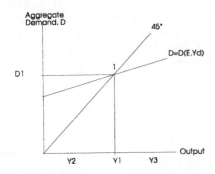

Figure 25.1

The equality of output and aggregate demand at point 1 sets short-run equilibrium. At this point, output settles at Y1. At a higher level of output, such as Y3, there is an excess supply of domestic output, and firms find themselves accumulating inventories involuntarily. As inventories start to build up, firms cut back on production, with the consequent regression of output to Y1. This analysis only applies in the short run because it is assumed that the money prices of goods and services are temporarily fixed. The relaxation of this assumption would place the analysis in the long run, where the real exchange rate has adjusted to equate long run output to aggregate demand. Therefore, long run output is determined only by the availability of factor supplies.

Output and the exchange rate in market equilibrium

Understanding the relationship between the exchange rate and output in the short run is critical to comprehend how an open economy operates. To build this knowledge, the determination of output is analyzed assuming variations only in the exchange rate; every thing else —including domestic and foreign prices— remains fixed.

Figure 25.2 pictures the effect of a depreciation of the domestic currency on domestic output. The depreciation lowers the price of domestic output. This value effect shifts the domestic and foreign demands from foreign to domestic output. The fall in the relative price of domestic output shifts the aggregate demand schedule upward from D1 to D2. On the D2 schedule, the demand for domestic goods and services is higher at each level of output. Firms respond to the excess demand for domestic output by expanding it from Y1 to Y2.

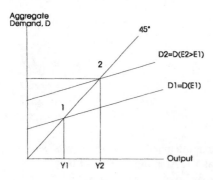

Figure 25.2

Deriving the DD schedule

To derive the relationship between output and the exchange rate - which is known as the DD schedule - we need to transfer information from the aggregate supply-aggregate demand dimension, pictured in Figure 25.2, to the exchange rate-output dimension depicted in Figure 25.3. At point 1 of Figure 25.2, the exchange rate E1 and output Y1 are both consistent with domestic equilibrium. However, the excess demand instigated by the depreciation of the exchange rate disrupts this equilibrium. At every level of the initially planned domestic output, there is an excess demand. To satisfy this unexpected excess demand prompted by the depreciation, firms expand output from Y1 to Y2. Given the exchange rate E2, domestic output Y2 is the new equilibrium output.

256

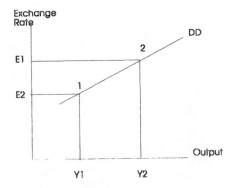

Figure 25.3

Transferring the information on the exchange rate and output from Figure 25.2 to Figure 25.3 leads to the DD schedule, which shows the various levels of output and the exchange rate consistent with short-term equilibrium. *The DD schedule shows combinations of output and the exchange rate such that the market for goods and services is in short-term equilibrium, with aggregate demand equal to aggregate supply.*

Economic policy and the position of the DD schedule

The position of the DD schedule -- a shift in DD schedule -- can be produced by: 1) changes in the level of taxes, government expenditures, and investment; 2) variations in domestic and foreign prices; 3) alterations in consumer's behavior; and 4) the substitution of foreign products by domestic goods and services.

Government expenditures and the DD schedule

To illustrate how an increase in autonomous expenditures affects the position of the DD schedule, Figure 25.4 depicts the effect of a temporary increase in government expenditures on the DD schedule. An increase in government spending from G1 to G2, assuming the exchange rate is fixed at E1, causes the aggregate demand schedule in the upper portion of Figure 25.4 to shift upward. All else remaining equal, output increases from Y1 to Y2 at the given exchange rate of E1. This, in turn, shifts the DD schedule from DD1 to DD2. The effect of other factors affecting the DD schedule is presented in Chart 2.

257

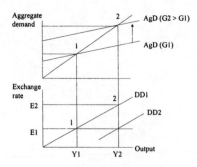

Figure 25.4

Chart 2
Factors affecting the position of the DD schedule

| | EFFECT ON | |
Policy Action	Aggregate Demand	The DD Schedule
EXCHANGE RATE POLICY		
A depreciation	Upward shift	A movement along the DD
An appreciation	Downward shift	A movement along the DD
FISCAL POLICY		
Increase government expenditures	Upward shift	Outward shift
A decrease in taxes	Moves counter-clockwise	Outward shift
OTHER DISTURBANCES		
An increase in autonomous investment	Upward shift	Outward shift
An increase in prices	Downward shift	Inward shift
An increase in autonomous consumption	Upward shift	Outward shift
An increase in autonomous savings	Downward shift	Inward shift

The consistent response of the DD schedule to the policies listed in Chart 2 suggests a pattern of behavior that can be summarized in the following rule:

258

Any variation that raises aggregate demand for domestic output shifts the DD rightwards. Any change that lowers aggregate demand shifts the DD leftwards.

Short-run equilibrium in the asset market

Equilibrium in the asset market is achieved simultaneously in the money market and the foreign exchange market when the prevailing interest rate satisfies both interest rate parity and equates the real domestic money supply to aggregate real money demand. Interest parity among two currencies such as the dollar and the yen can be expressed as follows:

$$R\$ = R¥ + [E^e\$/¥ - E\$/¥]/E\$/¥$$

where R\$ = current interest rate on one-year dollar deposits;

 R¥ = current interest rate on one-year yen deposits;

 E^e\$/¥ = dollar/yen exchange rate expected to prevail a year later;

 E\$/¥ = current price of a yen in terms of dollars (dollars per yen).

Equilibrium between real domestic money supply [ms = (MS/P)] and real money demand [md = Md(R\$,Y)] can be described as:

$$M_S = m_d(R\$,Y)$$

where *R$* is the interest rate on domestic deposits that satisfies both interest rate parity and money market equilibrium, and *Y* is output.

Behavior of the real demand for money

The demand for money rises when the interest rate falls because a fall in the interest rate makes interest-bearing bank deposits less attractive to hold. In contrast, a rise in the interest rate lowers the real demand for money. A rise in output increases the volume of monetary transactions that have to be completed to produce the higher level of income. These additional transactions compel individuals and corporations to increase their demand for real money. A fall in output diminishes the need to hold real money.

A rise in output and asset market equilibrium

With the analytical tools developed in the two previous sections, we are now ready to explore the dynamics of short-term equilibrium in the asset market. Interest and exchange rates associated with output in equilibrium for a given stock of real money supply, a given domestic price level, a given foreign interest rate, and a given value of the expected exchange rate are shown in Figure 25.5 at point 1.

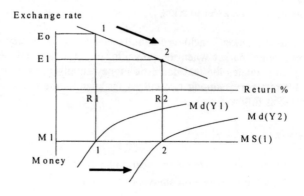

Figure 25.5

A rise in output from Y1 to Y2 shifts the real demand for money from Md(Y1) to Md(Y2). This, in turn, raises the domestic interest rate from R1 to R2. The rate of return on dollar deposits is relatively higher than the rate of return on foreign deposits because no change has occurred in the foreign interest rate, R2. This relatively higher rate of return on dollar deposits persuades holders of foreign currency deposits to try to sell them in order to "buy" the more profitable dollar denominated deposits. To induce dollar holders to trade, the holders of foreign currency deposits offer a better price for the dollars, causing a dollar appreciation. The appreciation of the dollar, however, is constrained to be just enough so that the increase in the rate at which it is expected to depreciate in the future offsets the increased interest rate of home-currency deposits.

Deriving the AA schedule

The information presented in Figure 25.5 provide the elements to derive the combination of output and exchange rates consistent with equilibrium in both the money and foreign exchange markets. This output-exchange rate schedule is commonly recognized as the AA schedule. If the information of Figure 25.5 is transferred to Figure 25.6, then it is possible to identify points A and B. Linking this two points permits the derivation of the AA schedule.

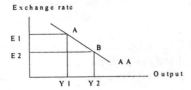

Figure 25.6

The DD-AA model and equilibrium

At this juncture, two separate schedules of exchange rate and output levels have been derived: the DD and the AA schedules. A short run equilibrium for the economy as a whole has to lie on both of them concurrently to be able to satisfy equilibrium on both the goods and asset markets.

The intersection of the DD and the AA schedules (depicted in Figure 25.7) is the only point meeting the general equilibrium criterion, since it is the only one commonly shared by both schedules. At this intersection, the levels of output and the exchange rate consistent with a short-term equilibrium for the economy as a whole are **Y*** and **E*** respectively.

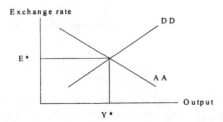

Figure 25.7

261

Effect of monetary and exchange rate policy on the position of the AA schedule

The AA schedule shifts in response to variations in the domestic money supply, foreign interest rate policies, and alterations in the expectations about the future level of the exchange rate. The effect of these and other policy changes are illustrated in Chart 3.

Chart 3
Factors affecting the position of the AA schedule

Policy Action	The AA Schedule
Monetary policy	
Increase in the money supply (expansionary)	Upward shift
Decrease in the money supply (restrictive)	Downward shift
Price targeting	
Reduction in the price level (deflation)	Upward shift
Increase in the price level (inflation)	Downward shift
Change in foreign monetary policy	
Increase in the foreign interest rate	Upward shift
Reduction in the foreign interest rate	Downward shift
Change in expectations	
Increase in the value of the expected future Exchange rate	Downward shift
Decrease in the value of the expected future Exchange rate	Upward shift
Other changes	
Outward shift in the demand for money	Downward movement along the AA
Inward shift in the demand for money	Upward movement along the AA

Monetary policy

A temporary increase in the domestic money supply and its effect on the AA schedule is illustrated in Figure 25.8. An expansion of the money supply lowers the domestic interest rate. This new interest rate does not satisfy the interest parity condition, since the return on local currency deposits is less than the return on foreign currency deposits. To clear the asset market, a depreciation of the local currency is needed. A depreciation of the local currency restores interest rate parity.

Using Figure 25.5 it is possible to show that the increase in the money supply shifts the AA schedule from AA1 to AA2. At the initial level of output, Y1, the exchange rate at point 2 does not clear the goods market. There is an excess demand for domestic output brought about by the depreciation of the local currency. To restore balance in the goods market, output has to expand. This output expansion, in turn, will feed back into the assets markets. After a series of

262

adjustments among the goods and the asset markets, the economy will finally settle at point 3. *In brief, an increase in the money supply can cause a depreciation of the domestic currency from E1 to E2 and an expansion of output from Y1 to Y2.*

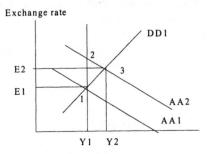

Figure 25.8

Fiscal policy

Changing the level of government expenditures for purposes of economic stability is known as *fiscal policy*. The following quotation from the *Financial Times* illustrates how government spending — under certain conditions — can stimulate aggregate demand:

> *Reacting to mounting pressure from home and abroad for steps to buoy Japan's sagging economy, the ruling Democratic Party proposed another package of stimulative measures. The package...features a supplementary budget to finance public-works spending and a variety of other measures... the Primer Minister...hoped the measure would create additional demand .....The US and other nations have pressed Japan to boost domestic demand so as to boost imports.*[4]

The excerpt suggests that this temporary increase in Japanese government spending should raise aggregate demand and worsen the current account. These assertions can be corroborated by the DD-AA just developed.

The DD-AA model predicts that a temporary increase in Japanese autonomous government spending should cause an upward shift in aggregate demand in Japan, and a rightward shift in the DD schedule as shown in Figure 25.9. These shifts expand Japanese output from Y1 to Y2 and force an appreciation of the yen from E1 to E2. The expansion of domestic output in Japan raises output from Y1 to Y2. This increase, assuming an unchanged money supply, shifts the demand for money. All these effects result, ultimately, in an appreciation of the yen. This appreciation induces Japanese consumers to shift their demand towards the relatively less expensive foreign goods, which eventually leads to a deterioration of both the Japanese trade and current account balances. In short, the predictive power of the DD-AA model developed in this technical note is, to a large extent, consistent with the assertions of the *Financial Times* article.

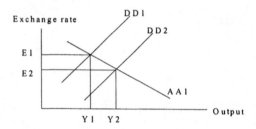

Figure 25.9

Notes

1 *The Financial Times*, December 30, 1998.
2 *The Financial Times*, December 30, 1998.
3 The results presented in Chart 1 are drawn assuming a fixed level of foreign income and a dominance of the volume over the value effect. Otherwise, the results presented in this chart will not hold true.
4 *The Financial Times*, December 29, 1998.

Problems

1. Departing from an initial situation of equilibrium, indicate the likely effect of a decline in domestic investment on the level of national income and the exchange rate.

2. Departing from an initial situation of equilibrium, indicate the likely effect of an increase in tariffs on the level of national income and the exchange rate.

3. Departing from an initial situation of equilibrium, indicate the likely effect of a permanent increase in government spending on the level of national income and the exchange rate.

4. Departing from an initial situation of equilibrium, indicate the likely effect of an increased money supply in either Germany or Japan on the US level of national income and the exchange rate.

5. Departing from an initial situation of equilibrium, indicate the effect of a depreciation of the local currency on the level of national income.

6. Departing from an initial situation of equilibrium, indicate the effect of an increase in the money supply on the level of national income and the exchange rate.

7. Departing form an initial situation of equilibrium, indicate the effect of a decrease in the interest rate of Japan or Germany on the US level of national income and the dollar.

8. Departing from an initial situation of equilibrium, indicate the likely effect of a reduction in the domestic demand for money on the level of national income and the exchange rate.

9. Assuming constant prices and a fixed stock of money, indicate the effect of a tax increase on the level of national income and the exchange rate.

10. A country is originally in a position of full employment equilibrium. Suddenly, that country experiences the loss of an important export market. What is the appropriate monetary policy to return the economy to a similar level of income in equilibrium?

11. A country is originally in a position of full employment equilibrium. Suddenly, that country experiences a shift in the demand from imports to domestic goods. What is the appropriate fiscal policy response to return the economy to a similar level of income in equilibrium?

12. Assume Canada was in a position of equilibrium at full employment before its free trade agreement with the United States. Suppose that, as a result of this agreement, the Canadians can shift a substantial portion of their aggregate demand from domestic goods to imports from the US.

a) What is the effect of this shift in aggregate demand on the Canadian level of national income and the Canadian dollar in the foreign exchange market?

b) What is the appropriate monetary policy to return the Canadian income and exchange rate to equilibrium?

13. Assume a country having a balanced budget -- tax revenues equal to government expenditures -- and a level of income in equilibrium which is below what the President and Congress believe is appropriate. Both Congress and the President agree to cut taxes to increase the domestic level of economic activity. The initial result of this policy is a government deficit. The citizens of this country believe that the government will finance this newly created deficit by increasing the money supply.

a) Using the DD-AA model, indicate the predictions of this model regarding the effect of tax cuts on the level of national income and the exchange rate.

b) Will the creation of money offset or neutralize the exchange rate effect of the tax cut?

26 The collapse of the Mexican peso

Introduction

By mid May of 1995, José Montes, Finance Director for Continental Grain in Mexico, was busy preparing for a meeting with top management about the company's strategy in Mexico. He was convinced that he should be ready to answer questions regarding the possible reasons for the crisis that had hit Mexico in December of 1994, the conditions existing in the Mexican financial markets in 1995, and the future peso/dollar relationship.

Political stability and the exchange rates

On the way back to the office, located in the heart of the financial district, Montes reflected on his last meeting with Felipe Díaz-Garza, a top political analyst. Díaz-Garza had provided him reliable information linking the excess demand for dollars in 1994 to the political assassinations of PRI presidential candidate Luís Donaldo Colosio on March 24, 1994, Catholic Cardinal Juan Posadas Ocampo on May 24, 1994 and Francisco Ruiz Massieu, General Secretary of PRI on September 28, 1994. The data also showed an acceleration in capital flights with the unfolding political events.

The economic foundations of exchange rate behavior

More economic-minded analysts, while acknowledging the importance of the political events, dismissed them as structural reasons for the peso crisis. They argued that the political events had only been a trigger mechanism that helped to cause a crisis built upon the exchange rate policies implemented by the Central Bank of Mexico during 1988-94 period. In their view, the roots of the crisis could be traced back to the poor policy response of the Bank of Mexico to peso appreciation in 1993 and 1994. Other factors listed as relevant by this group of analysts were the sizable current account deficits resulting from the real peso appreciation; and the government reliance on short-term debt to finance the current account deficits of 1993 and 1994. According to this group, the peso crisis was only a matter of time:

> *While the details could not have been predicted, something...was bound to happen. Without the Chiapas uprising or the assassination of Colosio, Mexico might not have hit the wall in December of 1994, but it probably would have not gone unscathed through 1995...*[1]

Rumors

Press reports attributed another view of the peso crisis to the former President Salinas, which the media labeled as "the Christmas mistake." According to Salinas, the crisis happened because of the erratic policies of the Zedillo administration and the challenges posed by the transition. If Zedillo had continued borrowing in November and December of 1994 to meet the excess demand for dollars that had hit the Mexican financial market in this period, the crisis would not have happened. Instead, Zedillo opted for a devaluation. This was interpreted to mean that the Mexican government was abandoning the commitment to fully support the convertibility of the large chunk of dollar-denominated Tesobonos due to mature in March of 1995. In Salinas' opinion, under the spell of the uncertainty introduced by Zedillo's policies, an investor's best response was to withdraw from the Mexican fund as fast as possible.

The Zedillo administration

A spokesman of the Treasury Department portrayed Zedillo as a victim of both exchange rate and monetary policies implemented by the previous administration. According to him, the monetary policy of the Central Bank had only served to finance the excess demand for dollars that had finally exhausted Mexico's foreign exchange holdings.

Banco de México, the Central Bank, which up to this point had remained on the sideline, quickly entered into the fray. Francisco Gil-Díaz, Vice-Governor of this institution, pointed out that:

> *[It] is somewhat perplexing that economists, journalists, and laymen devote so much attention to the public policies supposedly required to maintain the right, or, at least, a competitive real exchange rate when it is a market determined real variable and, therefore cannot be set by monetary, budget, or nominal exchange rate manipulation...Economic policy is everywhere distorted by diverse policy disturbances, but the task of the analyst is to try to identify fundamental causes of*

weaknesses that led to the 1994 crisis...We believe that analysis and the data are clear in pointing out that Mexico experienced a politically triggered speculative attack, not a crisis based on the misalignment of real phenomena.[2]

Notes

1   P. Krugman, "Dutch Tulips and Emerging Markets," *Foreign Affairs*, vol. 74, no. 4, 1995.
2   F. Gil-Díaz and A. Carstens, "Some Hypothesis Related to the Mexican 1994 - 5 Crisis," paper.

Table 26.1
Savings and investment

Year	Savings public	Savings private	Investment public	Investment private	Net savings (S – I) public	Net savings (S – I) private	Current account
1988	1.4	17.6	5.0	15.4	-3.6	2.2	-1.4
1989	3.1	15.6	4.8	16.5	-1.7	-0.9	-2.6
1990	6.7	12.5	4.9	17.0	1.8	-4.5	-2.7
1991	7.5	10.3	4.6	17.8	2.9	-7.5	-4.6
1992	7.1	9.5	4.2	19.1	2.9	-9.6	-6.7
1993	6.3	8.9	4.2	17.8	2.1	-8.9	-6.8
1994	5.0	10.7	4.5	19.1	0.5	-8.4	-7.9

Source: Banco de México, several issues.

Table 26.2
Total external debt and interest payments on Mexico's external debt

Period	Total external debt % of GDP	Total external debt % of total exports	Interest on external debt % of GDP	Interest on external debt % of total exports
1980	29.60	258.10	3.10	27.30
1986	78.40	356.10	6.50	29.60
1987	78.30	308.70	5.90	23.50
1988	58.00	248.90	5.10	21.90
1989	45.70	198.90	4.50	19.70
1990	43.60	196.70	3.00	13.80
1991	40.20	203.20	2.90	14.70
1992	34.70	188.00	2.30	12.70
1993	34.70	184.60	2.10	10.90

Source: World Debt Tables, 1994-1995.

Table 26.3
3-month interest rates
(Percentage)

Period	Cetes	Tesobono	US	Cetes-US	Tesobono–US
Dec-89	40.19	15.07	8.01	25.12	7.06
Dec-90	25.84	12.00	7.91	13.84	4.09
Dec-91	17.33	9.06	4.54	8.27	4.52
Dec-92	17.53	3.48	3.53	14.05	-0.05
Dec-93	11.71	5.09	3.08	6.62	2.01
Jan-94	10.89	4.87	3.02	6.22	1.65
Feb-94	9.13	4.34	3.21	4.79	1.13
Mar-94	11.97	7.27	3.52	4.70	3.75
Apr-94	16.45	7.75	3.74	8.70	4.01
May-94	16.54	7.05	4.19	69.49	2.86
Jun-94	16.49	6.95	4.18	9.54	2.77
Jul-94	17.19	7.25	4.39	9.94	2.86
Aug-94	13.82	7.24	4.50	6.58	2.74
Sep-94	13.10	6.79	4.64	6.31	2.15
Oct-94	14.35	6.85	4.96	7.50	1.89
Nov-94	14.76	7.50	5.52	7.26	1.98
Dec-94	31.99	10.49	5.50	21.50	4.99
Jan-95	38.00	24.98	5.75	13.02	19.23

Source: Banco de México and Survey of Current Business.

Table 26.4
Inflation and exchange rate changes, peso/dollar

Period (quarter)	Inflation (%)	Nominal exchange rate changes	Real exchange rate (1980 = 100)
1991-1	7.32	0.67	127.09
1991-2	3.61	1.22	124.88
1991-3	2.74	1.30	124.08
1991-4	4.60	0.90	120.61
1992-1	5.40	-0.03	115.50
1992-2	2.71	0.92	114.11
1992-3	2.00	0.10	112.83
1992-4	2.52	0.73	111.68
1993-1	3.27	-0.42	108.58
1993-2	1.85	0.19	107.69
1993-3	1.62	0.10	106.49
1993-4	1.66	0.30	105.80
1994-1	1.94	1.34	105.84
1994-2	1.54	5.51	110.66
1994-3	1.45	1.56	111.75
1994-4	1.85	5.95	116.76
1995-1	8.00	58.09	172.41

Source: International Financial Statistics, IMF, several issues.

Note: The real exchange rate is defined as RER = Nominal exchange rate*(Consumer price index, Mexico/Consumer price index, US).

Table 26.5
Financing of current account deficits
(Percentage)

Period (quarters)	Current account deficit	Capital account	Errors and omissions	Change in reserves
1993-1	100.00	144.42	-4.39	-40.02
1993-2	100.00	132.47	-3.93	-28.54
1993-3	100.00	104.48	-3.21	-1.27
1993-4	100.00	152.18	-14.23	-37.95
1994-1	100.00	157.17	-45.60	-11.56
1994-2	100.00	1.00	-29.28	128.27
1994-3	100.00	44.28	54.10	1.62
1994-4	100.00	-50.62	17.64	132.98

Source: Banco de México.

Table 26.6
Mexico, balance of payments, 1993-1994
(Dollars, million)

Period (quarters)	Current account result	Capital account result	Errors and omissions	Change in reserve
1993-1	-5,706	8,241	-250	2,283
1993-2	-5,761	7,632	-226	1,644
1993-3	-6,578	6,873	-211	83
1993-4	-5,345	8,134	-760	2,028
1994-1	-6,851	10,768	-3,124	792
1994-2	-7,366	73	-2,156	-9,449
1994-3	-7,839	3,471	424	-127
1994-4	-7,596	-3,845	1,340	-10,102

Source: Banco de México.

Table 26.7
Policy alternatives and outcomes

Domestic credit

		Tight	Loose
Exchange rate	Devalue	Adjustment with devaluation	High inflation
	Not Devalue	Adjustment with contraction	Actual policies

Table 26.8
Monetary base and its components
(Dollars, billion)

Period (quarters)	Monetary base	Foreign assets	Net domestic credit
1992-1	10.70	18.39	-7.70
1992-2	11.22	17.88	-6.66
1992-3	10.24	17.90	-7.66
1992-4	14.11	18.55	-4.44
1993-1	11.21	20.92	-9.71
1993-2	11.55	22.27	-10.72
1993-3	11.27	22.86	-11.60
1993-4	15.20	24.54	-9.34
1994-1	13.35	24.65	-11.30
1994-2	12.79	16.00	-3.21
1994-3	12.87	16.14	-3.27
1994-4	10.69	6.15	4.54
1995-1	8.53	8.98	-0.45

Source: Banco de México, *Indicadores Económicos*, February, 1995.

27 The international monetary system

Introduction

Governments often face a temporary balance of payments surplus or deficit and, with less frequency, they encounter structural external imbalances. To combat a temporary balance of payments deficit, a nation can simply draw down its reserves without adjusting the exchange rate or its monetary and fiscal policies. This policy is known as *temporary financing*. In the case of a temporary surplus, the monetary authorities can purchase the excess supply of foreign currency by printing local currency or by the sale of another asset, i.e. a Treasury bill. The first policy is a case of *unsterilized intervention* which means that the central bank, when buying the foreign currency, is permitting the resulting change in its assets to increase the commercial banks' reserves, change the money supply, the interest rates, and the exchange rate.[1] The second policy option is an instance of *sterilized intervention* because the central bank is offsetting the purchase of foreign exchange with the sale of another asset. In this last example, bank reserves, monetary policy, and the exchange rate remain unaffected.

A structural deficit, reflected in the persistence of trade deficits over sustained periods, may require a permanent adjustment in the exchange rate. Sometimes, however, the monetary authorities are unwilling to let the exchange rate adjust. In this case, monetary authorities are sticking to a *fixed exchange rate policy*. In a fixed exchange rate system, the government stands ready to buy and sell currency at official exchange rates. Fixed exchange rate systems are attractive to some countries because, if they can be maintained, they eliminate foreign exchange risks and reduce inflation risk. The shortcoming of this system is that, by standing ready to buy or sell currency at the stated exchange rate, the government is assuming the foreign exchange risk of its constituency. If the market value of a currency whose parity is fixed is less than the official exchange rate, the government is essentially subsidizing the currency traders by the difference between the market and the official value. This results in a transfer of wealth from the society at large to those businesses that would otherwise have had to purchase currency at their market value.

To maintain a fixed exchange rate system, the authorities may resort to a host of policies. For instance, authorities may apply a policy mix consisting of tight monetary and fiscal policies complemented with commercial policies that limit international trade. This package of policies helps countries to implement *fixed exchange rate systems*. This package is often labeled as *exchange rate control*.[2]

Theory and practice indicate that a fixed exchange rate system has at least two major weaknesses. First, it forces a direct link between domestic and foreign inflation rates. Secondly, it is prone to speculation when there is a perceived difference between official and market rates. In spite of these drawbacks and limitations, some countries and regions are still implementing fixed exchange rate systems. One noticeable experience is the European Exchange Rate Mechanism (ERM), which mandates a fixed parity within the members of the EC, where the currencies can deviate from the official exchange rate only within a small band of variation. Another interesting case is the pegging of the Argentinean peso to the US dollar, recognized as a Currency Board System. In the case of the EC, the country members want to create a truly unified EC market, say, similar to the one existing in the United States, where all the states adhere to a common currency. The case of Argentina is different. They stick to the Currency Board to avoid the hyper inflationary consequences that followed the parity adjustments of the Argentinean peso in the foreign exchange market.

In view of the exhibited weakness of the fixed exchange rate system, most countries prefer the implementation of a *freely floating* or *flexible exchange rate system* or some variant of it, such as a *managed float*, an *adjustable peg*, or a *dual-floating exchange rate system*. Under a floating system, currency values are allowed to fluctuate in relation to each other. This is the case of the Japanese yen, the British pound, the US dollar, and the German mark, among others. These currencies are not truly fluctuating freely because government intervention is constant and does have short-term impact on currency values.

Managed float systems are very similar to a flexible exchange rate system, except that under the managed float, the currencies are allowed to vary only within a pre-determined band. When the currencies threaten to surpass their upper or lower boundaries, the government intervenes. This system is often implemented because it allows the intervening government a certain degree of currency control while pursuing domestic policy objectives. The flip side of this flexibility is that it is often too costly to achieve, and only for very short periods. Government intervention may cost billions of dollars to maintain a band, and the effect is for short periods that may range from a few hours to few months.

Under a pegged system, the value of one currency is pegged to another currency, or to a basket of currencies, but it is allowed to fluctuate against the rest of the currencies. An example of the first type of "pegging" was the Guatemalan currency "el quetzal," which was fixed to the US dollar but was fluctuating against the rest. An example of the second form of "pegging" is the special drawing rights (SDR) and the European currency unit. The special drawing rights are an international currency created by the International Monetary Fund that is allocated on some pre-agreed proportion among the country members to reinforce their holdings of international reserves. SDRs are merely bookkeeping units that can be traded only among central banks of countries belonging to the IMF. Since 1981, the value of the SDRs has been determined by a basket of currencies whose composition is 41 percent US dollars, and 19 percent German marks, with the remaining 40 percent equally divided among the British pound, French franc, and Japanese yen. The value of the ECU is also determined by a basket of currencies. In this case, however, the ECU weights each member's currency by a measure of the associate's relative gross national product and volume of trading within the European common market. The most glaring disadvantage of the pegged system is that the system is still subject to speculation. Consequently, central banks often intervene to preserve the system.

Overall, floating exchange rates are considered a better vehicle to eliminate structural imbalances. However, the process to eliminate the imbalance can be delayed by sterilized interventions, multinationals' pricing policies aimed to preserve their market share in world markets, and the structural inability of the international firms to respond to new international trade opportunities.

Policy coordination under a fixed exchange rate system

From the previous discussion, it is obvious to conclude that there is not a perfect exchange rate system. Regardless of imbalance considerations, a country can always choose the international monetary system that best suits its national interest. However, to implement the system of choice with a certain degree of success, the local government needs the cooperation of its trading partners and a great deal of monetary and fiscal discipline. For instance, the creation of a fixed exchange rate system necessitates inter-country agreements on the initial level of the exchange rate parities, the degree of exchange rate variation to be allowed, and a clear definition of the procedure to settle balance of payments imbalances. To remain free of speculation, the system also requires a great deal of monetary and fiscal policy responsibility and strict discipline to operate within the system.

The international monetary system in a brief historical perspective

An overview of the historical development of the international financial system is a must to understand how alternative exchange rate systems affect asset value across national boundaries. This knowledge, in turn, is essential to manage value and financial risk within present and future exchange rate systems.

The gold standard

The first fixed exchange rate system formally established was the Gold Standard System in 1870. Under this system, the parity of each currency was fixed to gold, which was the only asset accepted to settle or defer a balance of payments deficit.[3] Under the rules of the Gold Standard, a nation running a balance of payments deficit had to settle it with a shipment of gold. Gold holdings by private parties were not allowed. Consequently, the inflow of gold had to be purchased by the central bank of the country running the surplus. In theory, the acquisition of gold had to result in an none sterilized intervention that would eventually increase commercial banks' reserves and the money supply. Sooner or later, the sustained increase in the money supply had to lead to a rise in the domestic price level which could not be accommodated by exchange rate variations. The only way to release the inflationary pressures created by the inflow of gold in the surplus country was by trading local currency for foreign goods —that is, by increasing imports which implied a reverse in the gold flows.

The previous description of the Gold Standard rules of operation suggest that the system was a self-correcting fixed exchange rate system where automatic variations in the money supply and free trade had a key role to play in preserving the stability of the international monetary system. Discretion to fine-tune the domestic economy had no part to play in this arrangement. The main criticism raised against this system was its heavy reliance on gold mining to provide world liquidity to the international payments' system. After World War I, the European countries had to struggle with a legacy of inflation and political instability that turned the Gold Standard into an unsuitable exchange rate system. After many years of unsuccessful experimentation with an uncoordinated float, the majority of the countries agreed in 1944 to the creation of a modified gold standard system named the Bretton Woods System.

The Bretton Woods system

Under Bretton Woods, the local currencies were fixed to the dollar, which was fixed to gold. Similarly to its predecessor, the Gold Standard, variations of the parity under Bretton Woods were limited to a very narrow band, unless the countries were suffering from a "fundamental disequilibrium." In that case, the country was allowed to change its rate to a new official par value considered to be sustainable. However, unlike the Gold Standard, under Bretton Woods, external imbalances could be settled with dollars. Therefore, in addition to having gold as part of their international reserves, the nations could also have dollars. An additional caveat was that the nations holding US dollars were entitled to trade, at any time, their dollar holdings into gold at the US Treasury. This was the famous "open window" clause. In this way, the liquidity of the international system was not subject to the availability of gold, but rather to the supply of dollars. This advantage of Bretton Woods turned out to be its main weakness. To provide liquidity to the world's payment system, the US had to run trade deficits continuously. An additional weakness of the system was its asymmetry. Under the rules of the system, a loss of reserves could force a devaluation of the currency of the country suffering the loss of reserves, but there was not a comparable pressure on surplus countries to appreciate their currencies.

The lack of fiscal and monetary discipline in the United States and her sustained balance of payments deficits in the late 1960s undermined the role of the dollar as a reserve currency and weakened confidence in the ability of the US Treasury to meet its open window responsibilities. France, fearing dollar inconvertibility, turned in its dollar holdings to the US Treasury Department. Other countries expressed the same desire. Under the threat of a massive convertibility of dollars to gold, President Nixon unilaterally suspended the gold convertibility of the dollar in 1971. In practice, this action put an end to the Bretton Woods system era.

The floating rates system

After President Nixon's announcement, the international monetary system entered a period of price instability. To cope with it, the leading industrialized nations led the way to the implementation of a coordinated floating exchange rate system. Negotiations to establish the new rules of the system started informally between finance ministers of the US, Britain, Germany and France. Japan joined later to create the group known as the G5. Subsequently, Canada and Italy were invited to join, and this group of countries formed the G7.

Under a floating exchange rate system, exchange rate parity is the result of the economic fundamentals of the currencies and the interest rate parity condition. Gross domestic product growth, inflation, interest rates, and the balance of payments are the key indicators to determine the fundamentals that shape long-term exchange rate trends. However, the day to day fluctuations of the exchange rates are better explained by the interest rate differential or interest rate parity condition. Neither the economic fundamentals nor interest rate parity is necessarily a consistent indicator. Often, economic fundamentals point to a currency devaluation, whereas the day-to-day variations of the currency may show a sustained appreciation induced by interest rate indicators. The discrepancy between the two indicators usually does not persist for long. Eventually, the currency fundamentals take precedence and deliver the appropriate market rates. In recent years, however, it has not been unusual to see the two indicators at odds for extended periods, from a few months to a few years in length. The most recent example was the sustained appreciation of the dollar from 1982 to 1985, in spite of the very large US trade deficit in this period.

The perceived advantage of a coordinated float over a fixed exchange rate system was its flexibility. Under a float, the nations are free to choose the monetary and fiscal policies that best suit their national interest. However, this freedom to choose is often abused. Countries running trade surpluses are frequently pressured by local industry boards to resist adjusting their currencies in order to delay the loss of their industry's international competitiveness. To prevent appreciation of the local currency, the central banks of the surplus countries repeatedly use foreign exchange intervention. In this way, without a formalized agreement, the international monetary system has gradually turned into a *"dirty float"* system, which is an exchange rate system characterized by considerable central bank intervention to maintain the currencies oscillating within a rather wide band of variation.

Governments of the European Economic Community desiring a higher degree of discipline within the EC, which has always been favored by Germany, agreed in December of 1971 to the creation of a fixed exchange rate system known as the "snake." Under this agreement, the EC countries set limits to the maximum range of movements for the most appreciated member currency versus the most depreciated member currency. There were also provisions for how much the currencies could oscillate within each pair-wise exchange rate. All the EC members initially supported the system; however, it collapsed in 1993, leaving behind a great deal of economic disarray.

The external debt crisis of 1982 forced some of the developing nations to adopt extreme measures to deal with the crisis. One measure often implemented was the creation of a *dual exchange rate system*. Under this exchange rate setting, two exchange rates coexisted: one was a market rate and the other a subsidized rate at which importers of key raw materials and technology could purchase currency from the central bank to import these items. The logic behind this currency subsidy was two-fold. First, it provided the local industry with the raw materials and technology required to maintain the operation of the plants and equipment. Second, it limited the price effect of a devaluation on the domestic cost of production of some industries considered "strategic."

To abate the inflationary consequences of the 1982 external debt crisis, the Mexican government instituted a heterodox economic program that has received different names over different periods. The latest package, operating since 1993, was labeled the "Solidarity Pact." The key element of this program was the implementation of a *"managed float."* Since the most important trading partner of Mexico is the United States, the Mexican government committed to pre-announcing the peso/dollar exchange rate and to maintaining the pre-announced rates. Given that the central purpose of this exchange rate system was to reduce inflation and to diminish the inflationary expectations of sustained devaluations, the government has gradually reduced the severity of the devaluations and the frequency of the announcements. This economic experiment is considered a success, since the rate of inflation has been reduced from hyperinflation to moderate levels approaching single digits, and the peso has regained respectability and stability in international financial markets. Currently, managed float is practiced to a great extent by developed and developing nations to prevent wide swings in the currency parities.

Floating versus fixed exchange rates

Any international monetary system invites trouble if it permits excessive speculation because this activity will make the system unstable. Some experts believe that a floating exchange rate system is more prone to speculation. This is true, however, only when countries operating under a fixed exchange rate are truly committed to keeping the exchange rate fixed. Otherwise, there is no strong theoretical or empirical evidence to rule out speculation under either of the two systems.

280

The floating system has been considered by many as inherently more inflationary than its counterpart, the fixed exchange rate system, on the grounds that it frees monetary and fiscal authorities from any monetary or fiscal discipline. This point has been especially important to conservative policy makers who are advocating a return to a fixed exchange rate system to regain that discipline. This point is, however, more a matter of theory than practice, since lack of discipline has existed under both systems. As a matter of fact, supporters of currency floatation have used the lack of discipline argument to support the freely fluctuating exchange rate system. They have argued that the lack of national commitment to a fixed exchange rate system is rather a benefit that has freed monetary authorities from the burden of maintaining reserves to "defend" the local currency from speculation due to "inadequate" levels of the central bank's reserves.

Floating exchange rate systems have been advocated as a system better suited to absorb external shocks. However, a fixed exchange rate is considered to be a superior method to assimilate domestic shocks. The arguments presented reveal that there is not strong empirical evidence to validate the superiority of one exchange system over the other. The practice indicates, however, that most of the nations currently favor the implementation of a managed float featuring the best of both worlds. That is a system where currencies can fluctuate within a pre-agreed band of variation wide enough to allow flexibility in the system, but narrow enough to warrant some acceptable degree of stability. Otherwise, the existence of an exchange rate has no meaning:

> *Increases of 50 percent and declines of 25 percent in the value of the dollar or any important currency over a relatively brief span of time raise fundamental questions about the functioning of the exchange rate system...What can an exchange rate really mean when it changes by 30 percent or more in the space of twelve months only to reverse itself? What kind of signals does that send about where a business should intelligently invest its capital for long-term profitability?*[4]

Notes

1 The creation of local currency to purchase foreign exchange, like any other open market purchase, increases bank reserves and, ultimately, the amount of money in circulation.
2 Exchange controls are usually implemented when a central bank restricts the availability of foreign exchange for imports, and forces firms to surrender their export revenues.
3 In practice, the system allowed fluctuations of the currency within a narrow band.
4 Paul Volcker and Toyoo Gyohten, *Changing Fortunes*, Times Books, Random House, New York, 1992, p. 246.

281

Appendix
Major exchange rate agreements since Bretton Woods

Date	Event	Content and Implications
1946	Bretton Woods	The US dollar was convertible into gold at the rate of $35 per ounce of gold. The remaining currencies were pegged to the dollar. The IMF and the World Bank were created to oversee and police the system.
1971	President Nixon suspends the convertibility of dollar into gold.	The dollar and the rest of the currencies are forced to float.
1972	Smithsonian Agreement	Dollar is devaluated to $38 per ounce of gold. The Group of Nine (Belgium, Canada, France, Italy, Britain, Germany, Japan, Sweden, and The Netherlands) agree to revalue their currencies and to maintain these new values within a 4.5 percent band of variation.
1976	European Joint Float	The European Economic Community adopts a pegged exchange rate system, with the pound falling out of the system.
1976	The Jamaican Agreement	The floating exchange rate system, already in place, is officially accepted.
1979	Creation of the European Monetary System	The European Exchange Rate Mechanism is set around a 2.5 percent band of variation. To complement the system, the ECU is officially introduced.
1985	The Plaza Accord	Group of Nine and the United States agree to cooperate on two items: 1) to control currency volatility, and 2) to depreciate the US dollar against the major currencies.
1987	The Louvre Accord	The United States and the Group of Four (France, Germany, Japan, and Britain) agree to cooperate to maintain the currency markets around the levels existing at that time. This accord was reached after the dollar had depreciated.
1991	The Treaty of Maastrich	A single European currency is proposed as the ultimate goal of monetary union. EC country members also agree to pursue a common agenda including a broad set of economic, financial, and monetary reforms.

Problems

1 During the Bretton Woods era, the exchange rate between the Japanese yen and the US dollar was as high as 300/$1. In the early 1980's that same rate stood at 260/$1. On November 10, 1987, the exchange rate moved to 134/$1. In response to those changes in the exchange rate, "Japan's trade surplus narrowed again in October of 1987, but surplus with the United States grew." Given the previous information on the exchange rate between the Japanese yen and the dollar and the quotation of *The Wall Street Journal*, can we concluded that both the world economy and the United States demand for imports have been shown to be highly exchange rate elastic?

2 The German mark has a central bank rate (in units per ECU) of 2.0583. The Dutch guilder has a central bank rate (in units per ECU) of 2.31943. Determine the mark price of the guilder.

3 Assume an international gold standard with the escudo (the Portuguese currency) fixed at Esc15,000 per ounce of gold. If an ounce of gold sells for $500, what is the escudo price of one dollar?

4 What is the most appropriate measure to force a depreciation of the dollar against the British pound?